AF560148

ECONOMIC THOUGHTS OF AMARTYA SEN

ECONOMIC THOUGHTS OF AMARTYA SEN

Editors

DR. INDERJEET SINGH
ANIL KUMAR THAKUR

Published on behalf of
THE INDIAN ECONOMIC ASSOCIATION

REGAL PUBLICATIONS
New Delhi - 110 027

ECONOMIC THOUGHTS OF AMARTYA SEN

ISBN 978-81-8484-149-7

First Published 2012
Reprint 2017

Typeset by
RAHUL COMPOSERS
358, Pocket-B, Phase-2, Sector-16B, Dwarka, New Delhi - 110 075

Printed in India at
MAYUR ENTERPRISES
WZ Plot No. 3, Gujjar Market, Tihar Village, New Delhi - 110 018

Published by
REGAL PUBLICATIONS
F-159, Rajouri Garden, New Delhi - 110 027 • Phone: 45546396
E-mail: regalbookspub@yahoo.com

Contents

Preface

The Indian Economic Association (IEA) organizes its annual conference every year. A conference work containing papers on all themes of the conference is published and distributed to its members. These themes are debated at length in the conference. After the conference, IEA publishes theme-wise work in the form of books. IEA held its Ninety-third Annual Conference at Panjab University, Chandigarh. This book is based on the contributions made to the conference theme, *"Economic Thoughts of Amartya Sen"*. The synoptic view of these papers is available in the opening chapter entitled, 'Introduction'. We hope that the readers will find this book both interesting and useful.

We acknowledge and put on record, the contribution of Dr. Anil Kumar Thakur and Prof. Inderjeet Singh for making this book possible in a very tight schedule. Our thanks are to the authors of papers without whose cooperation this work could not have been published in time. Last but not the least; we are thankful to the publisher for bringing this book in time and in an elegant manner.

PROF. SUKHADEO THORAT
President
Indian Economic Association (IEA)

List of Contributors

A. Shanmugasundaram, Asst. Professor, Kandaswami Kandar's College, Velur-Namakkal (T.N.).

Agradoot Bhaduri, Director, Media Infotech, Academic Co-ordinator, Sikkim Manipal University, DE.

Ankita Das, 39, Raja Basanta Roy Road, Flat 4A, Kolkata (W.B.).

D. Rahul, M.A. Economics, Acharya Nagarjuna University (A.P.)

Deepak Parmar, Lecturer, Department of Economics, N.S. Patel Arts College, Anand (Gujarat).

Deepali Khanna, Research Scholar, Department of Economics, JMI, New Delhi.

Dr. Leela Bhaskar (Member), Associate Professor, Department of Economics, Ethiraj College for Women, Chennai (T.N.).

Dr. Arindam Ghosh, Associate Professor, Head of the Department of Commerce, Panihati College, Visiting Lecturer: Media Infotech, Sikkim Manipal University, DE.

Dr. Arun Kumar Sinha, Head and Reader, Department of Economics, J.N.L. College, Khagual, Patna (Bihar).

Dr. B.R. Sangle, Dean, Faculty of Commerce, University of Pune, Pune (Maharashtra).

Dr. C. Dhandapani, Reader in Economics, Research Department of Economics, Muthurangam Vot. Arts College, Vellore (T.N.).

Dr. Dhiraj Kumar Bandyopadhyay, Associate Fellow in Economics, CUES, Department of Economics, Calcutta University, Kolkata (W.B.).

Dr. E.J. Helge, Associate Professor (Com.) and Head, Department of Bus. Economics (Ex Offi. Principal), Shri Shivaji Education Society, Amravati's Jijamata Mahavidyalaya, Buldana (Maharashtra).

Dr. G. Jayasankar, Assistant Professor in Economics, Research Department of Economics, Govt. Arts College, Triuvannamalai (T.N.).

Dr. Geeta G. Pandya, Government Arts College, Ahmedabad, (Gujarat).

Dr. H.N. Kathare, Assistant Professor, Rajaram College, Kolhapur (Maharashtra).

Dr. Halima Sadia Rizvi, Department of Economics, J.M.I., New Delhi

Dr. Manish Dev, General Manager, Trident Flight Handlers, Terminal C-1, Indira Gandhi International Airport, New Delhi.

Dr. M.P. Shrivastava, University Professor, Department of Economics, Magadh University Bodh-Gaya (Bihar).

Dr. M. Vijaya Bhaskar Reddy, Asst. Professor, Department of Management Studies, Sreenivasa Institute of Technology and Management Studies, Chittoor (A.P.).

Dr. M.B. Mistry, Department of Economics, Poona College of Arts, Science and Commerce, Pune (Maharashtra).

Dr. Maheshwar Prasad Yadav, P.G. Department of Economics, M.U. Bodh Gaya (Bihar)

Dr. N. Kanakasabesan, Controller of Examinations, Associate Professor and Head, Department of Economics, Ramakrishna Mission, Vivekananda College (Autonomous), Chennai (T.N.).

Dr. R.S. Gadage, Chintamanrao College of Commerce, Sangli (Maharashtra).

Dr. S. Ahmed, Department of Economics, Poona College of Arts, Science and Commerce, Pune (Maharashtra).

Dr. Shaukat Haseen, Senior Lecturer, Department of Economics, Women's College, AMU, Aligarh (U.P.).

Dr. S. Suresh, Associate Professor in Economics, Presidency College, Chennai (T.N.).

Dr. S.E.V. Subrahmanyam, Professor and Head, Department of Management Studies, SITAMS, Chittoor (A.P.).

Dr. S.N. Sukumar, Associate Professor in Economics, RKM Vivekananda College, Chennai (T.N.).

Dr. Shakeel Ahmad Siddiqui, Director, Department of Management Studies, Ideal Institute of Technology, Ghaziabad (U.P.).

Dr. Shankar Sah, P.G. Department of Economics, J.P. University, Chapra (Bihar).

Dr. Shaukat Haseen, Senior Lecturer, Department of Economics Women's College AMU, Aligarh (U.P.).

Dr. Sita Ram Singh, Principal, Professor of Economics, B.D. College, (Magadh University Service) Patna (Bihar).

Dr. Srinivasulu Bayineni, Associate Professor, Department of Economics, Yogi Vemana University, Kadapa (A.P.).

Dr. Sushama Deshmukh, Associate Professor, Mahila Mahavidyalaya, Amravati (Maharashtra).

K. Rameela, Ph.D. Research Scholars, Kandaswami Kandar's College, Velur-Namakkal (T.N.).

K. Suresh, Ph.D. Research Scholar in Economics, RKM Vivekananda College, Chennai (T.N.).

Manzoor Alam, Research Scholar, Department of Economics Aligarh Muslim University, Aligarh (U.P.).

Md. Rehan Khan, Research Scholar Department of Economics Aligarh Muslim University, Aligarh (U.P.).

Ms. Supreena Narayanan, Ph.D. Scholar, Department of Economics, Ethiraj College For Women, Chennai (T.N.).

Parmod Kumar, Assistant Professor, Punjabi University, Patiala (Punjab).

Prof. Dhirendra Nath Konar, BB-41/7, Salt Lake City, Kolkata (W.B.).

Prof. K. Hariharan, Registrar (Retd.), Sri Muthukumaran Institute of Technology, Chennai (T.N.).

Prof. Kedar Karamunge, (Modern College, Shivajinagar, Pune.)

Rajesh Patel, Lecturer, Department of Social Work, N.S. Patel Arts College, Anand (Gujarat).

Reena Singh, Associate Professor, MMH College, Ghaziabad (U.P.).

Sana Naseem, Research Scholar, Department of Economics, A.M.U., Aligarh (U.P).

S. Sasikala, Ph.D. Research Scholars, Kandaswami Kandar's College, Velur-Namakkal (T.N.).

S.D. Chamola, Professor of Economics (Retd.), 254, Sector 15-A, Hisar (Haryana)

S.M. Jawed Akhtar, Associate Professor, Department of Economics, A.M.U., Aligarh (U.P)

Sanjay Bhattacharya, Lecturer, Calcutta Institute of Engineering and Management, 24/1-A, Chandi Ghosh Road, Kolkata (W.B.).

Shweta Agrawal, Research Scholar, Mahatma Gandhi Kashi Vidyapeeth, Varanasi (U.P.).

Vishal Pawase, Deogoan, Sangamner, Ahmednagar (Maharashtra).

Introduction

Amartya Sen was awarded, "The Sveriges Riksbank Prize in Economic Sciences in Memory of Alfred Nobel 1998" for his contributions to Welfare Economics". The works of Amartya Sen cover a very vast temporal and spatial canvas. To quote Amartya Sen, *"I was born in a University campus and seem to have lived all my life in one campus or another . . . and I have not had any serious non-academic job"*. Further he added, *"While I am interested both in economics and in philosophy, the union of my interests in the two fields far exceeds their intersection"*. Amartya Sen, born in 1933 at Santiniketan in the present province of Bengal, created a renaissance in the realms of economics that by then dealt with merely material gains and losses. The Nobel Prize citation said that Amartya Sen *"has restored an ethical dimension to the vital economic problems"*. This book is collection of research papers on economic thoughts of Amartya Sen.

He has made several key contributions to research in this field. Heavily influenced by John Rawls, he is known for his work on famine, human development theory, the economic well-being and the underlying mechanisms of poverty. Kenneth Arrow's "impossibility theorem" suggested that it was not possible to aggregate individual choices into a satisfactory choice for society as a whole. Sen's contribution to the literature was to show under what conditions Arrow's impossibility theorem would indeed come to pass as well as to extend and enrich the theory of social choice.

In 1981, Sen published *Poverty and Famines: An Essay on Entitlement and Deprivation*, a book in which he demonstrated that famine occurs not only from a lack of food, but from inequalities built into mechanisms for distributing food. Sen also demonstrated that the Bengal famine was caused by an urban economic boom that raised food prices, thereby causing millions of rural workers to starve to death when their wages did not keep up. Governments and international organizations handling food crises were influenced by Sen's work. His views encouraged policy-makers to pay attention not only to alleviating immediate suffering but also to finding ways to replace the lost income of the poor, as, for example, through public-works projects, and to maintain stable prices for food.

Sen's revolutionary contribution to development economics and social indicators is the concept of 'capability' developed in his article "Equality of What". His *capabilities approach* focuses on positive freedom, a person's actual ability to do something, rather than on negative freedom approaches, which are common in economics and simply focuses on non-interference. Sen's work in the field of development economics has had considerable influence on the formulation of the *Human Development Report*, published by the United Nations Development Programme. He wrote a controversial article entitled, "More Than 100 Million Women Are Missing", analyzing the mortality impact of unequal rights between the genders in the developing world, particularly Asia.

Sen has been a ground-breaker among late twentieth-century economists for his insistence on discussing issues seen as marginal by most economists. He mounted one of the few major challenges to the economic model that posited self-interest as the prime motivating factor of human activity. Sen, who devoted his career to such issues, was called the "conscience of his profession." His influential monograph *Collective Choice and Social Welfare* (1970), which addressed problems related to individual rights (including formulation of the liberal paradox), justice and equity, majority rule, and the availability of information about individual conditions, inspired researchers to turn their attention to issues of basic welfare. Sen devised methods of measuring poverty that yielded useful information for improving economic conditions for the poor. In this context, following is the synoptic review of research contributions to this book.

Arindam Ghosh and *Agradoot Bhaduri* have reviewed the life and works of Amartya Sen. *S. Suresh* has analyzed the thoughts relating to choice of technique. Papers by *A. Shanmugasundaram et. al.* and *H.N. Kathare* deal with Sen's economic ideas on welfare economics. *D. Rahul* and *Geeta G. Pandya* have analyzed a wide range of works of Sen from mainstream economics to philosophy of ethics.

Paper by *Halima Sadia Rizvi* and *Deepali Khanna* traces the origin of Sen's ideas to Adam Smith's works and relates it to Gandhian and Rabindranath Tagore's ideas. Sen's stimulus for empirical and theoretical work has been the analysis of Smith's ideas on 'necessities and conditions of living'. Tagore believed in perfect symbiosis between man and man and man and nature and as the man moved away from nature, he was immersed in consumerism and commercialization. Tagore emphasizes on deprivation caused by the evil habits of the sufferers; whereas Sen's emphasis has been on deprivation caused by economic inequality, social justice and improper governance. Gandhian and Sen's views are similar on the issue "empowerment as a means to enjoy freedom". Paper reviews various contributions to economics and lists down the challenges that are still unanswered.

In welfare economics, contributions of Amartya Sen vary from axiomatic theory of social choice over definitions of welfare and poverty indices, to empirical studies of famine. *C. Dhandapani* and *G. Joyasankar* advocate that the state must have a proactive positive role in development. Regarding social choice, welfare and poverty, it elaborates ten propositions given by Sen, *Leela Bhaskar* and *Supreena Narayanan* analyzes Amartya Sen's contributions to welfarism, utilitarianism, poverty and industrialization in economics. The utilitarian approach had been represented and used in economic literature till quite recent in the history. Sen described it, "nihilism has been the dominant in number of studies on welfare economics bearings, as Baumol puts it, 'an ill-concealed resemblance' to obituary notices". It is a review paper covering a wide canvas showing how Sen has been willing to tackle uncomfortable subjects and challenged the conventional paradigms of economics.

Shaukat Haseen, Md. Rehan Khan and *Manzoor Alam*, analyzing Sen's approach to welfare economics, concludes that Amartya Sen's development of a 'scholarly bridge' between welfare and economics is an important and innovative contribution that has methodological as well as substantive importance that provides a prototype and stimuli for future research. *B.R. Sangle* and *S.K. Dhage* analyze the works of Amartya Sen from the perspective of welfare economics. Paper assesses the ways in which Sen's research agenda has deepened and expanded the welfare economics discourse in the disciplines of ethics and economics. It examines how his work has promoted cross-fertilization and integration on the subject across traditional disciplinary divides. In the concluding part, assessment of the challenges in the field ethics research has been done. *Arun Kumar Sinha* has analyzed Amartya Sen's approach to welfare and collective choice. In this context, *Deepak Parmar and Rajesh Patel* review the economic and philosophical ideas with special reference to inequality.

Paper by *Dhiraj Kumar Bandyopadhyay* covers Sen's contributions to positive economics on planning, choice of technique and economic growth. Paper extends to cover the issues related to theory of justice and social choice theory of normative economics. Work shows how Amartya Sen has breached the ramparts of narrowly confined space of traditional welfare economics and choice theory; and allowing ethical considerations and interpersonal value judgments to enter the space. *S.D. Chamola* analyzes Amartya Sen's classic work on idea of justice in the context of various contemporary theories of justice. Development and freedom are intimately related. By freedom he means well-being in five categories: political participation, economic well-being, social integration, information access and personal security. Sen has innovatively integrated the economic theory with the theory of justice. *Ankita Das* briefly reviews the freedom and famine relationship envisaged by Amartya Sen.

Amartya Sen has been writing rigorously about development issues. In his approach, Sen explicitly rejects the three ethical perspectives: utilitarianism, libertarianism and

Rawlsianism. Implicitly he also rejects Posner's wealth maximization argument as a fourth alternative. In this context, *Sushama Deshmukh* briefly reviews the Sen's contributions to development economics. *Srinivasulu Bayineni* while analyzing Sen's contributions to development economics covers: freedom and human rights; and poverty and famine. Civil and political rights can reduce the risk of major social and economic disasters by empowering individuals to complain, ensuring that these views are disseminated, keeping governments informed and precipitating a policy response.

Sen's contributions focus on both economic development *vis-à-vis* human development. The growth should focus the employment creation and poverty alleviation. Almost all the famines of the world are manmade; famines have occurred despite the availability foodgrains in some other part of the country. In famines, only poor people cannot purchase the food because of lack of purchasing power, information, opportunity and other factors. In this context, *R.S. Gadage* analyzes the famine, poverty and entitlement-related issues. Starvation is not eliminated despite of significant rise in per capita availability of foodgrains. Starvation does not merely depend on food supply but also on its distribution; it is concerned to person's inability to establish entitlement to have enough food.

The poverty can be solved through redistribution of increased production, democracy, liberty, strong opposition party, etc. The state should play a proactive role in poverty alleviation. Poverty is deprivation, it has several connotations. Paper by *K. Hariharan* covers Sen's contributions to economics of poverty. It elaborates the poverty identification and aggregation problem with special reference to Indian setting. Paper by *Parmod Kumar* and *Reena Singh* explores various conceptual and empirical issues relating to Sen's index of poverty.

Shankar Sah has analyzed Sen's views on inequality. There are many faces of gender inequality. Focusing on South Asia, he discovers that there is a split in India: "social and cultural divide" with anti-female bias depicted by natal and per-natal mortality. There is a need to take a plural view of gender inequality and calling for a new agenda of action to combat and put an end to it. In consonance to this argument, *Shweta*

Agrawal covers different faces of gender inequality in the context of Sen's development economics setting. The inequalities are with regard to: mortality, basic fertility, opportunity, professions, ownership and household decision-making. *Dhirendra Nath Konar*, attempts to highlight the problem of missing women in the developing countries by using the sex ratio for India and West Bengal. It argues that, without proper awareness of masses, only legislation cannot work.

The choice of technology and its employment impact is a one of the key instruments of development strategy. In the development economics framework, *Maheshwar Prasad Yadav* and *Shakeel Ahmad Siddiqui* have analyzed the employment, technology and development in its policy perspective. Various model formulation and empirical level issues have been debated at length. *M.P. Shrivastava* and *Sita Ram Singh* have analyzed the socio-economic policy of Aamrtya Sen on gross domestic happiness capabilities, entitlement and sustainable development.

Although, the capability approach has its roots in the writings of Aristotle, Adam Smith, J.S. Mill and Karl Marx, but it got prominence only after the publication of pioneer works of economist and philosopher Amartya Sen. Later on, Martha Nussbaum gave the capability approach a new shape and dimension. Finally, the concept of capability approach was adopted by international development agencies such as World Bank and UNDP as human development approach to poverty reduction by placing greater attention to social sector infrastructure. The capability approach is a broad normative framework for the evaluation of individual well-being and social arrangements for the design of policies and proposals about social change in the society. Paper by *Manish Dev* analyzes contributions of Amartya Sen towards the development of capability approach. It gives a holistic view of Sen's capability approach, Nussbaum's contribution and finally the World Bank's adoption in the form of human development.

Paper by *E.J. Helge* presents an outline of the capability approach and its central concepts. Then it compares the approach with three existing approaches of social policy research: the income poverty approach; deprivation indicator's approach; and social exclusion approach. Paper suggests an operational concept of capability approach that is both feasible and adequate for requirements of social policy research. It argues that there are possibilities for using a capability approach to poverty analysis in the field of social policy; these are in identifying the terrain of analysis and linking the concept of poverty to wider notions of social need and well-being.

The very concept of development is critical, ambiguous and more significantly value oriented. An alternative school of thought made an effort to present a people-centered approach to development, relevant to all countries and explain its connotations for development practices in many areas. *Sanjay Bhattacharya* explores different dimensions of capability expansion as a control variable for economic development. Key issues relating to education have been highlighted. Education is a highly permeated with aspiration and spectacularly under-resourced for the least endowed. Education, especially the girl education, is a most powerful determinant of economic development. There is a need to go beyond the traditional income inequality approach. Paper by *K. Suresh* and *S.N. Sukumar* analyzes poverty and inequality with special reference to capability approach. It underscores the measurement issues, strengths and weaknesses of capability approach and comes with an alternative methodological framework.

In many market-oriented economies, government regulation of economic activity is all pervasive. It is also the case with the mixed economies like India. *N. Kanakasabesan* analyzes the food entitlement, public distribution system and rent seeking behavior in India. It explores that the rent seeking is widely prevalent in economies where there is heavy subsidization of goods in public welfare; this takes various forms from pilferage to smuggling. *Vishal Pawase* and *Kedar Karamunge*, in their attempt to analyze economic theory, freedom and human rights, elaborate the basic building blocks of Sen's approach in this regard.

S.M. Jawed Akhtar and *Sana Naseem* have analyzed the theory and relevance of Social Choice. Public policy has a role not only in attempting to implement the priorities that emerge from social value and affirmation but also in facilitating and guaranteeing fuller public discussion. The reach and quality of open discussion can be helped by variety of public issues such as press freedom, media independence, expansion of education and economic independence. *M.B. Mistry* and *S. Ahmed* discuss the social choice and individual behavior dynamics postulated by Amartya Sen. *M. Vijaya Bhaskar Reddy* and *S.E.V. Subrahmanyam* has explored the Sen's thought on globalization. They cover his ideas on international asymmetries and institutions and their impact on developing countries.

The book is expected to encourage discussion and research on the matter and will be useful for the academia. Often words are too weak to serve as a mode of expressing one's inner feelings, especially the sense of indebtedness and gratitude. We must place on record the sincerest gratitude to Indian Economic Association for giving us an opportunity to serve by editing this book.

INDERJEET SINGH
ANIL KUMAR THAKUR

CHAPTER

1

Professor Amartya Sen's Thoughts in Welfare Economics

C. DHANDAPANI AND G. JAYASANKAR

Professor Amartya Sen is one of the World's most important and influential intellectuals, one of its foremost thinkers. The award of the *1998 Nobel Prize for Economics* to the great economist was the best thing that happened to the Nobel Prize in this field. This long-overdue award was for Sen's contributions to welfare economics and, among other things, for restoring *"an ethical dimension to the discussion of vital economic problems"*. Prof. Amartya Sen's contributions to welfare economics, *the basic theory of how societies make choices that are both fair and efficient,* have become part of every graduate student's training in economic theory.

Welfare economics is closely related to social choice distribution of goods, services, benefits and poverty. Amartya Sen made several key contributions to the research on fundamental problems in welfare economics. The contribution vary from axiomatic theory of social choice, over definitions of welfare and poverty indexes, to empirical studies of famine. Prof. Sen was chosen for Nobel Prize in Economics in 1998 for his intellectual message starting from 1970. His message is to be seen in giving priority to education, health, nutrition, women's well-being and other aspects of welfare economics and human development.

Prof. Amartya Sen is a humanist and he believed that ethics, morality and humanism, value judgement should be the fundamental principles of economics. Welfare of men,. women and children must be taken into consideration by the economist, planners and policy-makers. The Government and the state must have a positive role in the economic development. Development means eradication for clothings, shelters and above all freedom. This is the philosophy of Sen in welfare economics. This paper also discuss about the Prof. Sen's social choice, welfare distribution, and poverty. Sen's Ten propositions in welfare economics and Sen's intellectual views.

SOCIAL CHOICE, WELFARE DISTRIBUTIONS, AND POVERTY

Prof. Amartya Sen has made several key contributions to the research on fundamental problems in welfare economics. His contributions range from axiomatic theory of social choice, over definitions of welfare and poverty indexes, to empirical studies of famine. They are tied closely together by a general interest in distributional issues and a empirical studies of famine. They are tied closely together by a general interest in distributional issues and a particular interest in the most impoverished members of society. Sen has clarified the conditions which permit aggregation of individual values into collective decisions, and the conditions which permit rules for collective decision-making that are consistent with a sphere of rights for the individual. By analyzing the available information about different individuals' welfare when collective decisions are made, he has improved the theoretical foundation for comparing different distributions of society's welfare and defined new, and more satisfactory, indexes of poverty. In empirical studies, Sen's applications of his theoretical approach have enhanced our understanding of the economic mechanisms underlying famines.

INDIVIDUAL VALUES AND COLLECTIVE DECISIONS

When there is general agreement, the choices made by society are incontroversial. When opinions differ, the problem is to find methods for bringing together different opinions in decisions which concern everyone. The theory of social choice is preoccupied precisely with this link between individual values and collective choice. Fundamental questions are whether—and, if so, in what way—preferences for society as a whole can be consistently derived from the preferences of its members. The answers are crucial for the feasibility of ranking, or otherwise evaluating, different social states and thereby constructing meaningful measures of social welfare.

MAJORITY RULE

Majority voting is perhaps the most common rule for making collective decisions. A long time ago, this rule was found to have serious deficiencies, in addition to the fact that it may allow a majority to suppress a minority. In some situations it may pay off to vote strategically (i.e. by not voting for the preferred alternative), or to manipulate the order in which different alternatives are voted upon. Voting between pairs of alternatives sometimes fails to produce a clear result in a group. A majority may thus prefer alternative a to alternative b whereas a (second) majority prefers b to c; meanwhile, a (third) prefers c to a. In the wake of this king of *"intransitivity"*, the decision rule cannot select an alternative that is unambiguously best for any majority. In collaboration with Prasanta Pattanaik, *Amartya Sen* has specified the general conditions that eliminate intransitivities of majority rule.

INDIVIDUAL RIGHTS

A self-evident prerequisite for a collective decision-making rule is that it should be *"non-dictatorial"*; that is, it should not reflect the values of nay single individual. A minimal requirement for protecting individual rights is that the rule should respect the individual preferences of at least some people in at least some dimension, for instance regarding their personal sphere. Sen pointed to a fundamental dilemma by showing that no collective decision rule can fulfil such a minimal requirement on individual rights and the other axioms in Arrow's impossibility theorem. This finding initiated an extensive scientific discussion about the extent to which a collective decision rule can be made consistent with a sphere of individual rights.

INDEXES OF WELFARE AND POVERTY

In order to compare distributions of welfare in different countries, or to study changes in the distribution within a given country, some kind of index is required that measures differences in welfare or income. The construction of such indexes is an important application of the theory of social choice, in the sense that inequality indexes are closely linked to welfare functions representing the values of society, Serge Kolm, Anthony Atkinson and somewhat later—Amartya Sen were the first do derive substantial results in this area. Around 1970, they clarified the relation between the so-called Lorentz curve (that describes the income distribution), the so-called Gini coefficient (that measures the degree of income inequality), and society's ordering of different income distributions. Sen has later made valuable contributions by defining poverty indexes and other welfare indicators.

POVERTY INDEXES

A common measure of poverty in a society is the share of the population, H, with incomes below a certain, predetermined, poverty line. But the theoretical foundation for the kind of measure was unclear. It also ignored the degree of poverty among the poor; even a significant boost in the income of the poorest groups in society does not affect H as long as their incomes do not cross the poverty index: P = H [I + (1–1). G]. Here, G is the Gini coefficient, and I is a measure (between

0 and 1) of the distribution of income, both computed only for the individuals below the poverty line. Relying on his earlier analysis of information about the welfare of single individuals, Sen clarified when the index can and should be applied; comparisons can, for example, be made even when data are problematic, which is often the case in poor countries where poverty indexes have their most intrinsic application. Sen's poverty index has subsequently been applied extensively by others. Three of the axioms he postulated have been used by those researchers, who have proposed alternative indexes.

WELFARE INDICATORS

A problem when comparing the welfare of different societies is that many commonly used indicators, such as income per capita, only take average conditions into account. Sen has developed alternative, which also encompass the income distribution. A specific alternative—which, like the poverty index, he derived from a number of axioms—is to use the measure y. (1–G), where is income per capita and G is Gini coefficient.

Amartya Sen has pointed out that all well-founded ethical principles presuppose equality among individuals in some respect. But as the ability to exploit equal opportunity varies across individuals, the distribution problem can never be fully solved; equality in some dimension necessarily implies inequality in other. In which dimension we advocate equality and in which dimensions we have to accept inequality obviously depends on how we evaluate the different dimensions of welfare. In analogy with his approach to welfare measurement, Sen maintains that capabilities of individuals constitute the principle dimension in which we should strive for equality. At the same time, he observes a problem with this ethical principle, namely that individuals make decisions which determine their capabilities at a later stage.

WELFARE OF THE POOREST

In his very first articles Sen analyzed the choice of production technology in developing countries. Indeed, almost all of Sen's works deal with development economics, as they are often devoted to the welfare of the poorest people in society. He has also studied actual famines, in a way quite in line with his theoretical approach to welfare measurement.

ANALYSIS OF FAMINE

Sen's best known work in this area is his book from 1981 : "Poverty and Famines: An Essay on Entitlement and Deprivation". Here, he challenges the common view that a shortage of food is the most important (sometimes the only) explanation for famine. On the basis of a careful study of a number of such catastrophes in India. Bangladesh, and Saharan countries, from the 1940s onwards, he found other explanatory factors. He argues that several observed phenomena cannot in fact be explained by a shortage of food alone, e.g. that famines have occurred even which the supply of food was not significantly lower that during previous years (without famines), or that famine stricken areas have sometimes exported food.

CONCLUSION

Prof. Sen has taken an active research interest in the Indian economy and Indian society since 1950's. In an article on India's achievement over 50 years of independence, he expressed the view that perhaps the biggest achievement of independent India was the maintenance despite threats of political democracy in the country, and urges that this be seen not only as an achievement in itself but be used as an instrument of political struggle for social and economic progress. Prof. Sen goes on to say that some contrast.

The *"Biggest failure"* in India, Sen says, is social inequality. It takes its toll both directly—in terms of the quality of life—and indirectly—in terms of reducing the economic opportunity that people have. Prof. Sen says it is illiteracy the lack of health care, the absence of land reforms, the difficulty in getting micro-credit if you belong to the rural poor and the pervasive gender bias between men and women that make the problem of social inequality so large in India.

Prof. Amartya Sen's welfare contributions are significant relevance in modern India, he is a idealist. His welfare economic thoughts is basically sound and is relevant to our modern times. Prof. Amartya Sen belongs to the future, and not the past.

References

Prof. A.K. Sen, Poverty and Famine; An Essay on Entitlement and Deprivation, 1981, Clarendon Press, Oxford.

Prof. A.K. Sen, Choice, Welfare and Measurement, 1982, Oxford, Blackwell.

Prof. A.K. Sen, On Ethics and Economics 1987, Oxford Blackwell.

Prof. Nussbaum, M. and A.K. Sen (eds.), The Quality of life, 1993, Oxford Clarendon Press.

The Frontline Magazine, 24th Oct.-06th Nov. 1998.

Southern Economist, 1st August 2006 and 15th August 2010.

Prof. S. Neelakandan, Prof. Amartya Kumar Sen : A Brief Appraisal, at 30th Annual Conference of AET, Trichy.

CHAPTER

2

Economics of Amartya Sen

HALIMA SADIA RIZVI AND DEEPALI KHANNA

INTRODUCTION

Philosophy has never been so closely entwined with the study of the human conditions in a country inhabited by innumerable poor masses, as has been done by Dr. Amartya Sen. He stands with the worldly credit of a beautiful amalgamation of philosophy, ethics, and economics, in the process of tackling some of the most critical themes of development. Development as seen in a growing economy like India, was largely held as separate from achieving higher incomes and growth rates. In a multi-cultural and multi-linguistic country as India, it has been recognized by Sen, that the social and economic issues need to be like two sides of the same coin.

Amartya Sen was born in November 1933 in Bengal, then part of British India. His family was residents of Dhaka, now the capital of Bangladesh. As a child, he studied at

Santiniketan, where he was heavily influenced by the school's founder, Rabindranath Tagore, who had won the Nobel Prize for literature in 1913. Yet in the past 25-30 years, Sen's thinking has been largely in line with the 'Father of Modern Economics', Adam Smith.

ADAM SMITH AND AMARTYA SEN

Sen's stimulus for empirical and theoretical work has been the analysis by Smith of 'necessities and conditions of living'. He has not found good strength in the income measure of growth or even regarding income as the end. Rather he places great importance on the informational needs to dispel deprivation and oppression. There needs to be comprehensive and true information about the causes behind the socio-economic disorders, which become the malicious dark spots for any growing economy. Sen has reformulated the conventional picture of man as *homo economicus* to *homo socio economicus*. The *homo economicus* man was assumed to be acting in his self-interest. This proposition further got modified by contemporary economists as *rational behaviour*. Through the spectrum of varying ideas of welfarism to consequentionalism, Sen derived his idea of *homo socio economicus*. This forms the basis of his welfare economics of development engrained with a moral approach to meta ethical arguments. It is a value-laden approach to guide in the formulation of development programmes.

TAGORE AND AMARTYA SEN

Rabindranath Tagore believed in the traditional perfect symbiosis between man and man and man and nature. For him, as man moved away from nature, he was immersed in consumerism and commercialization. Tagore expressed pity for such men as for him this was not a move towards prosperity, but towards increasing concentration of wealth with a few at the cost of the majority. For development to be sustainable, Tagore advanced instilling self-confidence and initiative among the rural people, to help them fight problems typical to rural areas such as, land fragmentation, inadequate credit, lack of organized marketing and storage and the like. For Sen, issues such as ecology and sustainable development can enter as external variables within the market mechanism framework. He views deprivation in all forms such as food, health, gender rights, and child destitution; in terms of entitlements and capabilities. Tagore's emphasis is on deprivation caused by the evil habits of the sufferer; whereas Sen's emphasis has been on deprivation caused by economic inequality, social injustice and improper governance.

GANDHIAN ECONOMIC THOUGHT AND AMARTYA SEN

Gandhian economic views were seen by many to be utopian with flavours of "pastoral romanticism" as propounded by Rousseau and David Thoreau. This led him to a belief in the intrinsic goodness of all men, including one's opponents. Gandhiji believed in the wealth of a nation being embedded in it's people and labour as the main source of economic value. It was his firm belief in the efficacy of truth and non-violence, as influenced by Tolstoy that backed him during the freedom struggle. Gandhiji placed spirituality as over materiality for the welfare of the society above that of the individual. This was the backbone of *Satyagraha* which suggested self-sacrifice and resistance over pure self-interest. The idea of a traditional village economy was born with the compulsive requirement of self-sufficiency in newly independent India. However, the idea could not match with the growing economy, with greater private capital as compared to the sacrifice of material gains. Thus, in the contemporary conditions with evils in the economy, development an envisioned by Sen, was to accompany freedom to enhance the capabilities of people. Sen believed in creating a favourable national climate for development, in contrast to Gandhiji's belief at the micro-level of the village and the individual. Democracy provides freedom and development as freedom means to take advantage of the freedoms recognized by a government. Gandhiji's concept of economic development was not so much concerned with the raising of living standards as with the spiritual development of man. He was interested in economic development to the extent that it lifted the masses out of poverty. In this sense, his views are similar to Sen's views on "empowerment", as a means to enjoy freedom.

CONTRIBUTION TO ECONOMICS

How does Development Happen?

In consonance with the views of Peter Bauer, Sen believes that too much of emphasis on resource constraints, too less an emphasis on trade and under estimation of the role of institutions in shaping economic bahaviour; that made the policy-makers not design long-term sustainable development strategies. Trade, both domestic and international, contributes to the prosperity of the nation. It also brings about inequality. Thus, trade with shared opportunities and equitable benefits for all results in sustainable development. Similarly, institutions such as micro-credit, facilitate growth of production, distribution and consumption.

Freedom in Economic Theory

Sen asserts on the removal of unfreedom for development. Traditional economics has been bound by measurable economic capacities to remove poverty and to measure growth. Sen drifted away from the conventional approach to the more fundamental requirements of *entitlements, functioning and capabilities* of an individual. *Functionings* refer to the state of existence of a person, which may be from a basic elementary state to a complex one. *Capability* reflects the ability of a person to achieve various combinations of functionings in the form of the *beings* and *doings* he desires, with the *opportunity* or *freedom* to choose and have them. Sen has linked poverty and hunger with inadequate fundamental freedom and human rights. The 'outcome-independent' approach which suggests keeping socio-economic outcomes out of ethical evaluation, thus has been rejected. Sen has suggested the 'consequence-sensitive' approach to bring forth the importance of consequences such as life, death, starvation and nourishment in the exercise of freedom and human rights. Along with the physical and mental well-being of the person, the *agency* aspect, has also been put forward. It relates the goals of a person, as desired by him, to processes and outcomes in individual choice. An individual guaranteed with civil and political rights, with the freedom to express and move, is less vulnerable to economic and social maladies. Sen's research on "Missing Women" in many parts of the world demonstrates the role of social neglect and discrimination in abnormally high mortality rates and low survival rates among females.

The Problem of Choice

Sen has expressed rationality as a relationship between choices and preferences. With regards morality, it requires judgement about preferences which is unlikely in the case of rationality. Ruled by morality, if all behave moral rather than rational (by pursuing self-interests), it would be of common good to all, even if someone may have to sacrifice a little self-interest. Thus, for Sen, it is preferable to define a moral ordering on the basis of ordering of outcomes, rather than the space of outcomes.

Sen has called for widespread public communication in the use of social theory. When there issues of distribution, each individual tries to maximize his own share, regardless of what others get, then majority rule may tend to be inconsistent. But on issues of common national interest, there may be unanimity of opinion, let's say, on the failure a democratic government to provide relief from any natural disaster.

Amartya Sen's Idea of Justice

Amartya Sen highlighted that justice should not only be done, but it should be "seen to be done". This becomes important while assessing the level of development in any country. The market economy exists within many different ownership patterns, resource availabilities, social opportunities, other rules such as patent laws, anti-trust regulations, etc. Accordingly, the market economy itself would generate different prices, terms of trades, income distributions, and thus diverse outcomes. This does impact the prevailing levels of inequality and poverty. Yet, it does not suggest an abandonment of the market economy, but does require changes in the economic and social conditions surrounding the market and to determine what market solutions would emerge. Factors such as public health and education policies, taxation, land reforms, marketing systems, legal protections to various classes, etc. have a lasting influence on outcome of local and global economic relations and the effort to achieve justice and equity. The hallmark for all thoughts leading to banish injustice lies in reasoning, thereby arriving at means of reducing and dispensing justice. Sen has asserted on basing justice not in illusive ideas but on ones which coherent with actuality. He talks of institutions as catalysts of public discussion, he also places public reasoning in the centre of democracy, as being able to recognize the needs of people from various sections, and making their voices heard.

Sen has highlighted the divergent views of justice with the example of three children who fight over a flute. Anna claims that she should get the flute because she knows how to play it, Bob says he should get it because he is poor and has no toys of his own, and Carla says she should get the flute because she made it. This situation would have been dealt with by different theorists in different ways. The economic democratic who is committed to reducing social gaps might feel that Bob should get the flute because he is poor; an advocate of liberty would say that Carla should get the flute because she has made it; while the utilitarian may feel that Anne's pleasure would be greatest because she can play the flute.

According to Sen these divergent views guide principles that should govern allocation of resources in general. They are about creating social arrangements, selecting social institutions and about what social realizations are desired as the outcomes.

Sen has very finely struck a chord between merit and justice. Merit may be recognized under the *incentives* approach as, rewarding actions for the good they do and remunerating such activities that result in social good; or by the *action propriety* approach by the quality of the actions and not by their results. Though it is the incentive approach that tends to receive attention in contemporary economic debates. There is lack of normativism in the theory of merit, as it judges action on the basis of the good and bad as judged by the society. If antipathy to economic inequality is a part of the society's objective function, then the merit for reward has to judge in the light of such inequality. Despite this, due to the presence of the other elements of the objective function, merit-based rewards do generate considerable inequality. The presence of inequality and other drawbacks can lead to some psychological tension, especially since the rewarding of merit is not directly valued under the incentive approach.

Poverty and Famine

As asserted by Sen, poverty should be seen as deprivation of not just income, but also any inability to meet the needs of a basic desired lifestyle, which may be due to any social or environmental constraint. Formally, there could be reasons as; personal heterogeneities, environmental diversities, differences in social climate and different consumption patterns in different societies.

For measuring poverty, Sen has emphasized on the need to examine how much are the poor below the poverty line and how is the deprivation shared and distributed among the poor. The traditional "head count", H gives little indication of the severity of poverty: people may be close to the poverty line or far below. The sum of the shortfall from the poverty line, which may be expressed as the mean percentage shortfall, may be expressed as the poverty deficit, I, again evaluates equally all transfers to people below the poverty line irrespective of the seriousness of their poverty. Sen derived an alternative formulation where which weights each person's poverty gap by the person's rank in the ordering of the poor. This formulation means that a transfer from a person close to the poverty line to a person far below the line has the effect of reducing measured poverty, in a way that depends on the ranks of the people affected. The resulting "Sen Index" takes the form:

$$P = H\{I + (1-I)G\}$$

where G is the Gini coefficient of the income distribution of the poor.

Sen has examined deprivation in famines as being much bigger than absence of real incomes leading to starvation and death. It becomes important to seek information on entitlement to demand food rather than simply focus on food supply. This is due to the fact that famines can occur even without a significant decline in the food production. It may be due to decline in the real incomes of the wage earners due to a decline in the demand for labour or in the products produced by them. Thus, Sen has highlighted the income-sensitive approach to deal with starvation and hunger.

Hunger and Food Policy

Sen has called for understanding hunger and it's causes by understanding the process of acquiring food and consequences of the nutritional deprivation of the people. The basic cause underlying hunger is lack of income that destroys the capability to buy food. The general determinants are the level of employment and prevalent wage rates. A country cannot heavily rely on food imports and thus, food self-sufficiency helps to restore the capability to within the means. The rates of inflation also need to be stabilized to ensure food stability. There exist many distributional disparities which severely restrict the availability of the food even for the minimum nutritional requirements. Socially and economically unempowered women tend to bear high rates of fertility, thereby bringing more mouths to feed on the existing food supplies. Autocratic and military governments create obstacles in food entitlement, with no freedom of expression, movement and the journalist pressure. Too frequent wars limit the state expenditure on food production and distribution as well create a disincentive to expand productive activities. Early age undernourishment has it's adverse consequences throughout the life, not only on the well-being but also on the development of cognitive and mental skills.

To reach the otherwise left out vulnerable groups, a public distribution system directly targeted at such groups, needs to bring into the structure. The focus needs to shift from growth in national income to the freedom enjoyed by the freedom, such as the freedom to live a long and healthy life. The instrumental perspective of the food policy has to be extended from the freedom to earn profits to freedoms of broader kinds, including political freedom in the form of freedom of opposition, freedom of information and journalistic autonomy. The evaluation of the success of the policies needs to go beyond the numeric national income measures to the enhancement of the capabilities and freedom of the people.

Welfare Economics

The utilitarian approach has the elements of *act consequentialism* (evaluating a decision according to the resulting state), *welfarism* (evaluating a decision according to the levels of individual utility as covered under the social welfare function) and *sum ranking* sum of individual utilities). Sen's critique of sum ranking goes as follows:

> "Maximizing the sum of individual utilities is supremely unconcerned with the personal distribution of that sum. This should make it a particularly unsuitable approach to use for measuring or judging inequality". (Sen [1973], page 16).

According to Sen, the utility differences need to be comparable in order to have sum ranking; although the comparability may be partial rather than full. For him, a theory of welfare must be based on more than individual utilities, whether they are interpreted as pleasure, as fulfilment, or as revealed preference. He calls for sufficient information on health, morbidity and longevity. Sen's rejection of welfarism has been in line with the difference principle of Rawls (1971), Marxist theories of exploitation and Nozick's entitlement theory of justice (1974).

An alternative to welfarism has been provided by Sen in the "capabilities" approach. Capability refers to the freedom that a person has in terms of choice of functionings, which refer to what a person can achieve (such as being able to take part in the life of the Community).

Sen has argued that, in the chain

Commodities → Characteristics → Capability → Utility

it is "the third category—that of capability to function—that comes closest to the notion of standard of living" (Sen [III, 1983], p. 160).

The capability approach can be applied to arrive at a definition of poverty on the context of economic development. *Relative* deprivation in terms of income can lead to *absolute* deprivation in terms of capabilities. Thus, rising living standards in the community as a whole may lead to a poverty line that increases in real terms, which may over shadow the absolute deprivation in the space of capabilities. This approach has been of great significance in formulating the *Human Development Index* by the United Nations Development Programme.

CHALLENGES UNANSWERED

In examining the relationship between gender and the theory of social choice, Fabienne Peter, who engages with this field in her article, "Gender and the Foundations of Social Choice" poses two questions: how can insights from social choice theory benefit the study of women's well-being and gender inequality; and how can social choice theory benefit from insights from women's studies and gender studies? Peter suggests that research in social choice theory and related fields should investigate avenues that make social choice and evaluation more responsive to situated agency and thus to issues of participation and inclusion, building on but moving beyond the foundations for this laid by Sen's work.

Martha Nussbaum has been the most notable among feminist scholars who have engaged with, critiqued, and extended Sen's capability approach. She agrees with Sen that the capability approach for examining social justice is superior to utilitarianism, resource-focused analysis, the social contract tradition, or even to some extent of human rights. At the same time, she argues that to make the capability approach more useful for exploring social justice, Sen needs to take a more definite stand on which capabilities are important in our ethical judgments and our conceptions of justice. She also calls for specific lists of freedom, as freedom may have both good or bad dimensions attached to it.

According to Des Gasper and Irene van Staveren, the concept of freedom, as elaborated in Sen's book, *Development as Freedom*, has been overextended, in that all the capabilities that human beings could acquire are to be understood as freedom. They argue that freedom needs to be seen as one value among a number of other significant values, such as justice, respect, friendship and care. They stress the need for an alternative language to the language of freedom—one that also incorporates the importance of other values.

Sen has used normative evaluation in his capability approach as a critique to the informational bases. Despite finding considerable support for his treatment of substantive equality, many thinkers and practitioners have criticised Sen for his failure to be specific on which capabilities matter, which ones more than others, and why.

An idea of democracy that embodies individual participation in matters of social choice and public decision-making plays an integral role in Sen's capability approach. Sen places a central place to political freedom, so that one can freely participate in the decisions, values and standards of justice as set by the society. But there is little guidance as regards how to achieve political freedom. Deneulin argues that Sen takes a consequentialist approach, offering little criteria for decision-making sure that they are 'democratic' and help to expand valued individual freedoms (Deneulin, 2003:18). Sen's concept of democracy seems an idealistic one where political power, political economy and struggle are absent (Stewart and Deneulin, 2001:63-4). More needs to have been spoken about the preconditions to have democracy and the normative minima for democratic outcomes to be just. Sen's deep consideration for equality (Sen, 1999: Ch. 3), and his convincing arguments for the interdependence of capabilities (Sen, 1999: Chs. 1&2), necessitate that a full elaboration of what constitutes political capability.

References

Agarwal, B., Jane, H. and Ingrid, R., *"Exploring the Challenges of Amartya Sen's Work and Ideas: An Introduction"*, *Feminist Economics*, 9 (2-3), 2003, 3-12

Alkire, S. (2008), *Amartya Sen*, Draft Entry for the Elgar Handbook of Economics and Ethics, October 2008.

Amy Berg, *Gandhi and Sen: Visions of Leadership for India,* Kravis Leadership Institute, Leadership Review, Volume 7, Winter 2007, pp. 14-18.

Atkinson, A.B. (1999), *The Contribution of Amartya Sen to Welfare Economics,* Scandinavian Journal of Economics, Vol. 101(2), 173-90.

Basu, R.L. (2009), *Viewpoint : The Eco-Ethical Views of Tagore and Amartya Sen,* Culture Mandala: Bulletin of the Centre for East-West Cultural and Economic Studies, Vol. 8, Issue 2, December 2009, pp. 56-61

Jensen, H.E. (2001), *Amartya Sen as a Smithesquely World Philosopher: Or Who Needs Sen When We Have Smith,* The University of Tennessee, U.S.A.

Korner, S. (2002), *Amartya Sen: Choice, Orderings and Morality,* ed. Practical Reason. Basil Blackwell, Oxford, 1974, pp. 54-67.

Lal, V. (2006), *Sen, Argumentative Indians and Bengali Modernity, Economic and Political Weekly,* December 23, 2006.

Nachane, D.M. (2008), *Gandhian Economic Thought and Its Influence on Economic Policy-making in India,* Indira Gandhi Institute of Development Research, Mumbai, India.

Nozick, R. (1974), *Anarchy, State and Utopia,* Basil Blackwell, Oxford.

Rawls, J. (1971), *A Theory of Justice,* Clarendon Press, Oxford.

Sen, A.K. (1973), *On Economic Inequality,* Oxford Univ. Press, London.

———, (1980), *Equality of What?* in S.M. McMurrin (ed.) *Tanner Lectures on Human Values* (Salt Lake City: University of Utah Press).

———, (1982), *Choice, Welfare, and Measurement* (Oxford: Basil Blackwell).

———, (1987), *Food and freedom,* Sir John Crawford Memorial Lecture, Washington, D.C., October 29, 1987.

———, (1992), *Inequality Re-examined* (Oxford: Clarendon Press).

———, (1993), "Capability and Well-Being," in *The Quality of Life,* ed. M. Nussbaum and A. Sen (Oxford: Clarendon Press), 30-53.

———, (1997), *Hunger in The Contemporary World,* Discussion Paper, The Suntory and Toyota International Centres for Economics and Related Disciplines, London School of Economics and Political Science.

———, (1998), *The Possibility of Social Choice,* Nobel Lecture (December 8, 1998), Trinity College, Cambridge.

———, (1999), *Development as Freedom* (New York: Anchor Books).

———, (1999a), "Democracy as a Universal Value", *Journal of Democracy,* Vol. 10, n. 3, 3-17.

———, (2005), *How does Development Happen?,* Cato Journal, Vol. 25, No. 3 (Fall 2005).

Srinivasan, S., *No Democracy without Justice: Amartya Sen's unfinished Business with the Capability Approach,* Queen Elizabeth House, University of Oxford.

Stewart, F. and S. Deneulin (2002), "Amartya Sen's Contribution to Development Thinking".

Studies in Comparative International Development, Vol. 37, n. 2, 61-70.

Vizard, P. (2005), *The Contributions of Professor Amartya Sen in the Field of Human Rights*, Centre for Analysis of Social Exclusion, paper 91, London School of Economics.

Wallace, Laura (2004), *People in Economics : Amartya Sen*, Finance and Development, September 2004.

CHAPTER

3

Economics of Amartya Sen

E.J. Helge

INTRODUCTION

The Capability Approach, developed and pioneered by the economist Amartya Sen, provides a conceptual framework for analysing well-being and a strong critique of existing traditions in welfare economics. The central tenet of the approach is that the appropriate space in which to conceptualise and measure well-being is not in terms of primary goods or in utilities but rather in terms of a persons capabilities; that is, in the real freedoms that they have reason to value. While the development and initial application of the approach occurred in the fields of welfare economics and development, it is growing in popularity with academics from a wide range of disciplines. However, is the approach useful to those of us who are interested in social policy issues, and in particular to those interested in the conceptualisation and measurement of poverty, social exclusion and related issues? How great a departure does it entail from existing social policy traditions?

Furthermore, do well-known problems with operationalisation render it of limited use for applied policy analysis?

This paper comprises four sections. The first will present an outline of the capability approach and its central concepts. The second will compare the approach to three existing traditions of social policy analysis (i) the income poverty tradition, (ii) deprivation indicators tradition, and (iii) the social exclusion approach. Third, the paper will consider the most contentious of the concepts within the CA itself—that of capability—and suggest a potential operationalisation that is both feasible and adequate for the requirements of social policy research. Finally, the paper will consider the conceptual ground covered by the capability approach and will briefly consider how this can be reconciled within social policy analysis.

SECTION 1

THE CAPABILITY APPROACH

The primary concepts of the capability approach are functionings and capabilities. Sen's concept of functioning refers to the various things a person may succeed in doing or being that is, a person's achievements in terms of objective well-being, while capabilities refer a person's real or substantive freedom to achieve such functionings.

Thus, functionings can be viewed as the various outcomes a person may achieve, while capabilities refer to the real, as opposed to formal, opportunities to achieve these outcomes. The various capabilities a person may possess are components of their overall capability, which is conceived as a set which reflects the alternative combinations of functionings the person can achieve, and from which he or she can choose one collection. Thus, while rarely drawn as a clear distinction in the literature, a person may be seen as possessing a range of capabilities which, combined, comprise their overall capability. The distinction between functionings and capability is thus between achievements on the one hand, and freedoms or valuable options from which one can choose on the other and Sen views the process of development as a process of expanding the real freedoms that people enjoy. Despite the rather abstruse terminology, there is a clear link to a wider literature on outcomes and opportunities. For this reason, and to make this link salient, I will on occasion include outcomes and real opportunities in parentheses when discussing functionings and capabilities respectively.

In order to highlight the distinction that Sen makes between the capability approach and alternative approaches to well-being, it may be useful to draw further on the concepts of commodities and the characteristics. Any commodity is viewed a possess in a range of characteristics. For example, food may offer the characteristic of nutrients; a car the characteristic of transport. Thus, recurring amounts of these commodities gives the person command over the corresponding characteristics that the goods provide. However, even if we know the commodities possessed by individuals, this does not tell us what individuals are able to do with these commodities; that is, the functionings that they are able to achieve because the rate at which individuals are able to convert these characteristics into functionings will vary due to differences in individual, social and environmental factors. For example, a fixed amount of food will provide different levels of functioning to a child compared to an adult. Furthermore, the functionings themselves may also result in utility, such as the enjoyment that a person may derive from cycling a bike. Given that our interest in commodities is of instrumental importance in comparison with the intrinsically important nature of functionings, it may be argued that to focus on commodities rather than on what they can allow us to do or be is succumb to commodity fetishism while utility is deemed to be an inadequate measure due to its adaptive nature and limited relationship to objective well-being. Thus in the chain from commodities—characteristics—functioning—utility, Sen argues that ethical evaluation should be concerned with a person's capabilities and functionings, which with the latter considered to be constitutive components of their well-being.

In conceptualizing capability as a set of the alternative combinations of functioning a person a person is able to achieve, Sen's concept is analogous to an opportunity set in the field of social choice theory. The vectors themselves contain only valuable functionings and the ability to exercise some choice is itself considered to have value. Thus, seen in this light, the value of a set can be reduced when the number of elements is reduced. Thus, functionings can be viewed as the various outcomes a person may achieve, while capabilities refer to the real, as opposed to formal, opportunities to achieve these outcomes. The various capabilities a person may possess are components of their overall capability, which is conceived as a set which reflects the alternative combinations of functionings the person can achieve, and from which he or she can choose one collection. Thus, while rarely drawn as a clear distinction in the literature, a person may be seen as possessing a range of capabilities which, combined, comprise their overall capability. The distinction between functionings and capability is thus between achievements on the one hand, and freedoms or valuable options from which one can choose on the other and Sen views the process of development as a process of expanding the real freedoms that people enjoy despite the rather abstruse terminology, there is a clear link to a wider literature on outcomes and opportunities. For this reason, and to make this link salient, I will on occasion include outcomes and real opportunities in parentheses when discussing functionings and capabilities respectively.

In order to highlight the distinction that Sen makes between the capability approach and alternative approaches to well-being, it may be useful to draw further on the concepts of commodities and the characteristics. Any commodity is viewed a possessing a range of characteristics. For example, food may offer the characteristic of nutrients; a car the characteristic of transport. Thus, [S]ecuring amounts of these commodities gives the person command over the corresponding characteristics that the goods provide. However, even if we know the commodities possessed by individuals, this does not tell us what individuals are able to do with these commodities; that is, the functionings that they are able to achieve because the rate at which individuals are able to convert these characteristics into functionings will vary due to differences in individual, social and environmental factors. For example, a fixed amount of food (nutrients) will provide different levels of functioning to a child compared to an adult. Furthermore, the functionings themselves may also result in utility, such as the enjoyment that a person may derive from cycling a bike. Given that our interest in commodities is of instrumental importance in comparison with the intrinsically important nature of functionings, it may be argued that to focus on commodities rather than on what they can allow us to do or be is succumb to commodity fetishism while utility is deemed to be an inadequate measure due to its adaptive nature and limited relationship to objective well-being. Thus in the chain from commodities—characteristics—functioning—utility, Sen argues that ethical evaluation should be concerned with a person's capabilities and functionings, which with the latter considered to be constitutive components of their well-being.

In conceptualizing capability as a set of the alternative combinations of functioning a person, a person is able to achieve, Sen's concept is analogous to an opportunity set in the field of social choice theory. The vectors themselves contain only valuable functionings and the ability to exercise some choice is itself considered to have value. Thus, seen in this light, the value of a set can be reduced when the number of elements is reduced

SECTION 2

RELATIONSHIP TO SOCIAL POLICY TRADITIONS

Despite the use of new terminology, we may legitimately question the extent to which the approach differs from some existing traditions in Social Policy. This section will attempt to briefly highlight some differences between three traditions of social policy analysis: the income poverty approach, relative deprivation/deprivation indicators approach, and the social exclusion approach.

Furthermore, while there may be advantages in an income measure, including its relative simplicity and summary nature, such a measure is inherently unidimensional and cannot recognise the plural nature of well-being. Indeed, such a measure may be particularly poor at highlighting situations where some dimensions of deprivation intensify despite rising income or where little relationship is found between income and a particular dimension.

While traditional relative poverty lines are genuinely relative and may provide information about a chosen standard over time, they have been criticised on the grounds that they do not relate to any concept of individual need, but remain popular largely due to their simplicity which may facilitate public discussion about the issues of inequality and poverty in the public domain more easily than more complex measures. The most common income poverty measure used in the social policy field is undoubtedly the head-count ratio, *H*, and Sen has been particularly critical of this measure, which he described as being obviously a very crude index and has criticised for being completely insensitive to the distribution of income among the poor. Indeed, there are many other widely appreciated problematic features of the head-count measure including that while it measures poverty elimination, it fails to register poverty alleviation in any way, and thus creates incentive effects for government to focus resources on the poor who are least in need, though the simultaneous use of a number of poverty lines may provide greater understanding of the income distribution than relying on one poverty line in isolation.

The second advantage of conceiving of capability as a set is that it allows us to understand the trade-offs that occur achieving certain functionings. For example, this may allow us to understand the extent to which functioning in one area cannot be achieved at the same time as others and that these choices are made explicit. However, this presents a rather counter-intuitive situation—both options of paid employment and caring may be in a person's capability set, despite being mutually exclusive options. Thus, while the conceiving of capability in terms of a set makes such trade-offs explicit, we require more information than simply observing that an outcome is included in a capability set before we can judge the extent to which it is truly feasible.

This shift from functioning to capability is often discussed as if it is one movement. However, I argue that this is best seen as consisting of two. The first shifts from functionings to capabilities; that is, from individual outcomes to individual opportunities. In order to exclude situations where particular outcomes occur as a result of choice, we look not at whether a person has achieved a particular outcome but rather at whether they had the real freedom to do so. The second shift is from individual capabilities to a persons overall capability, or from individual opportunities to a persons aggregate opportunity. Thus, it is argued by the author that one can accept that capability represents the real freedom of a person to do or be something that they have reason to value without necessarily developing the concept as analogous to an opportunity set. It may be useful to consider from a poverty perspective whether either or both of the aforementioned shifts are justified, with some consideration given to the burden of measurement that they imply.

The second consideration is the extent to which understanding trade-offs amongst important variables is deemed to occur. An example of this might be where a parent may choose to limit

SECTION 4

THE POVERTY CONCEPT AND THE CAPABILITY APPROACH

By now it should be obvious that suggested method of measuring capabilities has a clear similarity with the existing direct measurement of poverty and use of deprivation indicators. However, it is also a broader notion both in terms of the object of interest and the conditions of interest. There will undoubtedly be questions about whether this is really poverty at all, and it is an answer to this question that I begin to sketch an answer to here.

In *Poverty and the United Kingdom,* Townsend's deprivation indictators, as I understand them, were intended to examine the full range of conditions of living that were customary, or are at least widely encouraged or approved, in the societies in which they belong. Indeed, this breadth was stressed by Townsend himself—in discussing the use of deprivation indicators to measure poverty, he noted that [i]n principle, such a list might be developed, as I have suggested, from an exhaustive analysis of the amenities available to, and the customs or modes of living of, a majority of the population.

While such an exhaustive list may always prove elusive, he notes that in terms of his own survey, we sought only to ensure that all the major areas of personal, household and social life were represented in out questionnaire. The breadth of the sixty indicators measured is indeed impressive: six items of dietary deprivation, four of clothing, four relating to fuel and light, nine relating to household facilities, four to household conditions and amenities, twelve to conditions at work, five to health, one to education, five were environmental, four related to the family, two to recreational activities and four to social activities.

We are not told a great deal about the process of reducing these sixty into a more manageable index of twelve items other than it sought to focus on those indicators which apply to the whole population However, this process is of some interest, because the resulting index is in no way representative of the original breadth: four items of dietary deprivation, two each relating to the family, recreation and social deprivation, one item of household facilities and one of housing conditions. Not a single item from the categories of conditions at work, health, education, environmental deprivation, fuel and light and clothing are included in the summary deprivation index.

My intention with the aforementioned discussion is not to criticise the selection but rather to demonstrate that poverty, and the original direct measurement of poverty in particular, did begin from a broad notion of that concept and situate it within wider considerations of well-being and need.

Furthermore, in terms of the conditions in which we are interested in deprivation, Piachaud's influential critique of Townsend led to a shift in the terms in which we understand deprivation, following his observation that doing without some of the items of the deprivation index might be as much to do with tastes as with poverty. Indeed, in attempting to draw a distinction between deprivation by choice and by constraint, he was making a similar distinction between the functioning and capability concepts provided by Sen. However, the result of Piachaud's critique was not just to remove preferences by focussing where this occurred due to constraint, but rather to focus on one constraint in particular: that of a lack of resources. While this makes sense in terms of the importance of resources for the concept of poverty, for activities at least—it created a false dichotomy between those who did not engage in certain activities because they could not afford them and those who did not engage in said activities because they did not want to. The other potential reasons for non-participation that we have noted were subsequently overlooked. Nonetheless, the dichotomy was seen to fulfil its purpose in terms of the definition of poverty adopted. In terms of social exclusion, where additional constraints beyond a lack of resources might be considered, this was at times recognised.

Indeed, the results of Poverty and Social Exclusion survey itself demonstrated these exclusions. Eighteen (18) percent of respondents reported lack of time due to childcare responsibilities as preventing them from common social activities. Similarly, fourteen (14) percent were prevented by being too old, ill sick or disabled, six (6) percent by having no-one to go out with and five (5) percent due to having no vehicle or because of poor public transport.

Furthermore, I would suggest that we should not limit our understanding of socially perceived necessities to deprivations that are particularly amenable to changes in income. These may be of particular interest to the poverty concept itself, but may also have the effect of limiting our understanding of need and wider deprivations.

THE ADDITIONAL CONCEPTUAL SPACE

Clearly, then, a capability approach to poverty analysis requires some additional conceptual space not provided for by the poverty concept, traditionally defined. It might be asked whether the capability approach measures something altogether broader in nature then poverty, *per se*, and we may thus question whether it has anything to offer poverty analysis. I do not disagree that the capability approach does indeed take a broader focus than much existing poverty analysis. However, I do not believe that this requires us to jettison our existing concepts in favour of some radically new concept of poverty.

In some ways, this distinction relates to the origin and purpose of the respective approaches. The initial exposition of the capability approach was in response to the equality of what? debate, where the central question was which informational space we should be focussing on in our moral analysis and our considerations of equality. Such a focus on an informational space perhaps renders it more suitable to questions of terrain rather than understanding one concept (what is poverty?). Sen's conceptual writings are used to develop a conception of well-being or at least a conception of well-being that would be suitable for social policy analysis—and the moral terrain or space under consideration is deduced from this.

There may be a subsequent step which includes diving the conceptual territory of analysis up between the relevant concepts—as Sen himself suggests when discussed the potential of viewing the social exclusion approach as a subset of the capability approach.

Conversely, the approach that poverty analysis has taken has often been rather different. This has been something of a search for the meaning of that concept and then attempt to operationalise and quantify whatever definition we agree on. In this approach, an initial decision is made that poverty is an important social problem worthy of analysis in order to understand its causes and to make recommendations for policies to eliminate same. The approach is largely an investigation of what poverty is and the concept is redefined as knowledge in the field accumulates. My contention is not that such developments are illegitimate, but rather that our analysis need not necessarily follow the boundaries of one concept in any uniform way. Thus, the two approaches that I have sketched here are in no way conflicting and can, indeed, be reconciled. The question of how this might occur is beyond the scope of this paper, but is, I believe, and important area for further work.

CONCLUSION

It is argued that there are possibilities for a capability approach to poverty analysis within the field of social policy. These are in identifying a terrain of analysis? and in linking the concept of poverty to wider notions of social need and well-being. A capability approach to poverty analysis need not be seen as an attempt to tear up existing concepts or to deny the importance of poverty, but rather as an attempt to locate existing concepts within a broader framework of moral analysis within social policy.

References

Sen, A. (1976). "Poverty: An Ordinal Approach to Measurement", *Econometrica*.

Sen, A. (1983). "Poor, Relatively Speaking". Oxford Economic Papers.

Sen, A. (1987). Commodities and Capabilities. New Delhi, Oxford University Press.

Sen, A. (1992). Inequality Reexamined. Cambridge, Massachusetts, Harvard University Press.

Sen, A. (1993). Capability and well-being. The Quality of Life. M.C. Nussbaum and A. Sen. Oxford, Oxford University Press.

Sen, A. (1999). Development as Freedom. Oxford, Oxford University Press.

Sen, A. (2000). Social Exclusion: Concept, Application and Scrutiny. *Social Development*.

CHAPTER

4

Economic Philosophy of Professor Amartya Sen

B.R. Sangle and S.K. Dhage

INTRODUCTION

When Amartya Sen received the Nobel Prize in 1998, the *Wall Street Journal* went ballistic, saying that Sen "was remarkable only for the extent to which his renown outstripped the quality of his work" and that "he has done little but give voice to the muddleheaded views of the establishment leftists who dominate his world".

This paper analyses the work of the Nobel Prize winning economist Professor Amartya Sen from the perspective of Welfare Economics. It assesses the ways in which Sen's research agenda has deepened and expanded Welfare Economics discourse in the disciplines of ethics and economics, and examines how his work has promoted cross-fertilization and integration on this subject across traditional disciplinary divides. The paper suggests that Sen's development of a 'scholarly bridge' between Welfare and economics is an important and innovative contribution that has methodological as well as substantive importance and that provides a prototype and stimuli for future research. It also establishes that the idea of fundamental freedoms and human rights is itself an important gateway into understanding the nature, scope and significance of Sen's research. The paper concludes with a brief assessment of the challenges to be addressed in taking Sen's contributions in the field of ethics forward. Following are some major areas which covered by Professor Amartya Sen's research.

HUNGER IN INDIA

According to Amartya Sen some positive things have certainly occurred. First, pre-independence India had a stagnating agriculture, and this has been firmly replaced by an imposing expansion of the production possibilities in Indian agriculture, through innovative departures. The technological limits have been widely expanded. What holds up Indian food consumption today is not any operational inability to produce more food, but a far reaching failure to make the poor of the country able to afford enough food.

Second, substantial famines that so plagued India until independence has been effectively eliminated. the last sizeable famine occurred in 1943 four years before independence. And yet this creditable record in famine prevention has not been matched by a similar success in eliminating the pervasive presence of endemic hunger that blights the lives of hundreds of millions of people in this country.

Indeed, India has not, it should be absolutely, clear, done well in tackling the pervasive presence of persistent hunger. Not only are there persistent recurrences of severe hunger and starvation in particular regions, but there is also a gigantic prevalence of endemic hunger across much of India. Indeed, India does much worse in this respect than even sub-Saharan Africa. Estimates of general undernourishment what is sometimes called "protein-energy malnutrition" are nearly twice as high in India as in sub-Saharan Africa. It is astonishing that despite the intermittent occurrence of famine in Africa, it too manages to ensure a much higher level of regular nourishment than does India. About half of all Indian children are, it appears, chronically undernourished, and more than half of all adult women suffer from anemia. In maternal undernourishment as well as the incidence of underweight babies, and also in the frequency of cardiovascular diseases in later life, India's record is among the very worst in the world. People have to go hungry if they do not have the means to buy enough food. Hunger is primarily a problem of general poverty, and thus overall economic growth and its distributional pattern cannot but be important in solving the hunger problem. It is particularly critical to pay attention to employment opportunities, other ways of acquiring economic means, and also food prices, which influence people's ability to buy food, and thus affect the food entitlements they effectively enjoy. It is also crucial to use the means of specialized delivery of food that particularly helps poor children, such as more extensive use of feeding in the school. This can not only increase the incentive of children to go to school, but also actually make them healthier and less undernourished. The Supreme Court has been judicious in emphasizing the importance of this right.

Further, since undernourishment is not only a cause of ill-health, but can also result from it, attention has to be paid to health care, in general, and to the prevention of endemic diseases that prevent absorption of nutrients, in particular. There is also plenty of evidence to indicate that lack of basic education too contributes to undernourishment, partly because knowledge and communication are important, but also because the ability to secure jobs and incomes are influenced by the level of education. Indeed, low incomes, relatively higher prices, bad health care and neglect of basic education are all influential in causing and sustaining the extraordinary levels of under nutrition in India.

THE CHALLENGE OF THE CAPABILITY APPROACH

Development as Freedom's basic proposition is that we should evaluate development in terms of "the expansion of the 'capabilities' of people to lead the kind of lives they value—and have reason to value" which is Sen's definition of freedom. Unlike increases in income, the expansion of people's "capabilities" depends both on the elimination of oppression and on the provision of facilities like basic education, health care, and social safety nets. Basic education, health care, and women's rights are themselves constitutive of development. Growth in real output per head is also likely to expand people's capabilities, especially at lower levels of income, but it cannot be considered, in itself, the ultimate yardstick of development or well-being. The contribution of the "capabilities approach" lies not only in its role in broadening the core definition of economic development, but also in its effective utilization of Sen's lifelong efforts to theorize the possibility and necessity of "social choice." Discouraged from focusing on social choice by Kenneth Arrow's brilliant analysis demonstrating the impossibility of consistent social choice results under what seemed like a quite reasonable set of conditions, economists have been understandably leery of emphasizing the importance of political debate and discussion in setting the goals of development.

Sen has attacked this reluctance with impressive effectiveness. First, he has used his skills at formal analysis to argue convincingly that increasing the amount of information taken into consideration in making a decision, for example, allowing even relatively crude interpersonal comparisons of individual utilities, returns social choice to the realm of possibility. Having shown that social choice is possible, he then goes on to suggest that it is necessary. There are two sub-parts to this argument. First, he argues that real incomes are an analytically inadequate metric for making welfare comparisons, and that the utilitarian efforts to reduce well-being (and therefore the goals of development) to "one homogeneous good thing" are equally inadequate. He goes on to argue that "there is thus a strong methodological case for emphasizing the need to assign explicitly evaluative weights to different components of quality of life (or of well-being) and then to place the chosen weights for open public discussion and critical scrutiny". Therefore, "we cannot in general take preferences as given independently of public discussion", and "a proper understanding of what economic needs are their content and their force requires discussion and exchange".

The upshot of Sen's argument is also two-fold. First, development as the expansion of citizens' capabilities implies a quite different set of allocation decisions and growth strategies than the traditional real-income framework. Second, it implies that choices about those allocations and growth strategies must be "democratic", not just in the "thin" sense of having leadership succession determined by a regular electoral process, but in the "thick" sense of messy and continuous involvement of the citizenry in the setting of economic priorities. And, this democratic imperative does not flow from the fact that "democracy is *also* a good thing." It flows from the fact that it is not possible to evaluate economic outputs without such full-fledged discussion and exchange.

COLLECTIVE CAPABILITIES

As in the case of Sen's other bases for freedom, the opportunity to join peers in collective action is valuable because of its "intrinsic importance" as well as its "instrumental effectiveness . . . to promote freedoms of other kinds". Some of the greatest intrinsic satisfactions in life arguably come from social interaction with others who share our interests and values friends, families, communities, and other groups. These sorts of interactions are not just sources of "utility," they are also central to the development of our identities, values, and goals. They are fundamental in our efforts to figure out what we "have reason to value". At the same time, opportunities for collective action are clearly of instrumental value in securing the other kinds of freedoms that Sen enumerates from transparency to social opportunities to protective security.

Of course, these other freedoms, in turn, enhance possibilities for collective action, but widespread opportunities for collective action cannot be taken for granted even when other freedoms are present Democratic elections and civil rights may be prerequisites for politically potent associational life. Naturally occurring forms of associational life as in families and neighborhoods may provide a basis for the construction of more purposive organizations. Nonetheless, families and neighborhoods, elections and civil rights even in societies where basic literacy is widespread are unlikely to be sufficient in them. Dense, diverse, organized collective action is necessary to exploit the opportunities created by elections and civil rights, and complement the dispersed efforts of groups and individuals. Public policy that explicitly acknowledges the importance of collective action, public mores that are open to contestation and collective struggles, and focused efforts to stimulate and sustain organizations that transcend primordial and parochial interests are all necessary components in the quest for development as freedom.

DEVELOPMENT AS FREEDOM

Amartya Sen (1999) has argued for an even broader concept of development focusing on the concept of freedom. He sees development as an integrated process of expansion of substantive freedoms. Economic growth, technological advance and political change are all to be judged in the light of their contributions to the expansion of human freedoms. Among the most important of these freedoms are freedom from famine and malnutrition, freedom from poverty, access to health care and freedom from premature mortality. In a telling empirical example, Sen shows that urban African Americans have lower life expectancies than the average Chinese persons or inhabitants of the Indian state of Kerala, in spite of much higher average per capita incomes in the USA.

According to Sen, freedoms are both ends and means. Thus, markets can be an engine for economic growth (means), but—what is sometimes forgotten—they constitute important freedoms in themselves, namely, freedoms to exchange or transact. One important area where freedoms have frequently been restricted is the labour market, where slavery, serfdom or other institutional arrangements can restrict the free movement of labour. Political freedoms can contribute to economic dynamism, but are also goals in themselves. Sen argues somewhat optimistically that all freedoms are strongly interconnected and reinforce each other. He also tends to underemphasize clashes between freedoms of different groups of people and the value choices that still need to be made. There is no objective definition of development and there may be basic differences of opinion about the goals of development, even including that of the very goal of freedom, which may not be the ultimate goal from a variety of religious perspectives. Nevertheless, his use of the concept of freedom as a normative yardstick for development is insightful. In his perspective economic growth remains important, but not as a goal in itself. It is important in its potential contribution to a wide range of freedoms. It is not enough in itself. Sometimes changes in other spheres such as education and health can be at least as important in the expansion of freedoms.

According to Amartya Sen there are five distinct types of freedom, seen in an "instrumental" perspective, are particularly investigated in the empirical studies that follow. These include (1) *political freedoms,* (2) *economic facilities,* (3) *social opportunities,* (4) *transparency guarantees,* and (5) *protective security.* Each of these distinct types of rights and opportunities helps to advance the general capability of a person. They may also serve to complement each other. Public policy to foster human capabilities and substantive freedoms in general can work through the promotion of these distinct but interrelated instrumental freedoms. In the chapters that follow, each of these different types of freedom—and the institutions involved—will be explored, and their interconnections discussed. There will be an opportunity also to investigate their respective roles in the promotion of overall freedoms of people to lead the kind of lives they have reason to value. In the view of "development as freedom," the instrumental freedoms link with each other and with the ends of enhancement of human freedom in general.

While development analysis must, on the one hand, be concerned with objectives and aims that make these instrumental freedoms consequentially important, it must also take note of the empirical linkages that tie the distinct types of freedom together, strengthening their joint importance. Indeed, these connections are central to a fuller understanding of the instrumental role of freedom.

In other words, the requirements for development can be described as an individual's ability to participate freely in the political process, the mechanisms and capacity to seek economic well-being, the networks and connections which make social integration possible, free access to reliable information sources, and structures which allow personal safety. Sen puts it as enhancement of human freedom is both the main object and the primary means of development. The objective of development relates to the valuation of the actual freedoms enjoyed by the people involved. Individual capabilities crucially depend on, among other things, economic, social, and political arrangements. In making appropriate institutional arrangements, the instrumental roles of distinct types of freedom have to be considered, going well beyond the foundational importance of the overall freedom of individuals.

The instrumental roles of freedom include several distinct but interrelated components, such as economic facilities, political freedoms, social opportunities, transparency guarantees and protective security. These instrumental rights, opportunities and entitlements have strong interred linkages, which can go in different directions. The process of development is crucially influenced by these interconnections. Corresponding to multiple interconnected freedoms, there is a need to develop and support a plurality of institutions, including democratic systems, legal mechanisms, market structures, educational and health provisions, media and other communication facilities and so on. The institutions can incorporate private initiatives as well as public arrangements and also more mixed structures, such as non-governmental organizations and cooperative entities. The ends and means of development call for placing the perspective of freedom at the center of the stage. The people have to be seen, in this perspective, as being actively involved given the opportunity—in shaping their own destiny, and not just as passive recipients of the fruits of cunning development programs. The state and the society have extensive roles in strengthening and safeguarding human capabilities. This is a supporting role, rather than one of ready-made delivery. The freedom-centered perspective on the ends and the means of development has some claim to our attention.

ETHICS AND ECONOMICS

Professor Amartya Sen has moved into philosophy, in particular ethics and political philosophy, as a discipline in its own right, with its own demands, with its own tradition, with its own stock of increasingly sophisticated arguments and counter-arguments. By moving into philosophy in this way, Professor Sen has rendered, and continues to render, both disciplines a very precious service. For he is one of the very few people who are able to convey to economists, in a language they find congenial, those philosophical insights they would be naive to ignore in discussing even the most concrete policy questions. He is also one of the very few people who are able to explain to philosophers, in a language they can understand, those elements of economic culture which they would be foolish to neglect even at the level of abstraction they enjoy keeping to. But being immersed in both cultures does not only make for an ideal communicator. It also provides an ideal position from which to contribute in a creative way to some of the most central questions of normative political theory.

When evaluating the performance of an economy or a society, there are two metrics which are standard used: the metric of goods or commodities, and the metric of welfare or utility. One uses the goods metric, for example, when discussing performance in terms of aggregate real income and its distribution, but also in terms of John Rawls' primary goods. One uses the welfare metric, for example, when discussing performance in terms of Pareto-optimality or in a classical utilitarian framework.

The goods metric is fundamentally inadequate because it fails to take into account people's very unequal abilities to turn goods into what he calls functioning. The welfare metric handles this particular problem far better, but it is nonetheless fundamentally inadequate for different reasons. It amounts, among other things, to penalizing the poorest for adapting their ambitions to their fates. To quote from Professor Sen's most recent book: "The hopeless beggar, the precarious landless labourer, the dominated housewife, the hardened unemployed, or the over-exhausted coolies may all take pleasures in small mercies, and manage to suppress intense suffering for the necessity of continuing survival, but it would be ethically deeply mistaken to attach a correspondingly small value to the loss of their well-being because of this survival strategy."

A logically coherent, ethically defensible theory of distributive justice requires that one should reject both the goods metric and the welfare metric. This question central to both normative economics as it has developed in the wake of the theory of social choice, and to political philosophy in the liberal tradition—has been the topic of much of Amartya Sen's recent work. Those who have heard him this afternoon will know the own answer is one which gives an irreducible role to achievements and freedoms, to functioning and capabilities. Whether right or wrong, this answer has stimulated and continues to stimulate many fruitful discussions by economists and philosophers alike.

CONCLUSION

Amartya Sen argues that development and freedom are intimately related. By freedom he means well-being in five categories: political participation, economic well-being, social integration, information access and personal security. This paper is an attempt to give confirmation of Sen's views by showing that people who are well-off are more likely to support democracy than those who are poor. While being generally appreciative of Sen's theory of capabilities, the point of this article has been to raise some conceptual difficulties that arise in addressing entrenched conditions of power and domination from the capability paradigm. The enhancement of people's capability prospects with regard to education, employment, decent living standards and political participation can empower them to challenge and to counteract various dominating conditions in society. It can also bestow a sense of self-confidence in people to stand up to discrimination that may arise from deep-rooted social practices and customs. Yet, the objectives of the capability theory would remain less secure as long as citizens' capability prospects are dependent and subjected to arbitrary power and domination. As we have suggested here, Sen's theory of capabilities can learn from and be enriched by republicanism particularly by seeking to reinforce certain basic capabilities through commonly recognizable institutional measures and by envisioning individual freedom and capabilities as part of the patrimony and common good of the political community as a whole.

References

Cameron, J., and Gasper, D. (eds.) (2000), "Amartya Sen on Inequality, Human Well-being, and Development as Freedom". *Journal of International Development,* 12(7).

Fine, Ben (2001). "Amartya Sen: A Partial and Personal Appreciation." Centre for Development Policy Research, School of Oriental and African Studies, University of London, Discussion Paper, No. 1601.

Pollock, Robert L. (1998), "The Wrong Economist Won." *Wall Street Journal,* 15 October (Editorial).

Sen, A.K. (1995), "Rationality and Social Choice." *American Economic Review,* 85(1): pp. 1-24.

———, (1999a), *Development as Freedom.* Oxford: Oxford University Press.

CHAPTER

5

Amartya Sen's Contributions to Welfarism, Utilitarianism, Poverty and Industrialisation in Welfare Economics

LEELA BHASKAR AND SUPREENA NARAYANAN

AMARTYA SEN AND WELFARE ECONOMICS AND WELFARISM

Amartya Sen was awarded the Nobel Prize "for his contributions to welfare economics". Sen, and the Nobel Committee, interpret "welfare economics" broadly, but we begin with the narrower definition current forty years ago. The fact that we now view the subject differently is, to no little extent, a tribute to the influence of his writing. That we need to go beyond welfarism may now seem obvious, but it has not always been so.

In the 1950s, the utilitarian approach was still represented in economics, as demonstrated by its powerful use by James Meade in his Trade and Welfare (1955), but Lionel Robbins', An Essay on the Nature and Significance of Economic Science (1932), and the subsequent New Welfare Economics, had led to a state where, as Sen himself described it, "nihilism has been the dominant note in a number of studies on welfare economics bearing, as Baumol (1965) puts it, 'an ill-concealed resemblance to obituary notices'".

"Nihilism" is, as already noted, alien to Sen's nature, and his approach to welfare economics has been to seek positive steps forward from traditional utilitarianism. This was the trademark of his Collective Choice and Welfare [1970], which has dominated the field, and of his subsequent books, including On Economic Inequality [1973] and Inequality Reexamined [1992]. His aim has been to provide both a critique and an alternative.

AMARTYA SEN AND UTILITARIANISM AND PARETO EFFICIENCY

For Sen, the utilitarian approach can be factored into three elements:

(a) act consequentialism, so that a decision is evaluated according to the resulting state,
(b) welfarism, in that decisions are evaluated according to a social welfare function defined over the levels of individual utility, and
(c) sum-ranking, in that the criterion is the sum of individual utilities.

Although few economists today candidly admit to being utilitarian, implicit assumptions of this kind lie beneath many policy prescriptions. Even if macro-economists avoid (c) by positioning indistinguishable representative agents with dynastic utility functions, their policy prescriptions, such as "Golden Rules", are absolutely welfarist and consequentialist.

AMARTYA SEN AND POVERTY STUDIES

The bottom of the income distribution has been singled out for meticulous attention in studies of poverty. This is a controversial subject in many respects, as well as the definition of the poverty line itself. Even however if we are agreed on the appropriate cut-off (and on other matters such as the appropriate equivalence scales), there remains the difficulty as to the choice of poverty indicator. The almost universal practice is to count the percentage of the population below the poverty line: the "head-count", H. A good illustration is the widely quoted statistic, in the 1980s, of 50 million poor in the European Community.

Suppose that we presume that the marginal utility of income declines with income, thus not including the head-count. What then are the candidates? One is the poverty deficit, which is the sum of the deficit from the poverty line, which may be expressed as the mean percentage shortfall. The marginal value of a euro is then the same for all incomes below the poverty line, which led Sen to criticise the poverty deficit in turn for evaluating equally all transfers to people below the poverty line irrespective of the seriousness of their poverty: like the head-count, it is "blind to distribution among the poor".

The option proposed by Sen is derived from an axiomatic structure where the key axiom is that which weights each person's poverty gap by the person's rank in the ordering of the poor, parallel to the inequality axiom described above. In answer to the question—why should the severity of a 1,000 euro shortfall from the poverty line depend solely on how many people are ahead of you?—Sen cites, "relative deprivation": "the lower a person is in the welfare scale, the greater his sense of poverty". This axiomatisation means that a transfer from a person close to the poverty line to a person far below the line has the effect of reducing measured poverty, in a way that depends on the ranks of the people affected. The resulting "Sen index" takes the form:

$$P = H\{I + (1-I)G\}$$

where G is the Gini coefficient of the income distribution of the poor.

Sen's article was the means for the theoretical analysis of poverty measures, and his index has been widely used in academic studies. It has however had less impact on official statistical practice. In the voluminous United States poverty statistics, calculations are made of the income deficit (for example, Dalaker and Naifeh (1998), table D), but the great majority of the results refer to the head-count. In the United Kingdom, there has been a immense improvement in the statistics produced by the Department of Social Security, Households Below Average Income, but these do not use alternative poverty indices. While there may be agreement on the need to use a measure sensitive to the strength of poverty, it has proved harder to convince policy-makers of the salience of the meticulous approach adopted by Sen, with its stress on a person's rank in the distribution.

AMARTYA SEN AND INDUSTRIALISATION

Amartya Sen has made his views on industrialisation in West Bengal well known to economists. To him, industrialisation is necessary for the development of the state, it is the only technique for income growth. How will industrialisation come about, where will it be located—most of these issues will depend on market, on the necessities of those who are going to invest. For example, investors may like to have their industries set-up near Kolkata. To make simple this some farm land may have to be sacrificed. Otherwise industrialisation will itself get in a weak position, which would involve a lost chance for the people of the state. It even means defeat for the farmers. Too many people are dependent on land, resulting in a restraint on their earnings. As long as these supplementary people are not moved away from farming by means of industrialisation, their lot will not get better.

The rulers of West Bengal and their sympathisers have lapped up these words. The impression they are creating is, "Now see for yourself, no less a person than Amartya Sen has specialized what we are doing is the right thing." Sen, however, had some unpleasant things to say about the reward as well.

Ignoring those should be the most intelligent thing to do. Incidentally, Sen often offers wise advice on primary education, public health, maternal nutrition. He vents annoyance at West Bengal's failure on these counts, but never have we seen the state government getting worked up as a result. Perhaps bitter truths are out of earshot to them.

But neither have the protests against Sen's views been rare. Criticisms of Sen have been healthy in newspapers and magazines, on the internet, in civil discussions and debates. Surely this will not surprise the author of The Argumentative Indian (2006). And he knows, in this regard, Bengalis come first. A Bengali loves to argue. One of his plus points is, he does not hesitate to answer back a great scholar. She does not get awed with "O, Amartya Sen!" On the contrary, she retorts with double the eagerness, "So what if he has got the Nobel? Surely one has a right to raise questions and criticise!" There are many facets of these discussions and questions. There are inanities such as, "What does a non-resident Sen know about our land?" There are necessary questions on comparing Europe with India on matters of industrialisation. Making a list of such criticisms will be useless. But there is a common thread running through these discussions. Many have asked, "Sen has written so extensively on human development, he has been saying so strongly for so long that rise in income does not guarantee rise in capability—but his present advocacy of industrialisation is one-dimensional. He is not dwelling much on if education, health, nutrition, quality of life will improve as a result of industrialisation! Is industrialisation the in thing, and human development out? Industrialisation sweeps away human development?" [an allusion to a memorable phrase in Bankimchandra Chattopadhyay's *Anandamath*].

A simple answer to this question is, Sen has not said anything new, his opinion on industrialisation springs from his own position. There is a sentence in his interview (*The Telegraph*, 23 July, 2007) which is significant. But it also creates job and income and if the income goes up, government revenues go up, so there is money available for education and healthcare and other things." It's a simple logic: market will create income growth, the government will use a part of the additional income for human development. To be sure, Sen will not assert that government alone is responsible for education, health, etc. He will be of the view, civil society may share the responsibility; it's better and an imperative that it does so. But he wants that the state should have the primary obligation to satisfy these conditions of human development. The state should make up for the deficits of the society in this regard. He has repeatedly underlined: many a time government ventures into doing things that it should not do (such as running factories or hotels), and does not do what it should do (setting up suitable system of primary education or public health). Industrialisation is the task for the market; government can merely create an environment for it. Therefore, he would consider support for industrialisation non-antagonistic to the philosophy of human development.

The theoretical structure which Sen espouses makes the above mentioned logical sequence natural, and appropriate. If one wants to raise questions, those questions should better be directed at the very structure itself. This structure is founded on a division—the division between production and distribution. The task-division between market and state that we have just mentioned also contends that production should be within the domain of the market. The state may have a welfare-oriented role to play in distributing income generated from production. This division is not particular explicitly in the development-related discourse of Sen, but his development theory is based on it. To him, capabilities which are born out of education, health, nutrition are necessary conditions for development. These are synonymous with development (Development as Freedom). To provide people with these components of capability are important responsibilities of society and state. He underscores the role of free media and multiparty democracy in encouraging or compelling the state in carrying out the accountability. But the discourse keeps silent on production. It is unreservedly assumed, once the harvest of development is reaped a part of it will be utilised in providing for human development.

CONCLUSION

Sen has been willing to tackle uncomfortable subjects, and to challenge conventional economics. Indeed, he does so with relish. In some cases, he has been highly influential, carrying the field before him. In the public arena, his research has greatly influenced the Human Development Report produced by the United Nations Development Programme. In his analysis of hunger, Sen has emphasized the importance of the press and public debate in securing effective action, and he, together with Jean Drèze and others, has contributed greatly to that debate. On the other hand, in some cases, he has not so far carried the day: for instance, the Sen poverty index has yet to be widely adopted in official statistics.

Within the discipline of economics, he has been extraordinarily successful in arousing the interest of the profession in the issues on which he has concentrated, notably affecting the evolution of the subject. Indeed, one of his key contributions has been to legitimize the investigation of certain topics—such as famine, poverty and welfarism—that had previously been regarded by many as outside the profession's concerns. His own innermost position in the discipline has meant that when he has ignored the conventional lines of demarcation then graduate students have had the courage to follow.

As far as Amartya Sen's works are concerned we observe and conclude that several governments and international organizations handling food crises were influenced by Sen's work. His views encouraged policy-makers to pay attention not only to alleviating immediate suffering but also to finding ways to replace the lost income of the poor, as, for example, through public-works projects, and to maintain stable prices for food. A vigorous defender of political freedom, Sen believed that famines do not occur in functioning democracies because their leaders must be more responsive to the demands of the citizens. He earnestly believed as a profound economic thinker that in order for economic growth to be achieved, he argued, social reforms, such as improvements in education and public health, must precede economic reform.

REFERENCES

Akerlof, G.A., 1981, "A Theory of Social Custom, of which Unemployment may be one Consequence". *Quarterly Journal of Economics*, Vol. 95, 749-75.

Arrow, K.J., 1995, "A Note on Freedom and Flexibility" in K. Basu, P. Pattanaik and K. Suzumura, editors, Choice, Welfare, and Development, Oxford University Press, Oxford.

Atkinson, A.B., 1970, "On the Measurement of Inequality", *Journal of Economic Theory*, Vol. 2, 244-63.

Atkinson, A.B., 1987, "Original Sen", *New York Review of Books*, October 22 1987, 41-41.

Baumol, W.J., 1965, Welfare Economics and the Theory of the State, G. Bell, London.

Dalaker, J. and Naifeh, M., 1998, U.S. Bureau of the Census, Poverty in the United States: 1997, Current Population Reports, Series pp. 60-201, U.S. Government Printing Office, Washington, D.C.

Dalton, H., 1920, "Measurement of the inequality of incomes", *Economic Journal*, Vol. 30, 348-61.

Dasgupta, P., 1972, "A Comparative Analysis of the UNIDO Guidelines and the OECD Manual", *Bulletin of the Oxford University Institute of Economics and Statistics*, Vol. 34, 33-51.

Drèze, J. and Stern, N.H., 1987, Handbook of Public Economics, volume 2, North-Holland, Amsterdam.

Gottschalk, P. and Smeeding, T.M., 1997, "Cross-National Comparisons of Earnings and Income Inequality", *Journal of Economic Literature*, Vol. 35, 633-87.

Klamer, A., 1989, "A Conversation with Amartya Sen", *Journal of Economic Perspectives*, Vol. 3, Number 1, Winter, 135-50.

Kolm, S.C., 1969, "The Optimal Production of Social Justice", in J. Margolis and H. Guitton, editors, Public Economics, Macmillan, London, 145-200.

Lindbeck, A., 1995, "Welfare State Disincentives with Endogenous Habits and Norms", *Scandinavian Journal of Economics*, Vol. 97, 477-94.

Little, I.M.D. and Mirrlees, J.A., 1972, "A Reply to Some Criticisms of the OECD Manual", *Bulletin of the Oxford University Institute of Economics and Statistics*, Vol. 34, 153-68.

Meade, J.E., 1955, Trade and Welfare, Oxford University Press, London.

Mirrlees, J.A., 1971, "An Exploration in the Theory of Optimum Income Taxation", *Review of Economic Studies*, Vol. 38, 175-208.

Nozick, R., 1974, Anarchy, State and Utopia, Basil Blackwell, Oxford.

OECD, 1997, Historical Statistics, OECD, Paris.

Osmani, S.R., 1995, "The Entitlement Approach to Famine: An Assessment" in K. Basu, P. Pattanaik and K. Suzumura, editors, Choice, Welfare and Development, Oxford University Press, Oxford.

Pigou, A.C. (1912), Wealth and Welfare, Macmillan, London.

Ravallion, M., 1997, "Famines and Economics", *Journal of Economic Literature,* Vol. 35, 1205-42.

Rawls, J., 1971, A Theory of Justice, Clarendon Press, Oxford.

Robbins, L., 1932, An Essay on the Nature and Significance of Economic Science, Macmillan, London.

Rothschild, M. and Stiglitz, J.E., 1973, "Some Further Results on the Measurement of Inequality", *Journal of Economic Theory,* Vol. 6, 188-204.

Solow, R.M., 1990, The Labour Market as a Social Institution, Basil Blackwell, Oxford.

Sugden, R., 1993, "Welfare, Resources, and Capabilities: A Review of Inequality Reexamined by Amartya Sen", *Journal of Economic Literature,* Vol. 31, 1947-62.

CHAPTER

6

Amartya Sen on Famine, Poverty and Entitlement

R.S. GADAGE

INTRODUCTION

A.K. Sen is the outstanding economist for his outstanding contribution in the literature of economic thoughts. His contribution focuses on both economic development *vis-a-vis* human development, which can be applied to the economic problems of developed and underdeveloped countries. The growth should focus the employment and reduction of poverty. GNP growth is ruthless if people are living with illiteracy, ill-health and backward. Adoption of globalization should be backed by adequate national policies. Sen has compared the Indian index of human development with China. China placed at higher scale because of adoption and strict implementation of domestic policies. Kerala achieved better human development despite low income in comparison with other states because of public action and not the policies of the globalization and liberalization. Opportunities provided by well functioning of the state may be difficult to use when a person is handicapped by illiteracy and health. On the other hand, a person with education and health may be unable to use abilities because of limitations of economic opportunities related to the absence of market, bureaucratic system, lack of finance, etc.

FOOD SUPPLY AND STARVATION

There has been always discussion is that, food supply falling behind the world population, but there is a little empirical support. In most of the countries except part of Africa, the food supply is faster than the expansion of population. Starvation is not eliminated despite of significant rise in per capita availability of food grain. Hence, starvation depend not merely food supply but also on its distribution. This also concerned to person's inability to establish entitlement to have enough food.

FAMINE AND HUNGER

Almost all the famines are man-made in the world. In the famines only poor people cannot purchase the food because of lack of purchasing power, information, opportunities, etc. In addition to famine of Bengal, he studied the famines of Bangladesh, Ethiopia, Korea, Sahara, China, etc. In most cases famines takes place in one region and food grains are in abundant in another region. Famines can be evaded with good democracy, liberty of press and sound opposition party. Control of food grain distribution system, action on black marketers and efficient transport system. According to Sen, poor people, poor old men and women are affected due to famines. As compared to high income group and the middle income group poor are affected due to lack of employment opportunities which results into low purchasing power and entitlement to earn income. Simultaneously lack of literacy, education, diseases and exploitation is also responsible for grim poverty.

According to Sen, poverty is of course a matter of deprivation which may be absolute or relative and also nation's inability to provide the commodities. The absence of sustained entitlements for certain section of societies resulting into inadequate command of real power to buy subsistence in the market.

POVERTY AND AFFLUENCE

In economic sense poverty means lack of income or consumption. Whereas, Sen defined poverty in terms of capability failures, i.e. failure to meet basic needs and also inability to pursue the well-being. If a person has high income but cannot manage finance properly and experiences deprivation cannot be called poor, i.e. failure to judge independently the possibilities of converting incomes into capability function. The person with diseases may have more income but still inadequate to convert income into functioning. Of course, the relationship of income and capability may be affected by age, location, epidemics. There may be high poverty in high income countries due to ill-health, crime and high cost of living. Being poor in rich societies itself is a capability handicapped. The capability concept is explained by the example of bicycle. It is of course a commodity. It has characteristics of transportation with other characteristics. Having a bike is an ability of a person moving to certain way with bike characteristics is a capability. That capability may give utility to the person. In this chain Sen argues that, commodities—characteristics capability utility. In this case, it can be said that, poverty is an absolute notion in the space of capabilities but it may take a relative form in the space of commodities or characteristics.

ENTITLEMENT AND OWNERSHIP

Some people not having enough to eat the food is called starvation, which is explained in terms of calories and commodity basket. Starvation relates to ownership of food by persons. And ownership relates to entitlement, considering a private ownership market economy, I own the loaf of bread because of paying money, i.e. exchanges. My ownership of money is accepted because of ownership of money, which is earned by selling bamboo umbrella. My umbrella is accepted because I made it with my own labour by using some bamboos from my land. The land belongs to me because of inheritance. This is called chain of entitlement. Entitlement approach has three interrelated basic bricks.

1. *Endowment Set*: Combination of tangible assets like land, equipments, animals and intangible assets like knowledge, skill, power or membership of a particular community.
2. *Entitlement Set*: Set of all possible combinations of goods and services that a person can legally obtain by using the resources of his endowment set. It means the food when men can get depends on their stock and claims. Stock covers landed and other property and labour power. Wages received by agricultural labours are regarded as their stocks, but their claims depend on food grain prices. If prices of food grains are increases then their food entitlement will be adversely affected. Famine, cyclone reduces the people's stock, crops agricultural employment and claims also. In famines food grains are directed to other markets. Under such circumstances government should enhance people's stock by ensuring through employment of government programs and public distribution system. So that, declining purchasing power can be mitigated.
3. *Mapping Set*: Shows the relationship between endowment set and entitlement set. It shows the rate at which the resources of the entitlement set can be converted into goods and services included in the entitlement set. And entitlement mapping have three components viz. a production component (production function) and exchange component made up of rates of exchange involved in trading and transfer component.

ENTITLEMENT FAILURE

A person is said to suffer from the failure of food

entitlement when his entitlement set does not contain enough food to enable him to avoid starvation. A person reallocates the resources to obtain the food but does not get minimum food to escape of starvation. This is called entitlement failure. It results into endowment loss and further leads to production failure, exchange failure and transfer failure. Sen described it direct entitlement failure. When exchange fails then entire channel of entitlement fails. The exchange entitlement faced by person depends on his position in the economic class structure and mode of production.

MEASUREMENT OF POVERTY AND INEQUALITY

Sen has traced two types of poverty lines viz. nutritional poverty line and cultural poverty line. The former identified the people who suffers from malnutrition and later refers to the level of income adequate for meeting established rule of decency of Adam Smith.

The poverty in Indian official approach considered the minimum for all in 1960-61. For this, policy was to achieve the real growth rate of income. But just to explain above and below poverty line is not sufficient to achieve the welfare. H = q/n (H = Head-count ratio, q = Total poor, n = Total population) techniques ignores the distribution of income, relative deprivation and welfare. Suppose poverty line is selected at Rs. 11,000 per capita per annum, all those whose income are below Rs. 11,000 would be counted as poor but it makes no distinction whether income is Rs. 10,999 or Rs. 599 or Rs. 199. But the income with Rs. 599 well of as a person with Rs. 199. Hence, H ratio makes no difference of such persons. It is not discriminatory and crude measurement. Hence, Sen considered the distribution of income/consumption to define above and below poverty line. Larger the skewed distribution of income then larger would be the poverty gap. Sen Produce the poverty measure, which is known as Sen's Index. P = [I+(1–I)G] H. Where P = poverty index, I = poverty gap ratio, 1 = measure of distribution, H = Head-count proportion of the people below poverty line.

The index explains the poverty line is independent of each other. A reduction in the price index would reduce the poverty and *vice versa*. Further increase in population of poor would reduce the mean consumption and the poverty line may go up. Such exercise may result same as wage good model.

POVERTY IDENTIFICATION AND AGGREGATION

The poverty can be identified through specified set of basic needs and inability to fulfil these needs as a test of poverty. So far, as aggregation, it is difficult to translate commodity characteristics into commodity requirements. It is also difficult to measure a calories practically because of dietary habits of population are not immutable. Consumption pattern varies family to family and also nutrition. In the aggregation exercise absolute deprivation may have to be supplemented by consideration of the relative deprivation. So both should be used for measurement.

COLLECTIVE SOCIAL WELFARE

It relates to welfare economics and collective decision-making. It analyses welfare of human beings or occurrence of famines during plenty or how famines can be avoided in democracy. Sen combined tools from economics, philosophy and ethics with economic problems. He apposed the views of Lionel Robbins about the neutrality of economics between means and ends and emphasized economics without values have no meanings and values in economics have no effects.

DEVELOPMENT ECONOMICS AND FREEDOM

Development has been shifted from growth to welfare in 80s and 90s. This change is due to contribution of economist. For state sponsored development programs Sen's methodology of evolution of projects on the basis of social cost benefits have helped in assessing the impact of development projects. In the development, deprivation and well-being excise of choice may be constrained by the socio-economic ills. In this case, functioning and achievements are very much important. In achievements, people must have to be succeed in achieving the better life.

The notion of functioning and capability associated with a freedom. Freedom means option to choose. Always more freedom does not mean well-being because of ill-developed market and the state social planner suffers from innumerable information constraints. The process of freedom should be involved decisional autonomy of choice to make an immunity from interference to others.

Sen's contribution also relates to vital sector like education and health. He advocated the positive growth and human development. Sen. challenged the automatic human development with growth. He compared Kerala to Hindi belt in respect of social development. For social development redistributive measure are to be applied where population is increasing.

CONCLUSION

Approach of poverty concern to endowment, entitlement and mapping set. The famines are man-made. Because famines have occurred despite sufficient availability of foodgrain productin in some part of the country. The poverty of the people can be solved through redistribution of increased production, democracy, liberty, strong opposition party, etc. Ultimately government should ensure the entitlement. China avoided the famine and starvation by giving entitlement of education, health and nutrition by the state. Government should move counter-productive to productive intervention to eradicate poverty. It is possible everywhere.

References

Sen, Amartya (1981), Poverty and Famines, Oxford University Press, Mumbai.

Sinha Ajitkumar and Sen, Rajkumar (2000), Economics of Amartya Sen, Deep & Deep Publications (P) Ltd., New Delhi.

Dreze Jean and Sen, Amartya (1998), Hunger and Public Action, Oxford University Press, Calcutta.

CHAPTER

7

Economics and Philosophy of Amartya Sen

D. Rahul

November 2009 : On 19th November, he attended an interactive session with a few Oxford economists and a couple of MPs from Conservative and Labour Party in UK. On the same day, he also delivered a public lecture titled *The Pursuit of Justice* in Oxford's Sheldonian Theatre followed by question and answer session with the audience. On 20th November, he interacted primarily with a few Oxford philosophers and political theorists, again followed by comments and questions from the audience. The focal point of his public lecture and interactive sessions was his new book *The Idea of Justice* that got published in July 2009. Sen, a Nobel Prize winner in Economics and a Lamont Professor of Economics and Moral Philosophy at Harvard University took an intelligent and pragmatic approach by pondering over the idea of 'enhancement of justice' by 'removal of injustice' instead of imagining an *a priori* perfect just society, or 'identifying perfectly just social arrangements' or 'just institutions' in his book. However, the book has several deficiencies, and in this article, we would try to point out those ontological, methodological and epistemological limits/ problems of Sen's *idea of Justice*. As Sen has rightly pointed out in his book that 'all disagreements need not to be overcome', let us put forward some disagreements with his Oxford lecture and the book, following his call of 'public reason' and the progressive legacy of 'public debates'. In the first place, before one starts with the question of theorizing about 'removing injustice' as Sen has tried to address in his book, it would be worth asking first about the ontological-*cum*-existential question of 'injustice' itself. That is to say, how injustices occur and exist in society? One can argue that injustices are the function of a certain kind of power relations in society, where the unjust conditions of plebs/underdogs/exploited/ oppressed/underprivileged/exluded/discriminated are the result or consequence of certain policies of the power bloc. Hence, *antagonism* is a constitutive part of any hierarchical and differentiated society. In this respect, we cannot address the question of 'justice' while focusing on 'removing injustice' without addressing, analyzing and *removing* 'antagonism', prevalent in our society.

Secondly, Sen has given a call for 'public reasoning' and 'public debates' for alternative versions/visions of removing injustice and thus Sen's idea of justice is pluralist in character with democratic engagement with varied positions on justice and yet we can arrive at certain common/collective outcomes. However, in this regard, one can ask the following questions: who would decide the 'rules and regulations' of public debates and public reasoning in a world market by corporate media? Who would win public debates in favour of 'justice' and against 'injustice'? Can there be such an 'ideal' situation of democratic engagement between say 'utilitarian', 'egalitarian' and 'no-nonsense libertarian' as Sen has portrayed in his ideal scheme of things, or the pragmatic reality can be very different of an *impossible dialogue* precisely because the very different positions on justice fundamentally disagree with one another and has an inbuilt narcissism within each one of them, claiming: 'our path is the right path', based on their 'reason'. In that case, 'the idea of justice' and 'ways to remove injustice' becomes a game of contesting positions struggling for hegemony. Therefore, setting the rules of such a game of contesting positions and the final outcome of such a game is depended on who wins and who loses the hegemonic struggle of contesting positions. Moreover, there cannot be any 'neutral authority' who can set the rules of 'public reason' and 'public debates' because *authority* by definition is linked with *power* and the historic experience of human existence shows us that 'power' is never innocent or impartial but has a motive to fulfil, and thus open to manipulation for such obvious parochial subjective goals. In this respect, Sen does not engage with the concept of *hegemony*, which actually derives from the antagonistic nature of human society. We can further clarify by saying that the struggle to ensure justice or removing injustice to arrive at relatively more just conditions in Sen's approach is intricately connected to the question of political struggle to win hegemony over the rest of the population in favour of justice. The population in a society can be politically convinced for a particular version of justice or ways of removing injustice by consultations, consent, democratic participations, etc. If a particular version of justice is superimposed from top then hegemony nonetheless can be established, but with coercive mechanisms, which in a way can also invite a resistance/challenge to the hegemonic formation/power bloc and thus can limit its scope of operation. In that case, the very notion of a hegemonic idea of justice and its moral authority that is established through an authoritarian imposition from above than hegemonic formation from below with people's consent and active participation in championing a version of justice can be questioned/collapsed with new possibilities of struggle for liberation from a repressive notion of justice. In the case of a repressive power, the normative idealism of 'just society' itself becomes relegated to redundancy with the emergence/prominence of realism, where only power, and 'remain seated in power' itself becomes an ideal. In such a case, the 'promise' and 'hope' of establishing a just society or removing injustices is a political project of the present, when the 'promise' of justice or removing injustice is made to the people at the current conjuncture ('now') for political mobilization at present to establish a relatively new just society in near future. Thus, ideals like justice or removing injustice in that case becomes only an illusionary veil to camouflage the hidden desire/goal of political act of achieving 'power'. In fact, the history of human existence has so far shown that no society has been absolutely just and even after eventful political transformations like Spartacus slave revolt, English Revolution, French Revolution, Russian Revolution, Chinese Revolution, Iranian Islamic Revolution, National liberation and decolonization, and post-war welfare state to the retreat of the welfare state with the emergence of neoliberal consensus, justice has not been ensured to significant sections of population in those societies and indeed we found new forms of injustices haunting the plebs. However, it can be definitely argued that some of the above mentioned political transformations have made some advancements in making societies relatively more just, while eliminating some injustices like abolition of slavery, disbandment of private armies of propertied classes, concentrated focus on social sectors like health and education. On the other hand, in the current neoliberal dispensation, we find just concerns for environment but at the same time, new forms of injustices with financial crisis, the retreat of welfarist policies, etc. Since, Sen's book is written for our times, he does not offer us any solution how we can make societies relatively just in the midst of neoliberal hegemony. Rather his arguments can well be sufficient to sustain a neoliberal hegemony as we will see next on the question of imperialism.

Thirdly, in page numbers 408 and 409 of the book, Sen argues that United Nations, NGO's and parts of the news media have a positive role to play in ensuring a 'global democratic state' characterized by 'global reasoning'. Now, it is not an ontological question at all, rather an ontical-*cum*-empirico-factual question that the UN, NGOs and media are more often than not, sold to corporate interests and has been the vehicles of US imperialism for quite sometime now, and how these are going to facilitate a 'global democratic state'! In this sense, Sen's idea of justice cannot be plural but *partial*, since the prevalent conditions of several forms of antagonism expressed in the phenomenon of poverty, inequality, illiteracy, health hazards, undemocratic international order are consequences of corporate model of neoliberal capitalism. In fact, institutions like UN, NGOs and media that Sen has so much hope and trust on them, have themselves contributed in sustaining the current unjust imperialist system. Thus, it can be argued that Sen's vision of global democratic state is not only partial and unjust but basically overlaps with the project of American empire. To be very precise, one can hear the sounds of the logic of empire in Sen's intellectual argument since his global democratic state would be mediated through imperialist agencies like UN, NGOs and corporate media. To balance such accusations of a pro-imperialist text, Sen difficultly tries to make a happy harmony, arguing in favour of a 'global dialogue' between imperialist power bloc alliance of Washington, London, Paris and Tokyo with 'anti-globalization protests' (p. 409). However, such a 'global dialogue' is impossible precisely because of antagonistic nature of global power relations and can only exist in the fancy imaginations of an idealist thinker, who ironically is not interested in providing a transcendental just perfect society. Even Sen's criticisms of US invasion to Iraq as 'mistaken' (p. 3) and American response to 9/11 'affecting hundreds of millions...in Afghanistan' (p. 402) carefully avoid using the term 'imperialism' which has perhaps now become old-fashioned in liberal intellectual circles because it embarrasses the imperialist power bloc. On the question of Taliban and 9/11, Sen in fact forgets to mention that it was America's own Frankenstein created as a strategy of Cold war politics, which is now haunting the empire. So, America has to account for much of the present crisis in the wake of 'global terrorism'. Similarly, Sen also does not assess America's unjust historic wrongs, most crudely expressed in decimating Hiroshima and Nagasaki with atom bombs, its military interventions and CIA sponsored coups in parts of Latin America and the Muslim world, and its proselytization of several third world nation-states with Fund-Bank market led economic policies that only sustained the problems of poverty, inequality, unemployment, lack of educational opportunities and health hazards. Today, this neoliberal consensus is facing a crisis of legitimacy owing much to the discredited economic agenda of global power elites in the face of a massive financial crisis in the West. In this context, Sen as one of the respected public intellectuals of our time stops short of advising the imperialist power bloc to 'reform' itself, and not to repeat its mistakes of historic wrongs and injustices to the world population. As a gentleman with liberal orientations he is also not telling the imperialist power bloc, 'look, you have no right to intervene in other's matters, nobody has given you that moral right or authority to bully and harm others, and your peeping tendency in other's houses is a violation of courtesy and can be seen as indecency, offensive and bad manners!' In other words, Sen is soft on the question of imperialism and avoids to vehemently criticizing it as a system of injustice. To summarize the above three fundamental disagreements with Sen, we can say that the questions of *antagonism, hegemony* and *imperialism* are absolutely missing in his book and one cannot comprehensively understand the notions of justice and injustice without addressing those issues.

Sen's book however, holds merit on a different count because it only seeks to find/search for an idea of justice rather than answering 'what is justice' and does not make a grand claim that 'this is justice'. Sen's approach as we have noted earlier is not to provide an 'ideal perfect just society theory' but to look at alternative ways of 'removing injustices' in comparative approaches as he claims in extending the legacies of Adam Smith, Jeremy Bentham, John Stuart Mill, Marquis de Condorcet, Mary Wollstonecraft and Karl Marx while differing with the 'transcendental institutionalism' of 'contractarian theorists' like Thomas Hobbes, John Locke, Jean Jacques Rousseau, Immanuel Kant and John Rawls. According to Sen, the contractualists believed in an ideal perfect just society theory on the basis of transcendentalism as an approach to find perfectly ideal just social arrangements while the theorists on the side of comparative framework were more interested in 'removing injustices' in varied ways. Now, we can notice sharpness in making an opposition between 'transcendental institutionalism' and 'comparative approaches' in Sen's idea of justice, but why these are or needs to be essentially different in Sen's approach is not clear. Moreover, Sen is rather focussing more on 'institutionalism' than the notion of 'transcendental' and in this case, an important question might be: why the idea of 'transcendental' is not valuable worth defending for Sen? Now Sen might not have anything against ideal theories and certainly not against ideal theories of justice portraying an ideal just society. Rather his approach is just to do things differently, and albeit exploring alternative ways of removing injustice is a different approach than to build imaginary castles in air by providing an ideal just society theory, which increasingly gets identified with ivory tower philosophy, losing connectivity with the ground level 'real' political praxis.

Sen's prime concern is not to construct a theory of perfectly ideal just society based on transcendentalism but how injustices can be minimised in different ways and how we can have a dialogue between varied points of view on the question of removing injustice. But then Sen's model itself is tied up with a normative ideal notion/position, where 'removing injustice' *itself* becomes an 'ideal' and thus can be transcendental as well. We would argue that since, 'removing injustice' is a central *idea(l)* for Sen, it has an implicit/subtle transcendentalism. Let us assume that in a society of A, we are witnessing injustices like 'poverty', 'inequality', 'unemployment', 'illiteracy', 'health problems', 'tyranny', etc. Now, Sen's approach would be to 'remove' some or if possible, all those injustices prevalent in the Society A without having a prior agenda of what would be an ideal perfect just society or how a perfect just society would look like. However, if we are successful in eliminating/eradicating some or if possible, all those injustices, then Society A loses its unjust identity and transforms itself into a different society, say Society B, by getting a new identity. Now, Society B is fundamentally *different* from the unjust conditions of Society A, and thus cannot be *identified* anymore with Society A. Therefore, after removing the injustices from an original unjust society, an altogether different society is waiting at the end of this *journey* from an *unjust* Society A to a *relatively more just* Society B. This particular journey or *transformation* from unjust Society A to relatively just Society B with Sen's approach of 'removing injustices' cannot be distinguished from the approach of transcendentalism. So, even if Sen distance himself from the idea of 'transcendental institutionalism', if we actually take 'institutionalism' out of it, then the indivisible remainder of 'transcendental' is very much present in Sen. Thus, it is a fundamental *methodological problem* in Sen's approach that what Sen differentiates between 'transcendental institutionalism' and 'comparative approach' is actually intertwined on the question of transcendental(ism).

One can also ask Sen about the duality of political *versus* practical utility of Sen's approach and whether we can argue for a distinctive political utility for just society. If we can argue for such a case, then what would be the feasibility of any theory of justice? How do we address the gap between academic philosophy and political practice, which in a way, Marx tried to resolve the issue? Sen might argue that Marx's communism is not feasible and Marx treats humans as animals, than humans while Sen values 'reason' and treats human rationality as an important tool in dealing with both philosophy and practice of removing injustice. In this respect, particularly Sen's reading of Marx as a comparativist than an ideal perfect just society thinker is a misreading of Marx and therefore there is a profound *epistemological problem* in Sen's thesis. The reading and placement of Marx by Sen among the comparativist framework, who is more interested in removing injustice than having an ideal just society is a selective reading. It is not clear from Sen, why he decided to frame Marx, not as an ideal perfect just society thinker and rather chose to pose him as a thinker who is more interested in removing injustices? In his Bengali book, *Jibonjatra O Arthaniti* (Life and Economics), Sen has copiously quoted Marx's *The German Ideology* (1845), where Marx argues about his 'communist society' and 'true socialism'. Then we know about Marx's idea of distributive justice in a communist society: 'from each according to his ability to each according to his needs' in *Critique of the Gotha Programme* (1875), which can be seen as Marx's own justifications of perfectly ideal just social arrangements. Marx's ideal of communism can be seen in his several works but particularly elaborated as a desired ideal just society in *Economic and Philosophical Manuscripts* (1844), *The Communist Manifesto* (1848) as well as in *Capital Vol. 3* (1894). Sen's treatment of Marx in *Capital, Vol. I, Grundrisse, Critique of the Gotha Programme* as a thinker interested in removing injustice is true but as we all know, Marx was also interested in establishing an ideal just perfect society in his vision of communism. In this respect, we can call Marx as a quasi-transcendental thinker rather than a pure transcendental or a comparativist one that Sen has tried to argue. Marx had both the tendencies of constructing an ideal perfect just society and at the same time, he was also interested in removing the prevalent injustices of society, and these two approaches are *complimentary* to each other and not necessarily mutually exclusive as in the case of Sen. Now, on the question of gap between theoretical and philosophical premises/promises with that of practical political performances in ground realities at the grassroots, and how we can overcome this gap between academic engagements and real political activism, Sen's solution of a global democratic state mediated through UN, NGOs, media, etc. as we have discussed earlier is unimpressive. Although Sen argues in favour of activism but keeps short of telling us what kinds of activism and in which direction—whether political activism in favour of an imperialist *status quo* would ensure a relatively more just society by eliminating injustices or political struggle against the very form of imperialist order would do the same.

This is however not to deny/denounce the merits of Sen's approach to justice, which makes a distinguished contribution by differing with Kant's notion of 'perfect justice', Aristotle's 'universal justice' and Harvard school's preoccupation with justice and 'moral rights', by avoiding the question of 'transcendental'. For Sen, Justice is not the only virtue but it seems that he gives priority to justice as a virtue. In this regard, it would be a valid question that why Sen has only engaged with the enlightenment thinkers in dealing with the question of justice despite the fact that justice has been a concern for and a continuous search of political philosophy right from the days of Greco-Roman tradition. Greek Sophists were one of the first 'individualists' in political philosophy tradition concerned with the problem of justice. Stoics believed in 'justice' as one of the four cardinal virtues apart from 'wisdom', 'courage' and 'temperance'. Then we find Socrates discussing justice in Plato's Republic. We also know how Roman senator Cicero valued justice as a 'glorious virtue'. What we get from Sen is a complete silence on these ancient thinkers of justice. Sen does not even engage with Plato, who has a classic theory on justice and instead refers to Plato only on two occasions and that too via Adam Smith's illustration and quotation. Also, Sen does not engage with the theological traditions of justice. This theological tradition offers a concept of justice in the everyday affairs of human world besides having parochial interests in the 'Judgment day' in Life after death, particularly in monotheistic religions. In this regard, Sen does not even engage with medieval Christian theological tradition of justice as best articulated by St. Thomas Aquinas, or the Ancient Hindu cosmic-theological argument which equated justice with *Brahman* (which has been interpreted differently as absolute Truth, shapeless God, unchanging, infinite, immanent, and transcendent reality for divine ground of all matter, energy, time, space, being, and everything beyond this Universe), and hence, we can place/identify 'injustice' but cannot place/identity/define 'justice' nor does he take the Islamic view of justice which prescribes certain rules, regulations and practices to ensure justice in society or in a way organising just social arrangements. Even if Sen's interest to look at non-western sources for a theory of justice and particularly his engagement with ancient Indian schools of *nyaya* and *niti,* sources like *Bhagavatgita* and *Mahabharata,* and with illuminating Indian personas like Gautama Buddha, Kautilya, Ashoka and Akbar has merits, his disengagement with ancient European and theological traditions on justice only limits his scope of inquiry. On that count, what Sen alleges about the attention towards contemporary western 'pursuit of political philosophy in general and the demands of justice in particular has been...limited and to some extent parochial' (p. xiv) can be also true in his case precisely because of his *disengagement* with ancient European and theological commentaries on justice. Furthermore, what Sen calls 'our global heritage' (pp. xiii-xvi) by trying to bridge a dialogue between ancient Indian philosophy with modernist European enlightenment thinking, effectively defies/denies the global ancient and theological heritage with the exclusion of ancient Greco-Roman and medieval theological traditions on justice in Sen's book. There is no convincing justification from Sen, that why the starting premise of *The Idea of Justice* is the European enlightenment and then situating some selected Indian thought on justice by contrasting and complimenting the Enlightenment legacy while excluding the ancient European thought on justice and different theological traditions of justice.

'Justice' for Sen is a *relational* concept. That is to say, we cannot comprehensively address the question of justice without *relating* it with other normative concepts like 'liberty', 'equality', 'freedom', 'democracy', 'capability', 'reason', etc. But for Sen, justice can be also *relative*, as he demonstrates about the three children and the Flute story discussed in the introduction of his book while illustrating that relative notion of justice can disagree on utilitarian, egalitarian and libertarian grounds. For the readers, the story in brief is of the following: "[W]hich of three children—Anne, Bob and Carla—should get a flute about which they are quarrelling. Anne claims the flute on the ground that she is the only one of the three who knows how to play it (the others do not deny this), and it would be quite unjust to deny the flute to the only one who can actually play it...In an alternative scenario, it is Bob who speaks up, and defends his case for having the flute by pointing out that he is the only one among the three who is so poor that he has no toys of his own. The flute would give him something to play with (the other two concede that they are richer and well supplied with engaging amenities). If you had heard only Bob and none others, the case for giving it to him would be strong. In another alternative scenario, it is Carla who speaks up and points out that she has been working diligently for many months to make the flute with her own labour (the others confirm this), and just when she had finished her work, 'just then', she complains, 'these expropriators came along to try to grab the flute away from me'. . . . Having heard all three and their different lines of reasoning, there is a difficult decision that you have to make. Theorists of different persuasions, such as utilitarians, or economic egalitarians, or labour right theorists, or no-nonsense libertarians, may each take the view that there is one straightforward just resolution that is easily detected, but they would each argue for totally different resolutions as being obviously right. There may not indeed exist any identifiable perfectly just social arrangement on which impartial agreement. One can suggest an egalitarian notion of distributive justice to counter this problem of justice in the above example provided by Sen by arguing that the flute can be just simply shared among the three children with equal amount of time spend by them with the flute, lets say rotating eight hours of Flute to each one of the three: Anne, Bob and Carla in a particular day. To this solution, Sen can argue that this might not happen because each one of the children can argue that they have a 'right' to get the Flute and might not wish to *share* on the ground of their 'right' that comes from their reasoned claims. However, if we assume that we live in an ideal perfect just society of say Marx's communism, then justice can be achieved on two grounds. First, as Erich Fromm in his analysis of *Marx's Concept of Man* has shown that in Marxian philosophy, the transformation of society coincides/ converges with the transformation of human *being* resulting into the transformation of human *self* who would emerge as different *being*, and a socialist man would be different from the bourgeois man of individualist-selfish character. Thus, a person in a communist society would be more favourable to the idea of collective sharing and would be devoid of *envy*. Even today, if necessary, an ideal communist would be more favourable to *share* things than claiming a monopoly over a certain thing. Secondly, Sen's example deals with a society of scarcity (one flute but three claimants) whereas Marx's communist society is a society of abundance. So, in Marx's communism, each one of the three children would get their respective Flutes and can do whatever they like with their flute: Anne can play it while Bob and Carla would perhaps listen to her or get lessons how to play the Flute, while Bob might be sharing his happiness to both Anne and Carla that finally he got a toy to play, and Carla would be satisfied that she got the thing (flute), which she has herself made with rigorous labour efficiency and can give lessons to both Bob and Anne, how to make such a flute.

So, justice is 'relational' as well as 'relative' in Sen, but can justice be regarded as 'necessary' for human existence? Can 'justice' itself autonomously offer anything concrete and substantial? Can 'justice' be seen as an *illusion* but still a necessary political utopia/political myth, a kind of unsatisfied Lacanian 'desire' which is unachievable yet *necessary* for *political mobilization*? Can justice be regarded as both contented/value loaded and at the same time, content-lessabstract empty concept, which has nothing to offer except 'hope' and 'promise' and thus *necessary* for 'justifications' of either sustaining the *status-quo* or for a call of 'transcendentalism', and hence the rhetoric of ideal just society in both secular and religious ideologies as distinct as communism and Islamism? That is to say, a (neo)liberal *status quo* can *justify*, defend and sustain itself in the name of *justice* and thus it promises *justice* to the people and the people in turn might get politically convinced to defend and sustain the *status quo*, which is synonym to political mobilisation behind such a status quo. In an alternative situation, secular and religious ideologies like communism and Islamism might assert that the present state of affairs is unjust and hence can give a call for revolution, change or transform society into an ideal just one, which is a transcendental quest. Sen does not offer us any answers to these sets of questions, rather he avoids asking these questions which makes Sen's *Idea of Justice* neither a Marxist reading of justice nor an existential reading of justice but unsophisticatedly ends up as a partial liberal bourgeois reading of justice which has potentialities/possibilities to *justify* the current injustices occurring in an imperialist world disorder. The imperialist system as the manifestation of global capitalism is currently immersed into 'blood and dirt', 'dripping from head to toe, from every pore,' to use Marx's phrase in *Capital, Vol. I*. It is a morally degenerated system, somewhat like the tale of naked king, but unfortunately, a public intellectual like Sen, who has often claimed himself publicly, to be on the side of the Left, does not play the role of the innocent child as a 'rational' conscience keeper to speak up that 'the king is naked'!

Philosophy and economics (also the philosophy of economics) can be defined as the branch of philosophy which studies philosophical issues relating to economics or, alternatively, as the branch of economics which studies its own foundations and status as a moral science.

The first question usually addressed in any subfield of philosophy (the philosophy of X) is "what is X?" A philosophical approach to the question "what is economics?" is less likely to produce an answer than it is to produce a survey of the definitional and territorial difficulties and controversies.

Ontological questions continue with further "what is . . ." questions addressed at fundamental economic phenomena, such as "what is (economic) value?", "what is a market?". While it is possible to respond to such questions with real verbal definitions, the philosophical value of posing such questions actually aims at shifting entire perspectives as to the nature of the foundations of economics. In the rare cases that attempts at ontological shifts gain wide acceptance, their ripple effects can spread throughout the entire field of economics. Methodology and epistemology of economics

ECONOMIC METHODOLOGY

An epistemology deals with how we *know* things. In the philosophy of economics this means asking questions such as: what kind of a "truth claim" is made by economic theories—for example, are we claiming that the theories relate to reality or perceptions? How can or should we prove economic theories—for example, must every economic theory be empirically verifiable? How exact are economic theories and can they lay claim to the status of an exact science—for example, are economic predictions as reliable as predictions in the natural sciences, and why or why not? Another way of expressing this issue is to ask whether economic theories can state "laws". Philosophers of science have explored these issues intensively since the work of Alexander Rosenberg and Daniel Hausman in the 1970s.

GAME THEORY AND ECONOMIC AGENTS

Game theory is shared between a number of disciplines, but especially mathematics, economics and philosophy. Game theory is still extensively discussed within the field of the philosophy of economics. Decision theory is closely related to game theory and is likewise very strongly interdisciplinary. Philosophical approaches in decision theory focus on foundational concepts in decision theory—for example, on the natures of choice or preference, rationality, risk and uncertainty, economic agents.

ETHICS OF ECONOMIC SYSTEMS

The ethics of economic systems deals with the issues such as how it is right to keep or distribute economic goods. This area overlaps strongly with other disciplines. Approaches are regarded as more philosophical when they study the fundamentals—for example, John Rawls' *A Theory of Justice* (1971) and Robert Nozick's *Anarchy, State and Utopia* (1974). Utilitarianism, one of the ethical methodologies, has its origins inextricably interwoven with the emergence of modern economic thought. Today utilitarianism has spread throughout applied ethics as one of a number of approaches. Non-utilitarian approaches in applied ethics are also now used when questioning the ethics of economic systems, e.g. rights-based (deontological) approaches. Many political ideologies have been an immediate outgrowth of reflection on the ethics of economic systems. Marx, for example, is generally regarded primarily as a philosopher, his most notable work being on the philosophy of economics.

NON-MAINSTREAM ECONOMIC THINKING

The philosophy of economics defines itself as including the questioning of foundations or assumptions of economics. The foundations and assumption of economics have been questioned from the perspective of noteworthy but typically under-represented groups. These areas are therefore to be included within the philosophy of economics. Cross-cultural perspectives on economics: an example is the Buddhist-inspired Bhutanese "Gross National Happiness" concept. Amartya Sen is a renowned advocate for the integration of cross-cultural phenomena into economic thinking. It may be well asked why anyone should try to lecture the World Bank on culture." Related area: economic anthropology. The numerous reactions to Bernard Guerrien's essay is There Anything Worth Keeping in Standard Micro-Economics?" show that there is no consensus among heterodox economists concerning what constitutes "autistic" economics. In this article, I would like to initiate another but parallel debate by questioning the widely held opinion that Amartya Sen has made an important contribution to post-autistic economics. I wonder if he is really, as Geoff Harcourt implies, "a real force for good in our discipline and the award of the Nobel Prize to him is a positive signal, to be embraced, not belittled". Before examining Amartya Sen's theoretical system, let's recall that he was not awarded the Nobel Prize for his eventual "heterodox" research programme, but for his very mainstream contributions to "standard" economics—particularly for his work on Social Choice .

The Prize thus mainly concerns Sen's early work in which he tried to go beyond Arrow's "Impossibility Theorem" by weakening certain formal and secondary—conditions (see, for example, *Collective Choice and Social Welfare*, 1970). The 1998 Nobel Prize, therefore, does not reward Sen's possible "de-autistification" of economics. Some people may argue that although Amartya Sen oriented his early investigations to mainstream issues, a shift can be observed in his publications since the early 80's. Indeed, from 1982 on, Amartya Sen focused his efforts on building the so-called "capability" approach. For many economists (whether orthodox or heterodox), this new system constitutes real progress in economic theory: it "reintroduces" ethical and philosophical considerations into economics. I will argue, however, that although Amartya Sen's "capability" approach treats some philosophical issues (as do all economic theories), his underlying theoretical system remains undeniably neoclassical.

SEN'S CAPABILITY APPROACH

The concept of capability was introduced so as to overcome the deficiencies of what Sen considers to be the "rawlsian" and the "utilitarian" approaches. He defines his concept as each individual's freedom to achieve a particular life. As he puts it : "The expression [capability] was picked to represent the alternative combinations of things a person is able to do or be the various 'functionings' he or she can achieve. Functionings represent parts of the state of a person—in particular the various things that he or she manages to do or be in leading a life. The capability of a person reflects the alternative combinations of functionings the person can achieve, and from which he or she can choose one collection. The approach is based on a view of living as a combination of various 'doings and beings', with quality of life to be assessed in terms of the capability to achieve valuable functionings". In his last book, *Development as Freedom,* Sen explains that "a person's 'capability' refers to the alternative combinations of functionings that are feasible for her to achieve. Capability is thus a kind of freedom: the substantive freedom to achieve alternative functioning combinations

JUST A VARIATION OF STANDARD MICROECONOMICS

The theoretical approach proposed seems, at first sight, revolutionary. However, when Sen explicitly describes his system (particularly in *Commodities and Capabilities,* 1985), it becomes clear that it is just a variation of the mainstream approach. Instead of reasoning in terms of an n-dimensional space composed of "commodities" (goods or utilities), Sen proposes a space of "functionings". Sen starts from the standard model, and takes two steps. First, following an approach developed by Gorman (1959) and Lancaster (1966), he considers that it is useful to move to the space of the "characteristics" of goods, rather than that of the goods themselves. Second, Sen endows each individual with a set of "utilization functions" and with a set of commodities. The functionings of each individual will then depend on the choice of a particular commodity vector and of utilisation functisson. The capability of each individual is then given by all the possible functionings an individual can achieve. The formal presentation of Sen's system shows how similar it is with the standard model and contrasts sharply with his "literary" essays where he invokes his approach.

HIS EMPIRICAL INVESTIGATIONS

Some people seem to believe that the capability approach—as opposed to the standard approach—is particularly fruitful in empirical research. Yet, Sen never uses his theoretical construction when he examines concrete questions: he merely calculates correlations between certain basic indicators. One does not really need his theoretical framework to carry out these investigations. And I have not found, in any of Sen's publications, an empirical investigation that directly apprehends concrete economic and social issues using the "capability" concept. Everyone knows that *illiteracy, sickness, short life expectancy, high infant mortality*, etc., should be eradicated because they impede people from leading good and happy lives. Sen seems to believe that by giving these evils more sophisticated name some fundamental breakthrough is made in our understanding of the causes and remedies of these evils. At least that is the impression one gets in certain passages of his work. For example, in a book with Jean Drèze, it is said : "Poverty is, thus, ultimately a matter of 'capability deprivation', and note must be taken of that basic connexion not just at the conceptual level but also in economic investigations and in social or political analyses. This broader and more foundational view of poverty has to be kept in view while concentrating, as we often would in this monograph, on the deprivation of such basic capabilities as freedom to lead normal spans of life or the freedom to read or write.

HIS INTRODUCTION OF MORAL PHILOSOPHY INTO ECONOMIC ANALYSIS

Others may argue that although Sen has a "mainstream bias", he nonetheless reintroduces philosophy in economic analysis. Although this is partly true, one may question Amartya Sen's objectives in this domain by quoting Sen himself. In his last book, he says:

In the absence of such imperfections classical models of general equilibrium have been used to demonstrate the merits of the market mechanism in achieving economic efficiency. It is possible, however, to question whether the efficiency sought should not be accounted in terms of individual freedoms, rather than in utilities. I have, in fact, demonstrated elsewhere Markets and Freedoms: achievements and limitations of the market mechanism in promoting individual freedoms that in terms of some plausible characterisations of substantive individual freedoms, an important part of the Arrow-Debreu efficiency result readily translates from the space of utilities to that of individual freedoms, both in terms of freedom to choose commodity baskets and in terms of capabilities to function. In demonstrating the viability of this extension, similar assumptions are employed as are needed for the original Arrow Debreu result. With these assumptions, it turns out that for a cogent characterisation of individual freedoms, a competitive market equilibrium guarantees that no one's freedom can be increased any further while maintaining the freedom of everyone else. The basic result about market efficiency can, in this sense, be extended to the perspective of substantive freedoms.

This excerpt clearly shows two things. First, it indicates that Sen (like most neoclassical theorists) confuses the highly centralized "general equilibrium model" with the completely decentralized "market mechanism". Second, it shows that Sen indeed "introduces" some philosophical concepts into standard economics, but that he does not, however, depart from the mainstream approach. One may thus ask if he has enriched economics or if he has impoverished moral philosophy.

SEN AND MAINSTREAM ECONOMICS

Finally, I would like to highlight an important aspect of Sen's vision, his faith in the future of standard economic analysis and his optimism concerning the direction in which it is being enriched, broadened making it more and more capable of economic and social problems. The modelling of the market economy in the recent development literature has substantially broadened the rather limited assumptions made in the Arrow-Debreu formulation. It has particularly explored the importance of the economies of large scale, the role of knowledge, learning from experience, prevalence of monopolistic competition, the difficulties of coordination between different economic agents and the demands of long-run growth as opposed to static efficiency. On different aspect of these changes see Avinash Dixit and Joseph Stiglitz, Krugman, Rome, Lucas. These developments have very substantially enriched the understanding of the process of development and in particular the role and functioning of the market economy in that process. They have also clarified the insights of earlier economists on development. Similarly, in a book that on India's economic development, he declares :

> Recent work on economic growth has also brought out sharply the role of labour and the so-called 'human capital'. The economic roles of school education, learning by doing, technical progress, and even economies of large scale can all be seen as contributions—in different ways—to the centrality of human agency in generating economic expansion. In terms of economic theory, this shift in emphasis has provided one way of filling the large 'residual' that was identified in the basic neo-classical model of Solow, and recent growth theory has done much to bring out the function of direct human agency in economic growth, over and above the contribution made through the accumulation of physical capital.

CHAPTER

8

"Capability Approach" and Poverty Alleviation : Amartya Sen's Contribution

MANISH DEV

Poverty is a greatest challenge not only for the millions of poor living in third world countries, but also to the governments of those countries whose a large chunk of population is living under abject poverty. Several approaches have been tried for poverty alleviation. In the initial stages of development growth mediated approach has remained core agenda of majority of economists and policy-makers. The relationship between growth and poverty lied at the heart of development economics. While, many see aggregate growth as both necessary and sufficient for reducing poverty, and consequently focus their efforts on achieving the desired macro-economic outcomes, others stress that the benefits from growth may not be evenly spread. Critics of glabalisation often argue that growth in terms of higher growth rates of GDP and per-capita income may well have an adverse effect on the most vulnerable sections of the society. There is plenty of evidence suggesting that growth is important for poverty reduction (Deininger-Squire, 1996; Foster and Szekely, 2001; Dollar and Kray, 2002; Bourguignon, 2003). Kray (2005) disentangles the impact of growth on poverty reduction by identifying three potential sources of pro-poor growth in terms of significant reduction in poverty. These are : (i) a higher growth rate; (ii) a high sensitivity of poverty to growth; and (iii) a poverty reducing pattern of growth. Inspired by these theoretical premises, almost all the under developed countries adopted the growth mediated approach of poverty reduction despite certain well augmented empirical studies that did not confirm the above theory. In view of these conflicting arguments, Prof. Amartya Sen propounded the concept of 'Capability Approach' which further developed by Martha Nussbaum and many others. The concept paved the way for greater attention on human development at international and national level. UNDP developed certain indicators of human development (HDI, HPI-I, HPI-II, GDI, GEM) by incorporating some important basic functioning such as longevity in terms of expectancy of life at birth, knowledge in terms of adult literacy and GER and standard of living in terms of adjusted real GDP per capita.

Thus, the concept of Capability Approach is as relevant as ever to the design of effective policies to combat poverty and deprivation (Nussbaum, 1993). The Capability Approach has proved powerful tool in reshaping thinking about topics as diverse as gender, human security and climate change besides generalized policies on poverty reduction and inequalities eliminations.

The Capability Approach is a broad normative framework for the evaluation of individual well being and social arrangements, the design of policies and proposals about social change in society. The Capability Approach is used in a wide range of fields, most prominently in development thinking, welfare economics, social policy and political philosophy (Robeyns, 2003). Although the Capability Approach has its roots in the writings of Aristotle, Adam Smith, J.S. Mill and Karl Marx, but it got prominence only after the publication of pioneer work of economist and philosopher Amartya Sen (Sen,

1980, 1984, 1985a, 1985b, 1987, 1992, 1993, 1995 and Dreze and Sen, 2002). Later on Martha Nussbaum gave the Capability Approach a new shape and dimensions (Nussbaum, 1988, 1992, 1995, 2000, 2002a, 2002b). Finally the concept of 'Capability Approach' was adopted by international development agencies such as World Bank and UNDP as human development approach of poverty reduction, placing greater attention to social sector infrastructure-education and health. Thus, the Capability Approach remained in forefront of poverty reduction approaches in third world countries like India.

The present paper analysed Prof. Amartya Sen's contribution towards development of Capability Approach. The paper also gives holistic view of Sen's Capability Approach, Nussbaum's contribution and finally the World Bank's adoption in the form of human development.

PROF. AMARTYA K. SEN'S APPROACH TOWARDS CAPABILITIES : CONCEPTUAL FRAMEWORK

The conceptual foundation of the Capability Approach can be traced in Sen's critiques of traditional welfare economics on the following grounds.

Traditional welfare economics considers income and commodity demand as the main source and base of well-being of an individual as well as the society. Prof. Sen emphasizes that economic growth and expansion of goods and services are necessary for human development. At this point Prof. Sen seems agree with Adam Smith (Sen, 1983). Sen considers income as one of the core factor of well being, but not the only factor of well-being as different people and communities may differ in their capacity to convert income into valuable achievements (Sen, 1985, 1999). Well-being of different people cannot be compared merely on the bundle of commodities or the income available with them, because of lack of information, the traditional welfare economics lacks the foresightedness in the sense that it does not consider the well-being of the people in terms of their Capability to function with the goods and services *inter alia* the income, at their disposal (Clark, 2004).

Sen also questions the welfare or utility approach because it concentrates on happiness, pleasure and desire fulfilment.

Sen emphasizes that utility does not distinguish between different sources of pleasure and pain or different kinds of desire (Sen, 1984). Sen points out that there is more to life than achieving utility. 'Happiness or desire fulfilment represents only one aspect of human existence (Sen, 1984). Rights and positive freedoms and many other things of intrinsic value, that have been neglected under welfare approach, are also of great importance while considering the utility a criterion of well being (Sen, 1987, 1992, 1999). Sen criticizes economists on the ground that they use utility as the focal variable in theoretical work, but translate this into a focus on income in their empirical works. According to Sen, income can be an important means to acquire goods and services Akins to utility; it can only serve as a rough proxy for what intrinsically matters, namely people's Capability (Sen, 1990). Thus, it can be concluded that in Sen's view neither income and commodity demand nor the utility (in terms of happiness and desire fulfilment) adequately represent human well-being and deprivation.

In more specific terms capabilities represent the various combinations of functioning (beings and doings) that the person can achieve. Capability is a set of vectors of functions, reflecting, the person's freedom to lead one type of life or another (Alkire, 2004). A functioning is an achievement of a person: what she or he manages to do or be. It reflects, as it were, a part of the 'state' of that person (Sen, 1985a). Sen terms valuable beings and doings as functioning. Functioning has following characteristics (Alkire, 2004).

- Functionings are all the 'ends' of human life.
- Functionings can also be means.
- Functionings can be elementary such as escaping morbidity and mortality, nourishment and mobility.
- Functionings can be complex, i.e. self-respect, participation in community life, ability to appear in public without shame, privacy and dignity.
- Functionings can be general capabilities to be nourished and communicate.
- Functionings can be specific capabilities to enjoy a luxurious life.

A functioning therefore refers to the use a person makes of the commodities and/or the services at his or her command. Functioning has different meaning to different thinkers (Table 1).

Sen clarifies that a person's functioning and his/her capabilities are closely related to each other, but with different instincts. Sen says, "A functioning is an achievement, whereas a capability is the ability to achieve. Functionings are in a sense, more directly related to living conditions, since there are different aspects of living conditions. Capabilities in contrast, are notions of freedom, in the positive sense; what real opportunities you have regarding the life you may lead (Sen, 1987). Here is an example to differentiate between functioning sand capabilities. Consider the two persons, one suffering from hunger in Kalahandi (Orissa), and the second, a white color job activist decided to go on a hunger-strike at the gate of the factory for salary hike. Although both persons lack the functioning of being well nourished, the freedom they had to avoid being hungry is distinct. Although both lack the achieved functioning in terms of nourishment and hunger free, person on hunger strike has the capability to achieve this functioning which Kalahandi person lacks.

Sen uses the term 'capability' in a broader sense to the alternative combination of functionings the person can achieve from which he or she can choose one collection (Sen, 1993, 1992, 2005). So instead of describing specific abilities—such as being able to avoid hunger, the notion of 'capability' is effectively used a synonym for the capability set. Sen makes it clear that capability or freedom has intrinsic value and should be regarded as 'the primary informational base' (Sen, 1993).

Relationship between functionings and capabilities can best be understood.

Prof. Amartya Sen's approach towards capability is a pathbreaking approach and improvement over welfare economics. It has following merits:

- It is flexible and exhibits a considerable degree of internal pluralism, which allows researchers to develop and apply it in many different ways (Alkire, 2002b).

Table 1

Some Lists of Functioning (Philosophical Dimensions of Human Value)

Finnins (1980) : Basic Human Values	*Doyal & Gaugh: (1992) Intermediate Needs*	*Rawls: (1993) Political Liberalism*	*Nussbaum: (1998) Central Human Capabilities*	*Amarty K. Sen: (1999)*
(1)	*(2)*	*(3)*	*(4)*	*(5)*
• Bodily life-health vigour and safety • Knowledge • Skillful performance in work and play • Friendship • Practical reas-onableness • Self-integration • Harmony with ultimate source of reality	• Nutritional food/ water • Protective housing • Work • Physical environment • Health care • Security in childhood • Significant primary relationship • Physical security	• The Basic Liberties: ➢ Freedom of movement ➢ Freedom of association ➢ Freedom of occupational choice against a background of diverse opportunities ➢ Powers and prerogatives of office	• Life • Bodily health • Bodily integrity • Senses, thought, imagination • Emotions • Practical reason • Affiliation • Other specific play control over one's environment	• Political freedom • Economic facilities • Social opportunities • Transparency guarantees • Protective security

• Economic security • Safe birth control/ child-bearing • Basic education	➢ Positions of responsibility in political and economic institutions ➢ Income and wealth ➢ The social bases of self-respect

Sources : (i) Finnin's, J. (1980); Natural Law and Natural Rights, Oxford University Press.
(ii) Doyal Len and Gaugh, I. (1992); Theory of Human Needs, MacMillion, pp. 39-42, 50-55.
(iii) Rawls, John (1993); Political Liberalism, New York, Columbia Univ. Press, pp. 19-24.
(iv) Nussbaum, Martha (1998); Sex and Social Justice, New York, Oxford Univ. Press, pp. 29-47.
(v) Sen, Amartya K. (1999); Development on Freedom, Oxford Univ. Press.

- There is no definitive list of capabilities. Instead Sen argues that the selection and weighting of capabilities depend on personal value judgement. Although Sen on and often used the term as capabilities such as being able to live long, escape avoidable morbidity, be well nourished, be able to read, write and communicate, take part in literary and scientific pursuits and so forth (Sen, 1984), he never as 'objectively correct' for practical and strategic reasons.
- Sen's Capability Approach can be used to assess individual advantage in a range of different space. Capability Approach provides a wider concept of well-being and deprivation than the simple assessment of poverty.
- Capability Approach has also been adjusted to focus on inequality, social justice, living standards and rights and duties.
- Sen recognizes that the Capability Approach is not sufficient for the evaluation of all types of programmes (Sen, 1999). By itself the Capability Approach does not provide a complete theoretical view of justice or development. Other principles such as personal liberty, economic growth and efficiency should also be taken into consideration for evaluative purposes (Sen, 1983, 1992). In this way equally recognizes the importance of other quantitative and qualitative parameters to evaluate the usefulness of policies and programmes of human development.

FURTHER READINGS ON CAPABILITY APPROACH 'NUSSBAUM' CONTRIBUTION

Prof. Amartya Sen certainly created a new dimension is welfare economics in the form of Capability Approach with a theory of good to guide moral judgement. In continuation of Sen's approach many different ethics of human well-being and need have emerged in development studies, social sciences and philosophy. Alkire and Black (1997), Alkire (2002), Clark (2002), Desai (1995), Nussbaum (1990, 1995, 2000, 2003) and Robeyns

(2003) have all generated lists of human capabilities in an effort to apply Sen's framework. Out of these the outcome of Nussbaum's theory is the most important.

Marth Craven Nussbaum, a widely respected classicist and Aristotle scholar, embraced the 'Capability Approach' to human development. Nussbaum gave it a distinctly Aristotelian flavour.

A necessary component of Nussbaum's Capability Approach is the list of basic capabilities. She asks an Aristotelian question, "What activities characteristically performed by human beings are so central that they seem definitive of the a life that is truly human?" Two more precise questions are then formulated, "which changes or transitions are compatible with the continued existence of a being as a member of the human kind and which are not?" "What kinds of activity must be there if we are going to acknowledge that a given life is human?" Answer of these questions lies in the core list of Nussbaum.

Her list includes (Nussbaum, 1999) :

1. *Life* : Being able to live to the end of a human life of normal length.
2. Bodily health and integrity.
3. *Bodily integrity* : Being able to move freely from place to place; being able to be secure against violent assault, including sexual assault.
4. *Senses, imagination, thought* : Being able to use the senses; being able to imagine, to think, and to reason ....; being able to use one's mind in ways protected by guarantees of freedom of expression with respect to both political and artistic speech and freedom of religious exercise; being able to have pleasurable experiences and to avoid non-beneficial pain.
5. *Emotions* : Being able to have attachments to things and persons outside ourselves; being able to love those who love and care for us .... not having one's emotional developing blighted by fear or anxiety.
6. *Practical reason* : Being able to form a conception of the good and to engage in critical reflection about the planning of one's own life.

7. *Affiliation* : Being able to live for and in relation to others, to recognize and show concern for other human beings, to engage in various forms of social interaction; being able to imagine the situation of another and to have compassion for that situation; having the capability for both justice and friendship. . . . Being able to be treated as a dignified being whose worth is equal to that of others.
8. *Other species* : Being able to live with concern for and in relationship to animals, plants, and the world of nature.
9. *Play* : Being able to laugh, to play, to enjoy recreational activities.
10. *Control over one's environment* : (A) Political : Being able to participate effectively in political choices that govern one's life; having the rights of political participation, freedom of speech and expressions association, . . . and (B) Material: Being able to hold property (both land and movable goods); having the right to seek employment on an equal basis with others. . .

Nussbaum further classified capabilities into three types (Nussbaum, 1999). Basic capabilities are the innate equipment of individuals that is the necessary basis for developing more advanced capabilities. She points out that most infants have the basic capability for practical reason and imagination, though without a good deal more development and education they cannot use it.

Internal capabilities are states of persons that are . . . sufficient conditions for the exercise of the corresponding function (given suitable complement of external conditions). Most adults have the internal capabilities of use of speech.

Combined capabilities are defined as internal capabilities plus the external conditions that make the exercise of a function a live option. The aim of public policy is the promotion of combined capabilities; this requires two kinds of efforts : (1) the promotion of internal capabilities (Say, by education or training), and (2) the making available of the external institutional and material conditions.

In her treatment to capabilities, Nussbaum is more specific. Her exhaustive list of basic capabilities provides basic political principles that have been given due importance and place in constitutions of almost all the countries of the world. These factors have been guiding principles in human rights legislations and development policies. Fundamental rights and directive principles of state of Indian constitution have given due recognition to core capabilities of human well being much prior to western scholars' attempts in this direction. Be it John Rawls, Amartya Sen, Nussbaum, David Clark or many more western thinkers, their thoughts have due recognition in developmental policies in most of the countries. However, the issue of operationalising the Capability Approach is still of great importance because it is rather difficult to quantify certain vectors of human capabilities, which have been highlighted by Prof. Amartya K. Sen and others.

CAPABILITY APPROACH AND POVERTY REDUCTION

Although, the Capability Approach has not been developed basically as an alternative approach of poverty reduction, it got recognition later on as an effective tool to deal with multidimensional poverty. The Capability Approach, whether in welfare economics, development, or poverty reduction, is basically a normative framework for assessing alternative policies or states of affairs or options. The Capability Approach represents a major contribution to poverty analysis because it provides a coherent framework for defining poverty in the context of the lives of the people and the freedom they enjoy. This approach draws attention to a much wider range of causes of poverty and options for policies than the monetary approach.

The Capability Approach views poverty as a deprivation of these valuable freedoms and evaluations multidimensional poverty according to capabilities (Alkire, 2007). It needs to be emphasized that the Capability Approach engages with and draws upon a plethora of methodologies and analytical techniques. It does not compete with the techniques used to identify domains of interest, or different data for multidimensional poverty comparisons. The Capability

Approach can draw on quantitative, qualitative, participatory, or subjective data, as well as examine income data, although income data alone are perhaps the crudest form of measurement. Furthermore, the Capability Approach has been advanced by participatory methods. It has been represented by various indices and quantitative measures; it advocates empowerment and draws attention to the critical role of social, political, legal and economic institutions in advancing capabilities over time. Within quantitative approaches, the techniques used to measure capabilities range from factor analysis and principle component analysis-type tests, to fuzzy set theory, multidimensional indices, structural equation models, dominance approaches, equivalent income measures and beyond (Alkire, 2006; Kuklys, 2005; Robeyns, 2006). The Capability Approach is a coherent framework that enables researchers to utilize diverse approaches to analyse multidimensional poverty and well-being in a concerted and conceptually coherent fashion.

CAPABILITY APPROACH TRANSLATES INTO HUMAN DEVELOPMENT

Several attempts have been made to apply the Capability Approach in the policies and programmes of development in general and human development in particular. The concept of human development, as enunciated by World Bank and its subsidiaries, and various organizations of United Nations (UNDP, FAO, WHO, UNICEF, etc.) has its theoretical basis in the Capability Approach (Fukuda Parr, 2003; Fukuda-Parr and Kumar, 2003). Several indices have been developed on the basis of Capability Approach.

Expectancy of life at birth, education—as measured by adult literacy and gross enrolment ratio and adjusted real GDP per capita (taken as a proxy for a number of functionings with material pre-conditions, such as being sheltered and well fed), availability of safe and wholesome water, effective participation in economic and political decision-making, etc. are the core functionings of capabilities that have been discussed by Sen, Nussbaum and many others. These indexes provide a better understanding of development of a country/

region as compared to GDP-based index which is an imperfect indicator of human development. HDI ranking of countries paved the way for respective governments, of somewhat lower HDI, to reform their policies. The same has happened in a continental country like India. Although, these indexes consider just a few functionings and that too in crude manner, it is probably the application which has had the greater impact on policy-making. It shows the usefulness of the Capability Approach.

CONCLUSION

Prof. Amartya Sen provided a sound base for human development and reduction of poverty and inequality in the form of Capability Approach. Martha Nussbaum erected a edifice on it with clear-cut demarcations in the form of basic capabilities and ultimately the UN agencies and the World Bank beautified the concept in the form of Millennium Development Goals and certain specific measures of human development. These efforts established the usefulness of Capability Approach in poverty reduction and bridging the gap between haves and have not's. These theoretical developments brought qualitative changes in policy initiatives at micro and macro-level in third world countries. Despite many shortcomings on theoretical basis, the Capability Approach proved its worth in its empirical usefulness.

References

Alkire, Sabina (2002a); "Dimensions of Human Development". *World Development*, 30(2) : 181-205.

Alkire, Sabina (2002b); *Valuing Freedoms : Sen's Capability Approach and Poverty Reduction*, New York, Oxford University Press.

Alkire, Sabina (2006); Needs and Capabilities. In Reader S. Ed. *The Philosophy of Need*, Cambridge, Cambridge University Press.

Alkire, Sabina (2007); Choosing Dimensions : The Capability Approach and Multidimensional Poverty, CPRC Working Paper 88, University of Oxford.

Alkire, Sabina and Black, R. (1997); "A Practical Reasoning Theory of Development Ethics; Furthering the Capabilities Approach", *Journal of International Development*, 9(2).

Bourguignon, F. (2003); "Growth Elasticity of Poverty Reduction : Explaining Heterogeneity Across Countries and Time Periods". In T. Eicher and S. Turnovsky, Eds. *Inequality and Growth, Theory and Impliations*, 211-17.

Clark, David A. (2004); The Capability Approach : Its Development, Critiques and Recent Advances, GPRC-WPS- 032.

Deininger, K. and L. Squire (1996); "A New Data set Measuring Income Inequality", *The World Bank Economic Review*, 10 : 565-71.

Desai, Meghnad (1995); 'Poverty and Capability : Towards An Empirically Implementable Measure'. In *Poverty, Famine and Economic Development*, Aldershot, Edward Elgar, pp.185-204.

Dollor, David and Kray, Aart (2002); "Growth is Good for Poor?", *Journal of Economic Growth*, 7(3) : 195-225.

Finnins, J. (1980); *Natural Law and Natural Rights*, Oxford, Claredon Press and Oxford University Press.

Foster James E. and M. Szekely (2001); "Is Economic Growth Good for the Poor? Tracing Low Incomes Using General Means". Research Paper presented at the WIDER Conference on Growth and Poverty, Helsinki; May, 25-26.

Fukuda-Parr, Sakiko (2003); The Human Development Paradigm : Operationlizing Sen's Ideas on Capabilities. *Feminist Economics*, 9(2/3): 301-17.

Fukuda-Parr, Sakiko, and A.K. Shiva Kumar (2003); Readings in Human Development, Delhi : Oxford University Press.

Kray, Aart (2005); "Aid, Growth and Poverty", World Bank, Washington DC.

Kray, Aaart (2005); "When is Growth Pro-poor? Cross Country Evidence", *Journal of Development Economics*, 6(2) : 28-42.

Kuklys, W. (2005); *Amartya Sen's Capability Approach : Theoretical Insights and Empirical Applications*, Berlin, Springer.

Nussbaum, M. (1993); "Non-Relative Virtues : An Artistotelian Approach". In M. Nussbaum and Amartya Sen (eds.), *Quality of Life*, pp. 242-49, New York, Oxford University Press.

Nussbaum, Martha (1988); Nature, Functioning and Capability : Aristotle on Political Distribution. *Oxford Studies in Ancient Philosophy*, Supplementary Volume, 145-84.

Nussbaum, Martha (1992); Human Functioning and Social Justice. In defense of Aristotelian Essentialism. *Political Theory*, 20(2) : 202-46.

Nussbaum, Martha (1995); Human Capabilities, Female Human Beings, In *Women, Culture and Development*, edited by M. Nussbaum and J. Glover. Oxford; Clarendon Press.

Nussbaum, Martha (1999); Sex and Social Justice. Oxford University Press.

Nussbaum, Martha (2000); Women and Human Development : The Capabilities Approach, Cambridge University Press.

Nussbaum, Martha (2002a); Beyond the Social Contract : Towards Global Justice. In *Tanner Lectures on Human Values*, Canberra.

Nussbaum, Martha (2002b); Capabilities and Social Justice. *International Studies Review*, 4(2) : 123-35.

Nussbaum, Martha (2003a); Capabilities as Fundamental Entitlements; Sen and Social Justice. *Feminist Economics*, 9(2/3) : 33-59.

Nussbaum, Martha (2005a); 'Well-Being, Contracts and Capabilities' in Lenore Manderson (ed.), *Rethinking Well-Being*, API Network, pp. 27-44.

Nussbaum, Martha (2005b); 'Women's Bodies : Violence, Security, Capabilities', *Journal of Human Development*, 6(2) : 167-83.

Robeyns, I. (2003); "Sen's Capability Approach and Gender Inequality : Selecting Relevant Capabilities:, *Feminist Economists*, 9(2-3), 61-92.

Robeyns, I. (2003); "The Capability Approach : An Interdisciplinary Introduction", draft written for the Training Course Preceeding the 3rd International Conference on the Capability Approach, Parna, Itlay, p. 5.

Robeyns, I. (2006); The Capability Approach in Practice, *Journal of Political Philosophy*, 17(3) : 351-76.

Sen, Amartya (1979); Personal Utilities and Public Judgements; Or What's wrong with welfare economics? *The Economic Journal*, 89 : 537-558.

Sen, Amartya (1980); Equality of what? In *The Tanner Lectures of Human Values*, edited by S.A. McMurrin, Salt Lake City.

Sen, Amartya (1983); "Development which Way Now?", *Economic Journal*, 93.

Sen, Amartya (1984); *Resources, Values and Development*, Oxford, Basil, Blackwell.

Sen, Amartya (1984); Rights and Capabilities. In *Resources, Values and Development*, Cambridge, Mass : Harward University Press.

Sen, Amartya (1985a); Commodities and Capabilities. Amsterdam; North Holland.

Sen, Amartya (1985b), Well-being agency and freedom. *The Journal of Philosophy*, LXXXII(4): 169-221.

Sen, Amartya (1987); The Standard of Living. In *The Standard of Living*, edited by G. Hawthorne, Cambridge; Cambridge University Press.

Sen, Amartya (1988); The Concept of Development. In *Handbook of Development Economics*, edited by H. Chenery and T.N. Srinivasan; Elsevier Science Publishers.

Sen, Amartya (1990a); Gender and co-operative conflicts. In *Persistent Inequalities*, edited by I. Tinker, New York, Oxford University Press.

Sen, Amartya (1990b); Justice; means versus freedoms. *Philosophy and Public Affairs*, 19 : 111-21.

Sen, Amartya (1992); Inequality Re-examined. Oxford, Clarendon Press.

Sen, Amartya (1993); Capability and Well-being. In *The Quality of Life,* edited by M. Nussbaum and A. Sen, Oxford, Clarendon Press.

Sen, Amartya (1995); Gender Inequality and Theories of Justice. In *Women, Culture and Development : A Study of Human Capabilities,* edited by M. Nussbaum and J. Glover, Oxford, Clarendon Press.

Sen, Amartya (1997); Maximization and the Act of Choice. *Econometrics,* 65(4) : 745-79.

Sen, Amartya (1999); Development as Freedom, New York, Knoft.

Sen, Amartya (2002); Response to Commentaries. *In Studies in Comparative International Development,* 37(2) : 78-86.

Sen, Amartya (2005); "Human Rights and Capabilities", *Journal of Human Development,* 6(2).

CHAPTER

9

Economics of Amartya Sen

DEEPAK PARMAR AND RAJESH PATEL

INTRODUCTION

It is but natural for Indians to feel elated that Amartya Kumar Sen is the first Indian, nay Asian to receive Nobel Prize for economics, in 1998. Many subjects dealt by Sen—inequality, poverty, famine—are close to the common people's heart. While analyzing these subjects and the attendant policy-related issues, Sen has supported specific state intervention in economic development. The theoretical issues tackled by Sen, a long-functioning of economics and philosophy, concern economics, ethics, and politics. His analysis of famine is well-known. However, societal-joint, cementing various subjects such as collective choice, inequality and poverty, women's problems, developmental indices have been about people's welfare. On considering the way the science of economics has evolved, there is apparently little reason to blame the public belief that economics is a 'calamitous' science concerned exclusively with money and material things. However, classical economists like Adam Smith, and Karl Marx did not hold the view that only material concerns are economic subjects, ethical aspects being beyond the pale of economics.

In course of time, mainstream economics started acknowledging public welfare truly as a part of welfare economics. Sen strove to widen the boundaries of this sidelined subject. He commenced his professional career by addressing the riddles faced by developing countries. Initially, he handled the problems of adequate rate of savings, proper production technology and later adopted welfare economics as the main focus. Sen advocated the essentiality of including an individual's liberty with ability while addressing social welfare, thereby loosening the straight jacket of traditional welfare economics. Another economist and Nobel Prize winner, Robert Solow, described Sen as "the guardian of the conscience of economics" indicating that Sen's insistence for taking human welfare as the focus started getting recognized by contemporary economists. The changes proposed by Sen in the nature of economics are reformative. While indicating the limits of traditional economics he did not give up the conventional framework. By resorting to the method of neoclassical economics itself, he succeeded in highlighting the imperative changes therein. The Nobel Prize is an index to his achievement.

OBJECTIVES

- To know about Amartya Sen
- To know about Welfare of Amartya Sen
- To know philosophy of Amartya Sen
- To know views of Amartya Sen regarding economic inequality

About Amartya Sen

Proper production technology is one of the crucial enigmas for the underdeveloped countries: for good's production whether capital-centred or labour-oriented technique should be deployed. In under-developed countries, characterized by scarcity of capital and excess of labour, the social cost of generating new industrial employment was regarded as zero, since the diversion of a person from agriculture to industry would not affect the farmer's productivity. In such a scenario, extensive resort to labour-oriented technology was regarded as justifiable. Electing this subject for his doctoral thesis, Sen pointed out that the reckoning of social cost of labour as zero would hinge on the savings rate. Only if the savings rate is adequate, extensive deployment of labour-intensive technology would be justifiable. Given the inadequate rate of savings, resort to capital-based technology would accelerate production growth. Thus, the determination of labourer's actual social cost would depend on the objectives. With the sole aim of increasing employment, resort to labour-centred technology, presuming social cost of labour as zero, would be advisable. However, if production is to accelerated with augmenting volume, futuristically capital-centred technology concomitant with increasing savings would be the answer. Blind championing of labour-centred technology would be inappropriate. This principle was elucidated by Sen through illustration of *"Ambar Charkha"* (i.e. spinning wheel).

Another crucial point made by Sen as regards sufficient savings is 'isolation paradox'. Though the need for enhancing savings rate is universally acceptable, given freedom to all, the personal savings rate would be less than the universally agreed rate. This highlighted collective remedies for improving savings rate through public policy (e.g. taxation).

Agricultural sector in underdeveloped countries has been an enigmatic challenge for economists. The "standard" economic principles have been evolved in the context of capitalist system. On the contrary, traditional agriculture was pre-capitalistic. In this sector, cultivation is arranged by family labour. According to the Indian Government data, small scale farming was running at a loss. Instead of regarding this as denoting farmer's illiteracy, Sen held the farmers' aim to be different—i.e. increasing production and not profit. The criteria of their achieving this goal are understandable. Sen considered on theoretical plane the way equipments are utilized in conventional agriculture. He also theorized about labour utilization in cooperative management. The motive of labour assumes criticality in co-operative institutions. He thought about utilization of labour in cooperative arrangement when wages are defrayed according to work or need. This view by Sen was published when 'cultural revolution' had started sweeping over China.

Given the core theme of economics as the satisfaction of material needs by people, human behaviour would have criticality on par with material matters. Ethics deals with objectives of human life and the way of living. Therefore, ethics and economics would have close correspondence though in conventional economics, human welfare was confined restrictively to welfare economics. As welfare economics accorded importance to utilitarianism, the gulf between economics and ethics kept widening. Sen's contention is that since human behaviour is the common thread in both economics and ethics, the integration of the two disciplines would fortify both.

About Welfare of Amartya Sen

With the basic assumption of traditional economics that a person strives to maximise utility, individual welfare would hinge on the utility experience. Social welfare would be a collation of all individual welfares. In another way, utility—the commodity's attribute of meeting human needs—can be thought of as the satisfaction a person gets. The same commodity would yield differing satisfaction to diverse persons. In case of governmental dispensary for poor supported by taxation, the tax payer's utility would be curtailed at the cost of the availers of medical aid. The relative utility loss of the tax payer *vis-a-vis* utility gain of the availer of the service would determine whether the relative governmental action in question is to the societal benefit or not. Economics has abjured the comparison of utilities of different persons being incapable of objective treatment. Pareto adequacy was proposed for ascertaining social welfare in such a situation. This principle regards that if at least one person's utility can be augmented without lessening that of even a single person, social welfare would stand enhanced. But, recognizing Pareto adequacy as the relevant norm would amount to rendering poverty and inequality irrelevant as also regarding as defenceless in the situation where welfare of a large number of poor is concomitant with the damage to one affluent person's welfare. Normally, conventional welfare economics has been rather mute as regards actual welfare of human society.

The assumption regarding human behaviour is another enigma. Whether persons always think only about their individual benefit and regard that it depends solely on their utilization of articles? Individual benefit and other objectives could not be totally independent. The reckoning of a person's success would contend with his efforts for others along with personal pleasure though both are not identical. Despite such an intricacy of actual human behaviour conventional economics assumes that: (i) An individual's benefit depends only on his utilization of commodity, (ii) A person's objective always is maximization of his benefit only, (iii) A person's every selection is solely in deference to his objective uncontaminated by the achievements of others. Owing to these assumptions, human behaviourial intricacies do not emerge to the front. Transgressing these assumptions, it would be cogently understood that a person does not confine self-help exclusively to the utilization of commodities. Taking into account other objectives also along with self-benefit, one would have to cooperate with others for attaining self-goals. Conventional economics has treated human behaviour straight-jacketedly. By discarding these blinkers, human welfare can be perceived meaningfully in economic exposition. It is Sen's submission that such an approach would only bridge the gulf between economics and ethics. Through his writings, Sen has endeavoured to attain precisely this. If every individual has equal right of selection, the riddle about collective option of determining collective selection through volitions of diverse persons would obviate.

Welfare economics conceptualised social welfare as summation of individual welfares. It was, therefore, implicitly presumed that collation of individual choices would yield collective selection. Nobel Prize winner, Kenneth Arrow, established that assumptions of realistic rules about individual priorities would not yield collective choice-order from diverse individual priority-orders. Amartya Sen's contention was that though Kenneth Arrow's terms are logically valid, they are much vexatious with reference to real group-life. Improbability withers away to the extent these terms are loosened. Generally, nature is blamed for calamities like famine or heavy downpour which damage food production, spurting foodgrains' prices. Of late, such famine-deaths have become rarer because of advanced means of communications and feasibility of fighting inflation through swift indigenous/foreign imports. In Sen's opinion, the aftermath of famine ought to be viewed not as a natural calamity but as a social failure.

Philosophy of Amartya Sen

Sen propounded two concepts: endowments and entitlements in today's context. The food men can get depends on their stock and claim. Stock covers landed and other property and labour power. The wages received by agricultural labourers and other artisans are to be regarded as their stock. Their claim would hinge on foodgrains prices. If their stock remains unchanged but claim declines, i.e. prices of foodgrains shoot up, their food entitlement will be adversely affected. Famine curtails people's stock, crops, agricultural employment and claims also, as foodgrains prices too get escalated. On analysing massive famines in Bengal, and Ethiopia, with statistics Sen showed that for want of demand in famine-affected areas the available foodgrains therefrom were directed to other markets. In such a situation, if government, acting properly—enhances people's stock, e.g. ensuring employment through employment generation programmes—the decline in people's purchasing power can at least be mitigated and deaths for want of food could be avoided.

In the context of social welfare, consideration of inequality cannot be avoided. Presuming that utility can be measured and that of different persons can be compared, Sen showed that equality can be examined. For comparing utilities of two persons, his remedy was to imagine oneself in their place and ponder as to who, one would prefer to be out of the two. Even if the thought about equality is brought within the orbit of welfare economics, the riddle of the basis of income distribution remain: whether it should be according to human needs or according to contribution to community production. The first way prioritises welfare and vide the second, one who works more will get more remuneration. But the possibility of those with lesser potential getting disregarded remains. The first way would be accepted as an ideal. But would it be practicable? Karl Marx had held work according to ability and remuneration according to needs, as the ideal. In his book of 1973, Sen preferred income distribution according to needs.

To Know Views of Amartya Sen Regarding Economic Inequality

As regards measurement of inequality also, on thinking deeply, Sen held integrated treatment of poverty and inequality as crucial, de-emphasising the extent of below-poverty-line. Income distribution *inter se* between the people below poverty line is not germane. If some income from less poor is given to more poor, inequality will be curtailed but the number of people below poverty line would remain the same. The Sen-index of reckoning income distribution amidst the poor has been utilised by many researchers while measuring up poverty.

While considering social equality, various kinds of human divergence have relevance. Individual differences vary according to age, sex, health and needs vary accordingly. Nature-ordained causes are responsible for this distinctness, so also social ones. In this context, the disparity *vis-a-vis* women can be quoted as an example. Despite being factors of the same family, available opportunities regarding education, and health diverge for men and women. Women are prone to be sidelined. In such a situation, while viewing human benefit, income per head cannot be regarded as the sole crucial item.

On international plane too, the constraints of index of per head income are explicit. A country like Sri Lanka is much behind western countries as regards income per head. But when such criteria as literacy, average life-span, infant mortality are being considered, Sri Lanka is comparable with western countries. These indices vivify important aspects of societal life which are overlooked by the income per head criterion. It is Sen's contention that while considering human interest, human competence—opportunities for its development in its totality should be taken into account. Acceptance of this idea would imply the definition of poverty as 'insufficient income' and not 'less income'.

The difference between less and insufficient income might appear as word-splitting; but the inadequacy of a person's income can be thought of in the context of his caliber and this concept is more appropriate than the one of less income. Caliber cannot be considered in isolation since it won't be full-fledged without freedom. While considering personal/societal interest in the context of caliber and freedom, the point of equality becomes pertinent for 'equality of what?'. If equality is insisted upon for income, inequality for caliber and ability would have to be regarded as acceptable. Different thought processes have insisted for a certain type of equality and the answer to the question whether equality is desired or not has to be obtained via the question of 'equality of what?'

CONCLUSION

Sen has dealt more explicitly with policy matters, especially for India in his book co-authored with Jean Dreze, which presents a different view about India's fifty years of post-independence economic advancement. Though a lot has happened during recent past, the progress is much inadequate as regards goals as also the possibility of achievement. Sen examined his view with reference to India that while viewing interest of individual and society, it won't suffice to think of only income per head but of man's ability (e.g., indices regarding education, health). The progress in education and health, indicative of life's important dimensions, is significant in itself. Though for progressing in the direction of income per head also, the criticality of factors like education and health enhancing human ability is evident.

REFERENCES

Bardan, Pranab (1994): Rational Fools and Co-operation in a Poor Hydraulic Economy in K. Basu and Others (ed.), *op. cit.*

Basu, Kaushik (1995): The Elimination of Endemic Poverty in South Asia: Some Policy Options in The Political Economy of Hunger (ed.) by Dreze, Sen and Hussain.

Patnaik, P. and Suzumura, K. (1995): Choice, Welfare and Development, Oxford University Press.

Chakrabarty, Achin (1998): Amrtya Sen and Our World of Exaggerated Opposites, *EPW*, Vol. XXXIII, No. 51, p. 3241.

Cohen, G.A., (1993): Amrtya Sen's Unequal World, *EPW*, Vol. XXXVIII, No. 40, p. 2156.

Minhas, B.S. Jain, L.R. and Tendulkar, S.D. (1991): Declining Incidence of Poverty in India in the 1980s, *EPW*, July 6-13.

Patnaik, Prabhat (1998): Amartya Sen and the Theory of Public Action, *EPW*, Vol. XXXIII, No. 45, p. 2855.

Singh, Ajit Kumar (1998): Human Development and India, Indian Economic Conference Volume.

Vaidyanathan, A. (1995): The Indian Economy: Crisis, Response and Prospects, Orient Longman.

Dreze, Jean and Sen, Amartya (1966): Indian Development: Selected Regional Perspective, p. 5.

CHAPTER

10

Expanding Capabilities : A Cause Worth Fighting

SANJAY BHATTACHARYA

I. INTRODUCTION

The very concept of "development" is critical, ambiguous and more significantly value-oriented. An alternative school of thoughts made an effort to present a people-centred meaning of development, relevant to all countries, and to explain its connotations for development practice in many areas. Regardless of any particular framework, many would view 'development' as a multi-dimensional and multi-sectoral process, involving social, economic and political change aimed at improving people's lives. In this context, many development agencies think economic growth and productive investment are the major concerns of economic development. Other similar conceptualization regarding development adds concerns for public health and education as key ingredients for a more dynamic economy and higher material prosperity. A different view of development is facilitating people to live the life they put worth-investment, employment and prosperity are some avenues of providing people such reach, even if they are certainly not the end in itself. The common thread underlining all these understanding is—they are normative.

While designing public policy for development one critical question pops up that should public policy aim at increasing economic growth only or it should offer equal weightage for providing people more social goods, promotion of gender equity and balanced ecosystems. These are questions correlate the value judgements to what should be done. Policy-makers must be able to envisage the locus of change in certain ways, although the different approaches about development are all interconnected and positive and predictive analyses is required for any normative assessments and *vice versa*. Nevertheless this writer strongly believes that normative analysis is fundamental and in some cases precondition predictive and positive analysis. Like for analysing poverty positively, the analyst must make a value judgement regarding the conceptualization of the problem—If it is conceived as 'lack of income' instead of 'inability of fulfilment of basic needs'—the impact will be different in the planning and execution end. The basic logic is normative approaches are the key pins of structuring of developmental policy, though may not be sufficient to conclude the discussions.

II. CAPABILITY AS A MEANS OF DEVELOPMENT

Now let us gaze to an approach to development in which the objective is to expand what people are able to do and be—what might be called their real freedoms. It is obvious that this approach 'puts people first'. In this view, the state of economy is considered examining the factors that enables people to enjoy a long and healthy life, a quality education, a satisfactory job, physical safety, democracy, etc. It has two significant shifts from the income-based approach: first, the analysis swings from the economy to the person. Second, the measure of assessment shifts from money to the things people can do and be in their lives.

But the policy distinctly must consider on the target population for distribution and the period of time to prioritize (dynamics). In this approach, there are also trade-offs to the diversified dimensions of human life. They are not disjoint; they overlap. Those who focus on people's lives are also imperatively concerned with economic growth, macroeconomic stability, income poverty reduction and other means of improving people's lives. On the other hand, those stressed on sustained growth still concern themselves with healthy, educated and skilled workers, and some degree of peace and stability. This is where the normative frameworks and ideas have enormous practical repercussions.

Amartya Sen defines a capability as "a person's ability to do valuable acts or reach valuable states of being; [it] represents the alternative combinations of things a person is able to do or be" (Sen, 1993). Thus, capabilities are opportunities or freedoms to achieve what an individual philosophically considers valuable. The significance of this idea rests on the judgmental stance regarding what is just or fair in the distribution of resources. Taking reference to Immanuel Kant, Sen opined that the over-weightage on the expansion of real income and on economic growth as the characteristics of successful development can be precisely an aspect of the mistake against which Kant had warned. There are cases where countries with high GNP per capita can however have astoundingly low accomplishments in the quality of life, with the mass of the population being subject to premature mortality, escapable melancholy, overwhelming illiteracy. Discussing economic inequality (1973), Sen has taken note of human diversity and its effect on inequality measurement. Capability Approach is his contribution to the link of human diversity. The theme question was equality of what? The approach dealt with questions of the balance between freedoms and equality that have characterized work on social justice since the late eighteenth century. As he explains, all time-tested egalitarian theories pose the issue of equality of something, for example, of income, welfare levels, rights, or liberties. This writer is strongly inclined to confine the discussion of development relating to 'Capability' in the scale where 'people matters'. The capability of a person is a derived notion that reflects the various combinations of functionings (doings and beings) that he or she can achieve. Thus, it reflects a person's freedom to select between diverse ways of living. The assessment of achievement and advantage of members of the society is always a focus of development analysis. It is keenly observed that the capability may be used to confirm the appraisal concerns of human development. Human development draws attention to 'what makes life worthwhile' to the people and the concept of human development rests fully on Amartya Sen's core idea of capabilities and agency. The fundamental importance of human capabilities provides a strong basis for evaluating living standards and the quality of life, and some general terms on which the problems of efficiency and equality can be discussed.

III. EDUCATION AS BASIC CAPABILITY

Education (should not be confused with schooling) brings empowerment. Without education, people can be ill-treated by the influential section of society. Resembling Marx, it can be said education is the crux of human flourishing. It not only opens the mind to further horizons, it also opens the ways to acquire other valuable capabilities.

(A) Human Capital and Capability

In the 1960s, ideas about the economic value of schooling were expanded upon. The famous idea of 'human capital' (Gary Becker, 1964) instigates from the study that schooling builds up certain qualities in people that enhance economic productivity and economic growth, just like the increment in physical capital or investment. This idea has stirred formidable discussions among planners as to how and why governments should arbitrate to social policy in connection to the social and economic desires of individuals, families and nations. It schedules that venture in human could be viewed as similar to venture in other means of production and just like investment in physical infrastructure, investing in human would yield a rate of return, which could be calculated. Theodore Schultz argued that education has an important economic value and that economic thinking has thus far tended to ignore the productive returns that education has had on economies (1963). But from the other polarity of the human development and capability approach, the value of an economy does not lie in economic growth but in its capacity to offer chances for human flourishing, i.e. for each human being to live a life he has 'reason to choose and value'. Comparing the two perspectives, Sen (1997) argues that human capital 'concentrates on the agency of human beings—through skill and knowledge as well as effort—in augmenting production possibilities'. In contrast, a capability approach to education 'focuses on the ability of human beings to lead lives they have reason to value and to enhance the substantive choices they have'. Though they may sound alike, however, there is also a crucial difference between the two approaches—a difference that relates to some extent to the 'distinction between means and ends'. The acknowledgement of the role of human qualities in promoting and sustaining economic growth evades the task of mentioning why economic growth is sought in the first place. If, instead, the focus is, ultimately, on the expansion of human freedom to live the kinds of lives that people have reason to value, then the role of economic growth in expanding these opportunities has to be integrated to the process of development as the expansion of the human capability to lead freer and more worthwhile lives. Sen (1992) has identified three distinct ways in which we can link the importance of education to the expansion of valuable capabilities: first, education fulfils an 'instrumental social role'. Literacy can encourage public debate and conscience about social and political arrangements. Next, Education also has an 'instrumental process role' in facilitating our capacity to participate in decision-making processes at the household, community or national level. Finally, it has an 'empowering and distributive role' in facilitating the ability of marginalized and excluded groups to organize politically. As without education, these groups would be unable to gain access to power and make a new case of launch of relocation of wealth. Indeed, education has a strong effect of repositioning between social groups, households and within families.

But it is not easy to decipher these broad ideas into simple Governmental or community policies and strategies. Even so, attempts have been made to go beyond the simple human capital concerns in international declarations such as the Millennium Development Goals (MDGs), Education for All (EFA), the Decade of Education for Sustainable Development (DESD) and the Beijing Declaration on Women. For example, the MDG targets have indicators not just for access to schooling, but for improvement of gender equity ratios in earning and political representation, eradicating hunger, support for sustainable development, and improved access to health and drinking water.

Martha Nussbaum expressed more philosophical concern with the nature of human flourishing and the role of education to develop it. In the fifth international conference of the Human Development and Capability Association held in Paris at UNESCO, Nussbaum (2006) argues that education is crucial to the health of democracy itself. She criticizes narrowly focused type of education for science and technology at the expense of the arts and humanities. She emphasized the role of education in forming the student's critical and imaginative capacities and she is more interested in the content of what is taught and the process of teaching. The substantial notion regarding what education should be is associated with her list of ten central capabilities that according to her should be the basis of constitutional guarantee. (Life, Bodily health, Bodily integrity, Senses, imagination and thought, Emotions, Practical reason, Affiliation, Other species, Play and Control over one's environment). Education in its bigger spectrum is an important constituent of nearly all the capabilities on the list.

(B) Education : Functionings and Capabilities

Another core idea in the capability approach is the distinction between capabilities and functionings (Sen 1980). Functionings are achieved outcomes—Reading, talking to children, taking part in the social life of a community—are all functionings. Capabilities are the potential to achieve these functionings. The difference between a capability and functioning is analogous to the difference between the scope to achieve and the actual achievement, between potential and outcome. It is significant to the extent that only functionings can give very little information about how well people are doing. Some cases may look as though the same functionings have been achieved but behind these equal outcomes there are different stories, which have relevance to the discussion of justice and equality.

Let us take a hypothetical case of two students who failed in a literature examination representing different section of society. One student, despite having a good schooling, having ample learning support and safe learning environment, one major reason for failure might be his choice to spend less time on learning process and more time with friends in leisure activities. The other is a girl from one of the poorest district of country. Despite her interest in learning and schoolwork, her results might be mainly due to the lack of availability of qualified teacher at her school. Her parents could not have afforded private tuition for all their children or they might have decided to prioritize their son and she might have little time to prepare for the examinations.

If we look only at functioning in this example—we see equal outcomes. But while the functionings of the students are the same, their capabilities are different. The capability approach requires that we do not simply weigh up the functionings but the real freedom or opportunities each student had available to choose and to achieve what they valued. Our evaluation of equality must then take account of freedom in opportunities as much as observed choices. The capability approach, therefore, offers a method to evaluate real educational advantage, and equally to identify disadvantage, marginalization, and exclusion.

(C) Girl's Education Through Capability Lens: A Case of Bangladesh

Gender and education in Bangladesh are seen in terms of enrolment rather than the freedoms that education can foster. Concentrating to education, Walker argues that the value of the capability approach is that it "enables us to ask a different set of questions about education . . . about what education enables us to do and to be" (2006). There is empirical evidence in this country which compels to conclude that education cannot be regarded as a basic capability unless it specifically addresses the process of developing the capabilities necessary to live a life one has reason to value. One particular interest was MDG

3, aimed to "promote gender equality and empower women". The target was to "eliminate gender disparity in primary and secondary education preferably by 2005 and in all levels of education no later than 2015" (United Nations, 2000). It was reported that Bangladesh had already achieved MDG 3 (e.g. News from Bangladesh, 2005; Zia, 2005). Unfortunately, despite some development in some areas in Bangladesh, the claim was simply untrue. The term capability, as used by Sen, has rarely been used in connection with education policy and practice in Bangladesh.

The claim that Bangladesh had achieved the MDG of "eliminating gender disparity in primary and secondary schools" (Zia, 2005), was based on statistics showing that there was approximate parity of enrolment in primary and earlier secondary years in Bangladesh. It is notable that the claims relating to the target of eliminating gender disparity in education rather than the goal of endorsing gender equality and empowering women. Therefore, even if the target has been reached, the goal has not. In addition, Bangladesh once again scored extremely poorly on UNDP's overall Gender Empowerment Measure (79th out of the 80 countries included—UNDP 2005). Again, measurement of empowerment does not have to be restricted to education, as can be seen from the much more sturdy statement on the promotion of gender equality in the resolution adopted at the 2005 World Summit.

Figure 1 indicates that girls' and boys' enrolment is about on a par at primary and early secondary level, but with a significant gap opening up by higher secondary school, where girls are only 40 percent of the school population. The gaps widen further at tertiary level, with only about a quarter of university students being women and even wider gender gaps in the Islamic schools and colleges and in specialist technical and vocational education schools.

Another area of progress toward parity can be easily measured in examination results. As example, the scholarship examination taken at the end of primary school is open to all school children but in practice, only the most privileged are entered. In 2001 (DPE, 2002) girls were only 44.8 percent of the total entries, and only 41.15 percent of the total number of children who passed, leading to a gap of nearly 18 percent.

FIG. 1

Gender Inequalities in Enrolment in Bangladesh

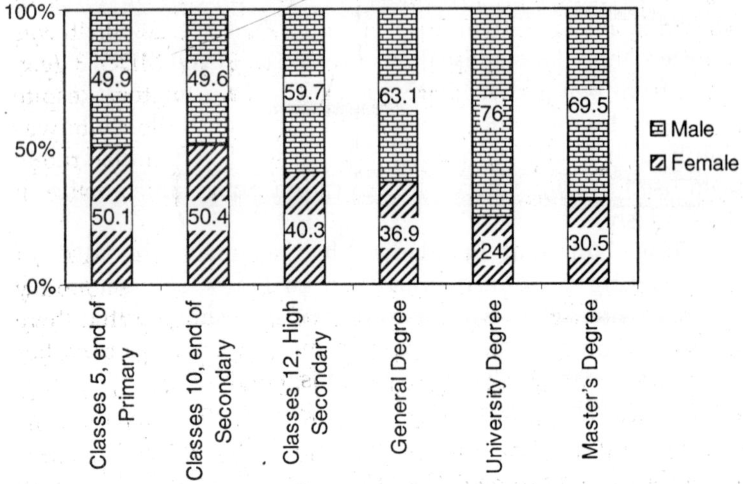

Source : Data extracted from BANBEIS, 2006.

These disparities start early, and present throughout the education system. As it is now almost universally accepted that girls are as capable as boys, we need to know more about the gaps, and what can be seen as a capabilities failure. Moving toward equality and empowerment, we need to identify the ways the education system assists or hinders the development of girls' capabilities.

IV. CAPABILITIES 'REEXAMINED'

The Capability approach has been criticized from different point of views and the most well known set of criticisms relate to the extent of operation of the framework. (Sugden, 1993) The first of these criticisms concerns with supplementation of the framework with distinct valuable capabilities. Sen is criticized for insisting too hard that certain capabilities simply are valuable (1992). Few criticisms cast doubt on the usefulness of the approach for making inter-personal comparisons of well-being in the presence of potential disagreements about the valuation of capabilities including the relative weights to be assigned to these capabilities (Beitz, 1986). However, Sen is notably positive about achieving agreement about evaluations and has also proposed a range of methods including 'dominance ranking' and the 'intersection approach' for extending incomplete orderings (Sen, 1985; 1993; Saith, 2001). Moving from functioning to capability obscures the exercise severely as additional information is required on counterfactual preferences (that cannot be observed) as well as actuals. But despite these critiques the approach surpasses resource-based approach on the ground that "it focuses on ends rather than means, can better handle discrimination against disabled, is properly sensitive to individual variations in functionings that have democratic import, and is well-suited to guide the just delivery of public services, especially in health and education" (E. Anderson, 2006). The most well-known and influential attempt to supplement the capability approach was done by Martha Nussbaum. Meanwhile Sen (1999; 2004; 2005) has advocated a more direct approach for extracting relevant information about the formation of human values, which emphasizes the constructive role of democracy and the importance of public participation and discussion. He argues 'it is the people directly involved who must have the opportunity to participate in deciding what should be chosen, not local elites or cultural 'experts' (1999). Thus the goodness of the capability set should be judged in terms of the quality as well as the quantity of available opportunities.

V. CONCLUSION

In this paper efforts are made regarding the capability approach, providing help to think about some key issues in education and schooling. There is no doubt that it has connotations to the Aristotelian notions of human flourishing but the capability approach is elementary in combining normative idea with practice, not just in education but in a wide band of political, economic, and social spectrum relating to education. Education is highly permeated with aspiration and spectacularly under-resourced for the least-endowed. We must acknowledge the genuinely comprehensive ideas for education in the capability approach, not only for its concern with heterogeneity, but also its call for both redistribution of resources and opportunities; valuing identically for diversity through traverse axes of gender, social class and race, ethnicity and thus integrating distributional and process elements of justice.

References

Banbeis (2006): *National Education Survey (Post-Primary)—2005*, Final Report, Dhaka: Bangladesh Bureau of Educational Information and Statistics.

Becker, Gary (1993): *Human Capital*, University of Chicago Press, 3rd edn., pp. 23-24.

Beitz, C.R. (1986): *Amartya Sen's Resources, Values and Development'*, *Economics and Philosophy*, 2(2).

Clark, David A. (2005): *The Capability Approach: Its Development, Critiques and Recent Advances*, Global Poverty Research Group, University of Manchester, UK.

Deneulin, Séverine and Sahani, Lila (2009): *An Introduction to the Human Development and Capability Approach—Freedom and Agency*, Human Development and Capability Association (HDCA), Earthscan, UK.

DPE (2002): *Primary Education Statistics in Bangladesh—2001*. Dhaka: Primary and Mass Education Division, Government of Bangladesh. http://www.gprg.org

Nussbaum, Martha C. (2000): *Women and Human Development: The Capabilities Approach*, Cambridge: Cambridge University Press.

Raynor, Janet (2004): *Education and Capabilities in Bangladesh*, Amartya Sen's Capability Approach and Social Justice in Education, (ed.) Melanie Walker and Elaine Unterhalter, Palgrave Mcmillan.

Saith, R. (2001): *Capabilities: The Concept and its Operationalisation*, QEH Working Paper Series, University of Oxford.

Schultz, Theodore (1963): *The Economic Value of Education*, Colombia University Press.

Sen, Amartya (1973): *On Economic Inequality*, Clarendon Press, Oxford.

Sen, Amartya (1980): *Equality of what?* In The Tanner Lectures on Human Values, edited by S. McMurrin, Salt Lake City: University of Utah Press.

Sen, Amartya (1985): *Commodities and Capabilities*, Oxford: Elsevier Science Publishers.

Sen, Amartya (1989): *Development as Capability Expansion, Journal of Development Planning*. New York, pp. 41-58.

Sen, Amartya (1992): *Inequality Re-examined*, Oxford University Press, Oxford.

Sen, Amartya (1993): *Capability and well-being*. In Nussbaum and Sen, *The Quality of Life.*

Sen, Amartya (1997): *Human Capital and Human Capability,' World Development*, Vol. 25, No. 12, pp. 1959-61.

Sen, Amartya (1999): *Development As Freedom*, Oxford: Oxford University Press.

Sugden, R. (1993): *Welfare, Resources and Capabilities: A Review of Inequality Reexamined by Amartya Sen, Journal of Economic Literature.*

UNDP (2005): *Human Development Report, 2005*: International Cooperation at a Crossroads—Aid, Trade and Security in an Unequal World. New York: UNDP.

United Nations (2000): *UN Millennium Development Goals (MDG).*

Walker, Melaine (2006): *Higher Education Pedagogies*, Open University Press, Buckingham.

Walker, Melanie and Unterhalter, Elaine (2007): *The Capability Approach: Its Potential for Work in Education*, Amartya Sen's Capability Approach and Social Justice in Education, (ed.) Melanie Walker and Elaine Unterhalter, Palgrave Mcmillan.

Zia, Begum Khaleda (2005): *High Level Plenary Meeting of the UN;* http://www.un.org/webcast/summit2005/statements/ban050914eng2.pdf

CHAPTER

11

Food Entitlement, Public Distribution System—Rent Seeking Behaviour

N. Kanakasabesan

INTRODUCTION

In many markets-oriented economies government regulation on economic activity is all pervasive. It is also the case with the mixed economies like India. Such restrictions give rise to rents of variety of forms. For these people compete among themselves. Some such competition is perfectly legal. In other instance, it takes other forms such as bribery, corruption, smuggling and bulk marketing. The most important forms in which government create rent is by issuing license or permits. In the case of food grains it takes the form of the ration card, which enables one to have and access and also entitlement to buy a certain quantity at subsidised rates from the Public Distribution System (PDS).

The Right to Food, as envisaged by the Food Security Bill follows other rights such as the Right to Information (RTI), the Right to Employment (NREGA) and the Right to Education (RE). In a way all these are nothing but entitlements. The Right to food involves a number of issues such as coverage, known as Targeting, and enhancement, procurement, storage and distribution.

In order to facilitate physical access, 28375 Fair Price Shops (FPS) are established across the State under the norm that no cardholder should travel more than 2 kms to draw his supplies and each such shop should Cater to 1000 cards in urban and 800 cards in rural areas. These FPS service to 1.89 crores card holders of whom 1.78 crores card holders buy rice at a nominal price of Re. 1 kg which involves a subsidy to the tune of about Rs. 3000 crores.

It is in this context an attempt is made to study the working of PDS in the State of Tamil Nadu. A significant feature that distinguishes TN PDS from most other states is its universal coverage. In this paper an attempt is made to study the phenomenon of Food Subsidy, PDS are rent seeking. An attempt is also made to develop the rent model.

PUBLIC DISTRIBUTION SYSTEM—AN OVERVIEW

The system of rationing of essential articles and goods has been prevalent during the Second World War. In those periods, items like cloth, tea and other necessities were on the list. This system however was withdrawn for reasons known to administrators in the early 1950's.

It was in the year 1964 that the state government started the implementation of the Public Distribution System, making available commodities like rice, wheat, kerosene, sugar and edible oil. This was provided through a wide range of FPS, where these commodities were supplied to the consumers at prices below the market price. In the beginning all the consumers had free access to such shops and there was no distinction made between the consumers on the basis of economic status.

As time progressed, the Nation began to face a series of droughts. This resulted in a chain reaction causing the supply bottleneck. In 1997, a revamped PDS was brought in (Targeted Public Distribution System (TPDS)) with two tier subsidized pricing structure for families Below Poverty Line (BPL) and for families Above Poverty Line (APL). The BPL families were to receive rice and wheat at highly subsidised prices and the APL families to receive the same at prices closer to the economic costs. For easy identification they were issued with yellow and pink cards respectively.

PUBLIC DISTRIBUTION SYSTEM PRICING

The universal PDS meant access to all. However, there were quantity restrictions. The details are presented below.

Sl. No.	*Number of members in the family*	*Quantity issued per month*
1.	One adult (one unit)	12 kg.
2.	One adult + one child (1+1½ units)	14 kg.
3.	Two adults or one adult and two children (2 units)	16 kg.
4.	Two adults and one child or one adult with three children (2 + ½ or 1 + 1½ units)	18 kg.
5.	Three adults and more (three units and above)	20 kg.

Source : Policy Note 2004-05, Government of Tamil Nadu.

Thus, the minimum supply is 12 kg., the maximum is 20 kg. In essence, it means that PDS is intended to meet the requirement only partially.

In fact, quantity restriction had been a phenomenon from the era of complete rationing of 1964. The quantity issued then was 1.6 kg. per adult per week and 0.8 kg. per child per week. This norm prevails even today. It is obvious from the above table.

Similarly, the price was also fixed by the Government, but then it had been revised time and again. Prior to 2000, two varieties of rice viz.; Common and fine and Superfine; were sold in the PDS at Rs. 2/kg. and Rs. 3.75/kg. respectively. From 2000, the price has been uniform at Rs. 3.50/kg. for both the varieties.

During the period October 2002 to August 2003, the Government of Tamil Nadu experimented with two part pricing. While the first part of the entitlement of 10 kgs. was sold at Rs. 3.50/kg., the remaining part was sold at Rs. 6/kg. From September 2003, uniform pricing is re-introduced. This can be summarised as under.

Year prior to	*Price/kg.*	*Quantity/kg.*
Oct. 2002	3.5	12, 14, 16, 18 and 20
Oct. 2002	3.5	For the first 10 kg.
Aug. 2003	6.0	For the rest up to a maximum of 10
Sep. 2003	3.5	12, 14, 16, 18 and 20

Source : Policy Note 2004-05, Government of Tamil Nadu.

SUBSIDY—THE CONCEPT

The word subsidy is of utmost importance when one deals with the scenario prevalent in the Public Distribution System in Tamil Nadu. The verbatim meaning for the word is "Monetary assistance granted by a government to a person or group in support of an enterprise regarded as being in the public interest". This subsidy pricing may be targeted or aimed at creating and increasing social benefit for the society as a whole. In practice a subsidy seems to be mainly targeted for those categories of people who need financial leverage or those who are economically weak.

TREND IN SUBSIDIES

Food subsidy, being a major component, will be the highlight of the trend for subsidies. As historical perspectives always help in viewing a problem, the food subsidy data for 15 years (1991-2005) has been provided. (see table on the next page)

The chart clearly brings out the rising burden of food subsidy on the Tamil Nadu government and hence calls for an in-depth scrutiny.

Year	Food Subsidy (Rs. Crores)
1991-92	340
1992-93	360
1993-94	350
1994-95	340
1995-96	600
1996-97	845
1997-98	890
1998-99	900
1999-2000	1170
2000-01	1560
2001-02	1200
2002-03	1200
2003-04	800
2004-05	775

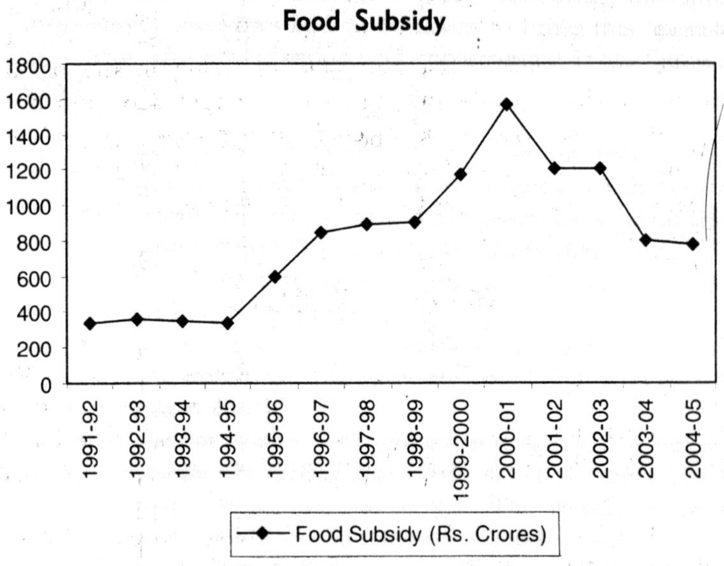

Sources : 1. White paper on Tamil Nadu Government's Finances.
2. Policy Note 2004-05, Government of Tamil Nadu.

PUBLIC DISTRIBUTION SYSTEM SUBSIDY— AT A GLANCE

The Public Distribution System is that network that works as a tool for the disbursement of all the subsidies allocated to it. It is through this framework that the commodities like Rice and Wheat are made to reach the final consumers at a highly subsidized cost. As the quantum of subsidy keeps increasing a method must be adopted to contain this movement. Measures must be taken to reduce the subsidies.

In Tamil Nadu alone, there is no difference in the pricing structure between the BPL and the APL families. Even though the Government of India brought about a two tiered system through the TPDS, Tamil Nadu has been following a Universal PDS. This clearly accounts for the consistent rise in the subsidy figures. The burden of universal PDS is obvious from the table given below.

Essential Commodity	*Rice*		
Source of Procurement/ Allotment	*GOI BPL Allotment*	*GOI APL Allotment*	*Decentralised procurement system in state*
Cost	Rs. 5.65/Kg.	Rs. 8.30/Kg.	Rs. 12.30/Kg.
Issue Price from PDS outlets (APL and BPL)	Rs. 3.50/Kg.		Rs. 3.50/Kg.
Subsidy per BPL card	Rs. 2.15/Kg.		Rs. 8.80/Kg.
Subsidy per APL card	Rs. 4.80/Kg.		Rs. 8.80/Kg.

Source : Policy Note 2004-05, Government of Tamil Nadu.

It gets clear from the above table that the Tamil Nadu Government bears out of its allocation the extra amount of Rs. 2.15/Kg for BPL and Rs. 4.80/Kg for APL. In case of State procurement, it is at uniform price of Rs. 8.80. This equality in pricing between the BPL and the APL families talks on the health of the Tamil Nadu economy.

FACTS STRIKING ON THE 'STATE'S BELLY'

- Due to non-classification of the PDS pricing into BPL

and APL categories, by the Tamil Nadu Government, the food subsidy provided by the Government benefits every one including those above the poverty line.

- Since the issue price of rice from the PDS outlets has been fixed only at Rs. 3.5 per kilo, the average monthly subsidy expenditure of the state turns out to a figure more than 120 crores.
- The total subsidy borne by the State on a BPL ration card for the purchase of one kilo of rice is Rs. 2.15, whereas the actual subsidy for the purchase of the same quantity of rice on an APL ration card is Rs. 4080. This is almost double the subsidy on a BPL card. The same in monthly figures for a 20-Kilo pack is Rs. 13 for the BPL family and Rs. 90 for the APL family.

MEASURES TO REDUCE SUBSIDIES

As the state subsidies were reaching mammoth proportions, measures had to be taken to bring this 'monster' in control. This was planned and implemented in the following ways :

- *Option-based family cards*—Under this scheme different family cards were issued to families that adopted for rice and other essential commodities. Families opted to purchase commodities other than rice. In fact, those who opted out of rice were given additional quantity of sugar.
- *Re enumeration*—A complete re-enumeration was attempted in August-September 2001 to weed out bogus cards.
- *Coupon system*—This measure was taken in order to drastically bring down the level of subsidies by reducing the misuse of the PDS off-take. Coupons were issued to the ration cardholders and they were to be exchanged for rice. Initially, for the allotted 20 kilos, two coupons of 10 kilos each were issued on a monthly basis. This system was further altered to

bring in easy exchange. The allotted 20 kilos were split into five coupons of 1, 2, 2, 5 and 10 kilos respectively.

- *Physical presence of the Family heads*—In view of targeting the PDS off-take to the right persons, it was enforced that the family heads of the respective families must physically be present for receiving their share of the public good.
- *Differential pricing*—The Tamil Nadu government follows a system of universal pricing in their PDS system. No differentiation is made in regard to the pricing of produce to the BPL and APL families. This made a significant dent in the state finances. To mitigate the negative effect of this subsidization, the Tamil Nadu government came up with a system of differential pricing. Under this system, the card holders are given rice at Rs. 3.5 for the first 10 kilos and Rs. 6.0 for the rest 10 kilos
- *'H' Cards*—This was an extreme measure taken so as to concentrate all the benefits of the subsidies to the 'needy' or the BPL category people. All those card-holders who earned a monthly income of 5000 and above were classified under the 'H' category, thus preventing them from benefiting through the PDS system. This measure was solely aimed at increasing BPL family welfare.

PUBLIC DISTRIBUTION SYSTEM IN PRACTICALITY

It does seem, from the above, that the Tamil Nadu government, by adopting a universally applicable PDS price, has done good to the people but at the cost of the exchequer. Reality is slightly different. The beneficiaries from the above subsidised structure seem to be the people, not because they consume the off-take but because they seek 'Rent' from this facility of PDS. This 'Rent seeking Behaviour' of the people turn the table's altogether.

Before delving into the actual model for the Rent seeking Behaviour in the Public Distribution System, let us browse through some economic literature on the subject.

RENT IN ECONOMIC LITERATURE

- *Rent or Economic Rent*—A payment to a factor in excess of what is necessary to keep it to its present employment. For example, if a man is earning 10,000 pounds in his current job and his next best alternative pay is 9000 pounds. This definition of rent stems from Pareto and can be contrasted by that developed by Ricardo, Mill and Marshall, which sees rent as the difference between what a factor receives as the payment which would be necessary to entice it into employment in terms of the above example, if a man would remain unemployed if offered less than 3000 pounds, but would supply his labour at this figure, the Ricardo-Mill-Marshall definition stems from Ricardo's view of the rent of lands, since he regarded all payments to land as the unnecessary surplus on the ground that had no alternative use.
- *Quasi Rent*—The income of a seller is a good or service over and above its opportunity cost, unless the good is temporarily in fixed supply.
- *Rent Seeking*—The use of real resources in an attempt to appropriate a surplus in the form of rent.

" . . . rent means the return to an asset in excess of its best alternative earning". It is "often called *economic rent* to distinguish from rent as conventionally defined. In the literature on the political economy of development, *rent* is always short for economic rent. In fact one can go further and state that in this literature *rent* is short for economic rent created by government action."

". . . The most important way in which Government creates rent is by issuing licences or permits to engage in various forms of activity.

—*Gerald M. Meir and James E. Rauch*

"It is not more than fifty year ago that some of the countries in the neighborhood of London petitioned to parliament against the extension of the turnpikes roads into the remote countries. Those remoter countries, they pretend, from the cheapness of labour, would be able to sell their grass and corn cheaper in England than themselves, and thereby would reduce their rents and ruin their cultivation."

—*Adam Smith*

Rent Seeking Behaviour in the Public Distribution System

—*A Model*

Conditions

1. Access—Possession of ration card
2. Ability—Income
3. The commodity taken here is rice, but cah be applied to any other PDS commodity.

Rent is

$R = K\ (Mp - Rp)$

where:

R – Rent
Mp = Market Price
Rp = Ration Price
K = Fraction of Rent $(0 \leq K \leq 1)$

Further:

$K = f\ (Qn, Ql, u, Y)$

where:

Qn = Quanitity
Q1 = Quality
U = Use
Y = Income

CONCLUSION

To conclude rent seeking behavior is not just a theoretical concept. It is widely prevalent in economies where there is heavy subsidization of goods in public welfare. This takes different forms; from pilferage to smuggling. According to sources in the Food Department, heavy subsidies lead to large-scale smuggling of rice from the PDS to the open market. The problem is severe due to bogus cards, which is about 11 percent. As long as the PDS price stays pegged at Re. 1.00/kg, without any annual revision in the rates, it would be difficult to curb the diversion.

References

Balaji, R. and Varadarajan, V. (2003), *"Food Subsidy in Tamil Nadu"*, Tamil Nadu Economy since 1991, Department of Economics, Loyola College.

Blaug, Mark (1968), *"Economic Theory in Retrospect"*, Heinemann Educational Books Ltd.

Central Issue Price, Price and Food Management, *Economic Survey*, 2002-03, Government of India.

Citizens Charter on Targeted Public Distribution System, Government of Tamil Nadu.

FCI's economic cost, Price and Food Management, *Economic Survey*, 2002-03, Government of India.

Food Subsidy, Price and Food Management, *Economic Survey*, 2002-03, Government of India.

Government of Tamil Nadu (2004), *"Policy Note 2004-05"*, Demand No. 12, Fort St. George.

Government of Tamil Nadu (2003),*"Citizens Charter, 2003-04"*, Demand No. 12, Fort St. George.

Interest Payments as percentage of Revenue Receipts, Section V, White paper on Tamil Nadu Government's Finances, Government of Tamil Nadu.

Marshall, Alfred (1962), *"Principles of Economics"*, ELBS.

Meir, M., Gerald and Rauch E., James (2003), *"Leading Issues in Economic Development"*, Oxford University Press, Oxford, New York.

Management of the Food Economy, Price and Food Management, *Economic Survey*, 2002-03, Government of India.

Pearce, W., David, (1992), "MacMillan Dictionary of Modern Economics", ELBS, MacMillan London and Basingstore.

Production of Foodgrains, Price and Food Management, *Economic Survey,* 2002-03, Government of India.

Procurement of foodgrains, Price and Food Management, *Economic Survey,* 2002-03, Government of India.

Public Distribution System, Price and Food Management, *Economic Survey,* 2002-03, Government of India.

Singh, Bright D. (1984), *"Micro Economic"*, Emerald Publishers.

Smith, Adam (1937), *"The Wealth of Nations"*, Random House, New York.

Tamil Nadu Budget, 2004-05, Government of Tamil Nadu.

The Public Distribution System Network, Section V, White paper on Tamil Nadu Government's Finances, Government of Tamil Nadu.

Trend in Revenue Expenditure, Section V, White paper on Tamil Nadu Government's Finances, Government of Tamil Nadu.

'The Hindu', April 21, 2000.

'The Hindu', May 14, 2000.

Todaro, P., Michel, *"Economics for a Developing World"*.

CHAPTER

12

Amartya Kumar Sen on Freedom and Famine

ANKITA DAS

I. INTRODUCTION

Sen's life work has addressed questions of poverty, inequality, freedom, and intolerance, reaching far beyond the usual confines of economics. In an article in *Scientific American* he showed that life expectancy is not only lower for African Americans than for European Americans, it is lower for African Americans even than for the people of China or the state of Kerala, one of India's poorest. He also documented the fact that in much of the world including India, Bangladesh, China, Pakistan and the Middle East, female children do not have equal access to health care and nutrition. The result, he calculated, is that there are more than 100 million "missing women"—girls who did not survive their relative deprivation.

In India Sen is a powerful voice for religious tolerance and for addressing the health and educational needs of the poor.

Regarding anti-globalization protests, he has said: "In so far as [the] protesters focus on the huge inequities of the world, they deserve a careful hearing, not a roughing up by [the police]." But he is for the most part a scholar, not an advocate: "I am used to thinking of the word 'academic' as meaning 'sound' rather than . . . 'unpractical,' he remarked when accepting the Nobel Prize.

Like Ronald Coase, Amartya Sen is also motivated by concerns about the world as it really is, but Sen's contributions are of an entirely different nature. Addressing deep philosophical issues and often using advanced mathematical techniques, Sen has taken up precisely the questions of fairness that Coase set aside in his famous "theorem."

What does it mean to say that someone is "well-off" or "better-off" than another person? How can we measure these things? And how can policies help to establish conditions that allow most people to be well-off? Sen begins his paper "The Economics of Life and Death" with the following statements: "Economics is not solely concerned with income and wealth but also with using these resources as means to significant ends, including the promotion and enjoyment of long and worthwhile lives. If, however, the economic success of a nation is judged only by income . . . the important goal of well-being is missed." Well-being, to Sen, requires more than *having* things; it requires *being able to do* things, or what he terms *capabilities*. Of course, the goods and services that income can buy are crucial to well-being, not ends in their own right. More than income is required.

Sen points out that some very poor people—for example, the populations of China, Sri Lanka, and the Indian state of Kerala—are much healthier on average than are poor people in countries five times richer (by the standard of average income) such as Brazil and South Africa. The difference is due to two things. First, income is very unequally distributed in Brazil and South Africa, so the poor in those countries suffer severe deprivation of nutrition and other necessities. Second, Kerala, China, and Sri Lanka have adopted public health policies that address many of the needs of the most vulnerable members of their populations.

Rather than measuring the economic development of nations by such indexes as average income and then devising policies to raise income levels, Sen proposes that we make our concept of well-being explicit. He begins his book *Development as Freedom* with these words: "Development can be seen . . . as a process of expanding the real freedoms that people enjoy .... If freedom is what development advances, then there is a major argument for concentrating on that overarching objective rather than some particular means." Sen goes on to say that "Development requires the removal of major sources of unfreedom," including poverty, poor economic opportunities, systematic social deprivation, intolerance, neglect of public facilities, tyranny, and repressive states.

Given his concern for such values as freedom and tolerance, it is hardly surprising that Sen has explored the role of ethical norms in our individual behaviours. In contrast to the self-interested and amoral economic man that is the behavioral foundation of much of conventional economics, Sen observes that while selfish behaviour is common, people also regularly act out of a concern (sympathy) for others, even for strangers. We also honour commitments to uphold moral norms even in circumstances in which we could benefit from violating them. In a paper titled "Rational Fools," Sen declares: "The purely economic man is needed close to being a social moron."

In the above backdrop, this paper shows the contribution of Amartya Kumar Sen in the field of famine and poverty study. In Sections II and III, we are discussing Amartya Sen's contribution in the field of famine and poverty respectively. Section IV is the concluding observations.

II. SEN'S STUDY ON FAMINE

In one of his most influential works Sen asked the very practical question: why do famines occur? The conventional answer was simple: too little food and too many mouths. But Sen showed that lack of food is rarely the cause of famine. For example, the 1974 famine in Bangladesh occurred despite the fact that per capita food availability was higher that year than it had been in the previous two years or was in the next year. The cause of the famine was massive unemployment caused by a weather-related disruption of planting activities that usually provided employment for vast numbers of poor landless workers. Without wages, the unemployed could not buy the available food, and as a result thousands starved. Moreover, as starvation spread, more affluent people began buying and hoarding large amounts of food, driving up its price and making it even further out of reach for the poor.

Thus, Sen showed that the famine resulted not from a lack of food but from an extremely uneven distribution of food caused by a very unequal distribution of income. The famine could easily have been averted had government policies been used to support the buying power of the poor. A contributing factor was that U.S. food shipments were held up during the famine (due to a dispute about Bangladeshi exports to Cuba), but the main failures were those of the government of Bangladesh. The fundamental problem, Sen argued, was governmental indifference to the plight of the very poor: "Famine is entirely avoidable if the government has the incentive to act in time . . . No democratic country with a relatively free press has ever experienced a major famine."

III. SEN'S STUDY ON POVERTY

Researches on the economics of poverty led Sen (1973, 1976, 1981) to the specification of an axiomatic structure of a new poverty measure as a function of (a) the relative frequency of the poor members of the population, (b) a weighted average of the poverty gap, i.e., the aggregate shortfall from the poverty line of the poor population, and (c) the Gini ratio of the income distribution of sub-population with incomes below the poverty line.

In fact, the Sen measure evaluating poverty and assessing inequality combines three distinctive characteristics of the inter-personal profile of poverty:

1. The head-count ration H.
2. The income gap ratio I, as a proportion of the poverty line, and
3. The Gini-co-efficient G of income distribution among the poor derived on the basis of a Lorenz curve.

Ultimately, we have $S = H[I + (1-I)G]$

S (Sen's Index of Poverty) should vary between 0 and 1. When every individual earns an income above z, S = 0 as q = 0. Similarly, S = 1, when nobody earns anything so that M = 0 and q = n. Thus, this measure gives a measure of distribution of poverty among those below the poverty line.

It is interesting to note that Sen's (1976) introduction of an axiomatic system for social welfare interpretation of the Gini ratio based on the individual income ranking of the population has propelled economists to think over it. Following Sen, Kakwani (1980) for example, presented a social welfare interpretation of the Gini ratio as a function of income.

But the criticisms that are labelled against such type of scales measures of poverty as proposed by Sen, Kakwani and others, are: (i) these measures try to capture almost all in a single indicator, valid for all dimensions of poverty, for all countries, at all times, (ii) the weights used for the shortfall from the poverty line depends on the rank order that a poor person occupies among all the poor. In the second case, the problem comes when any one is lagging behind by a money amount (say Rs. 100) of the poverty line. Then one has to count how many poor persons are ahead of this person in question. In defence of this second criticism, Sen argues that "the lower a person is in the welfare scale, the greater his sense of poverty". However, Sen shows that this formula satisfies several desirable properties, viz. that (a) the measurement of poverty focuses on the incomes of the poor and excludes information on incomes of the non-poor; (b) the value of the poverty index rises (falls) if the income of any poor person is reduced (increases); (c) the value of the poverty index rises (falls) if the income is transferred from a poor person to one who is less (more) poor. The Sen Index thus has embedded within it the head-count ratio, the poverty gap ratio and a measurement of inequality among the poor such that the value of the index would rise if there was an increase in any of the following: the number of poor relative of population, their average income gap and their relative deprivation.

IV. CONCLUSION

The contributions of Amartya Sen described so far on some specific grounds belong to the realm of purely axiomatic theory as well as empirical studies. For example, he as a hard-core theoretician has approached the problem of poverty from a different angle—considering poverty as a matter of deprivation and hence a situation of entitlements to food and other bare necessities of life. From another style he as a keen and resourceful empiricist has established a new approach to the problems of starvation and famine, whatever the critics may have said or may say.

References

Kakwani, N. (1980), Inequality and Poverty: Methods of Estimation and Policy Applications, OUP.

Karmakar, Asim K. and Manab Sadhan Biswas (1999), "Amartya Sen in Search of the Roots for Poverty, Inequality and Mismatch in Educational Sector", *Uttar Karnic*, Book Fair Number.

Sen, A.K. (1976), Poverty: An Ordinal Approach to Measurement, *Econometrica*, Vol. 44, March.

Sen, A.K. (1976), Famines as Failures of Exchange Entitlements, *Economic and Political Weekly*, Special Number, August.

CHAPTER

13

Revisiting Economics of Amartya Sen—Moving from Positive Economics to Normative Theories of Social Choice and Justice

DHIRAJ KUMAR BANDYOPADHYAY

I. INTRODUCTION

Amartya Kumar Sen was given Nobel Prize in Economics by the Royal Swedish Academy of Sciences for his work on social choice theory, axiomatic welfare economics and individual decision-making. We know that this is the work that he had done from the mid-1960s to the late 1970s, mostly in Delhi and London. A part of this work is reported in his classic book, *Collective Choice and Social Welfare (CCSW)*. This is his most important book; it is a work of immense elegance that combines formal logic, welfare economics and moral philosophy. The book had many new theorems (or at least reported on new theorems which Sen had first published in journals) and lemmas, but more importantly it influenced the way one thought of welfare economics and collective decision-making.

Sen did not start out in welfare economics. As an undergraduate student at Trinity College, Cambridge University, where he was returned to be Master, Sen wrote a dissertation on the choice of techniques, a work that was influenced by Joan Robinson, Maurice Dobb and A.K. Dasgupta. Then the dissertation with small modifications, own him Ph.D. and in 1960 it was published as a book, titled as *Choice of Techniques* and soon became a celebrated book, which students of development, planning and growth welcomed. He contributed to growth theory, cost-benefit analysis and development. Sen's paper on surplus labour in the *Journal of Political Economy* of 1966 became one of the most cited papers in development economics. Sen has now been seriously engaged, at the same time, in a closer examination of the nature and structure of inequality in existing human societies by providing us his latest valuable book *The Idea of Justice.*

Having said this, in Section II we like to discuss Sen's contribution in positive economics on Planning, Choice of Techniques and Economic Growth. In Section III we shall deal with the issues related to Social choice theory of normative economics. Sen's theory of justice would be analysed in Section IV. Section V finally concludes our study.

II. SEN'S CONTRIBUTION IN POSITIVE ECONOMICS ON PLANNING, CHOICE OF TECHNIQUES AND ECONOMIC GROWTH

Amartya Sen's first professional contribution appeared in the second half of 1956 in the "The Economic Weekly" (EW) [Sen, 1956a] and he followed up with another article for the EW in the same year [Sen, 1956b]. These appearances in the EW provoked controversies, and Sen replied to his critics [Sen, 1956c, 1956d and 1956e). He contributed four articles to the EW in 1957. In the same year his paper on the' choice of techniques' was appeared in the *Quarterly Journal of Economics* [Sen, 1957], which made him well-known in the reputed economists of the world.

Sen's early work was a response to the challenge of thinking rationally about the demands of central planning in India, at a time when planning was taken seriously by the central government. Sen (1956a) tackled the problem of the choice of techniques, a subject on which he was to publish his first book [Sen, 1960]. In fact, in these articles and his book on the choice of techniques he criticized purely market-based criteria for choice of techniques. But he recognized that market prices and costs should shape planners' choices, when such prices could not be altered by the planner without imposing too high a fiscal burden or social cost.

Following to some extent of Galeson and Leibenstein (1955) and Maurice Dobb (1955), Sen formulated a possible criterion for the choice of techniques, viz. the maximization of the surplus with a view to maximizing the rate of growth of national income and eventually the rate of growth of consumption per capita (given the rate of population growth). He modified the application of this criterion by incorporating the influence of international trade, and choices between imports, domestic production, domestic consumption and exports. He also formulated the problem of choice when future income and consumption streams might grow unsteadily or change their pattern because of technological change or other unforeseen developments, and formulated the problem of maximizing an objective function defined over such income or consumption streams [Sen, 1960: Chapter VIII].

Working in Cambridge in the late 1950s, and in close personal contact with Joan Robinson, Piero Sraffa, Luigi Pasinetti and others, he was aware of the controversy surrounding the valuation of capital and its marginal productivity, but he was not primarily concerned with those issues in his book [Sen, 1960: Chapter I].

From the point of view of gaining a perspective on his later work, his citation of a second, though partly related, class of complications is far more significant [Sen, 1960:88]:

"Apart from the difficulty introduced by changes in tastes and preferences over time, there is the problem that the relative prices are not independent of the distribution of income. In a society with inequality, as most societies are, the relative prices may not therefore be very meaningful, and we should not attach too much importance to the aggregate figures, conventionally measured, as reflecting total flows of goods and services weighted according to their relative social usefulness. This is another thing that makes it difficult to have precise preference calculations" [Bagchi, 1998].

Finally, Sen sounded a note of caution prefiguring the direction in which much of his later research would move [Sen, 1960:80].

"A simple criterion of output or surplus-rate maximization at given prices is sure to involves some rather naive assumptions about economic facts or social values, as we have seen earlier. If we wish to know what we are doing when we are choosing a particular technique at a particular point of time we really have to work out all these things we have been discussing. If the approach is complicated it is because the real world is not simple" [Bagchi, 1998].

His later work concentrated on illuminating how social values can be fruitfully captured in the choices made by any decision-maker for a collectivity, be it cooperative run by workers [Sen, 1966/1984], be it a family of peasants deciding on who should work on the farm, and how hard, and who should seek fortune outside [Sen 1966/1984] or be it planners and policy-makers in any society. Sen rarely essentialised the nature of actual societies: he took on board differences in incomes, tastes, needs and requirements for providing opportunities for developing the capabilities of different persons, groups or classes (most of these preoccupations are captured in the essays collected in Sen, 1982 and Sen, 1984, but, of course, in many of his other writings, some of which we will refer to).

Sen's work on aggregative models of planned and capitalist growth, we can refer here as Raj-Sen model of unstable growth under capitalism that he presented in 1962 to the International Economic Association Conference on the theory of interest rates [Sen, 1965/1970]. We know that the Raj-Sen model dealt with the problem of how to allocate a given value of foreign exchange resource, in the presence of limited export possibilities. In this model four sectors are distinguished: the consumption goods sectors (symbolized as C), a sector producing raw materials and intermediate goods (R) and a sector producing investment goods for sector C (symbolized as R) and finally a sector M producing investment goods (i.e. machinery) for itself and for sectors I and R. Then the results obtained by Raj and Sen strengthened the general conclusion of the Feldman-Mahalanobis model of planning, viz, that a larger allocation of investible resources to the capital goods sector would raised the rate of growth of the economy. It also gave a theoretical underpinning to the contention of Mahalanobis and other top policy-makers around that time that, for instance, if we wanted to raise the rate of growth of agriculture (predominantly a consumption good-producing sector), under conditions of a binding foreign exchange constraint, it is better to allocate foreign exchange for importing machinery and technology to build up capacity for expanding the capacity for fertilizer production, than to import fertilizer-producing machinery, or fertilizers to boost agricultural production. However, with the relative values of parameters assumed in the model, the capacity of the sector producing intermediate goods might turn out to be the limiting variable, and slow down the adjustment to the eventual steady-growth state implied by a given allocation of foreign exchange resources as between the different sectors.

But Atkinson (1969) pointed out certain limitations to the posing of the problem of choice in the model. After taking into account allocation directed by shadow prices he obtained a solution characterized by a convex combination of the ratios of the surplus allotted to the different sectors, in place of the predominantly corner solution obtained by Raj and Sen (1961). Sen's reply to such was : it requires a careful consideration of welfare judgments and not just mechanical calculations of rates of growth implied by various combinations of savings, sectoral-output ratios and other constraints allowed for by the model-builders.

In his later paper on 'The Money Rate of Interest in the Pure Theory of Growth' Sen (1965/1970) tackled the issue of Harrodian instability. In this model he showed that in Harrod's model, if the price level was allowed to vary, but the money rate of interest was fixed by the authorities, then with a given rate of inflation, there exists a rate of rise of money wages that equalises the warranted rate to the natural rate. Sen's argument was that this way of resolving the Harrodian instability problem was an alternative to the neoclassical and the neo-Keynesian postulates for resolution of that problem. It is important to note that in the neoclassical Solow-Swan model, the techniques used vary in response to change in prices and thus equalization between warranted and the natural rates is guaranteed, by assumption. On the other hand in the Kalecki-Kaldor-Robinson models shares of wages and profit would change so as to equalise the savings generated to the rate of investment required to allow growth at the natural rate. However, Sen argued in his model it is the variation of money wages which equalizes the warranted and natural rates. Then, Sen pointed out that the Harrodian stability requires not just the equality of G_w (the warranted rate of growth) to G_n (the natural rate of growth) but also of G_w to G (i.e. the actual rate of growth). In a capitalist economy, however, G is driven by the actual investment decisions of atomistic investors. Let us suppose these investors have an investment function and do not simply passively adjust their investment to the savings required to equalise G_n and G_w. In that case whenever G_w ? G_n, Sen showed that G and G_w would move in opposite directions, "and the very process that will bring G_w towards G_n will take G away from G_w" [Sen, 1965/1970: 229]. What is more, the assumption of G_w being continuously equal to G means that whenever G_w rises (falls) with a rise (fall) in the rate of interest, "we find ourselves claiming that a rise in the Interest rate stimulate growth and a fall discourages it".

So, if growth theory is to have any relevance to policy, it can not do without an investment function, and once that is given a fair play, it is easy to recognize that anything that reduces the 'knife-edge' balance between G_n and G_w will tend to highlight the 'knife-edge' balance G and G_w [Sen, 11965/ 1970:230]. Sen was also bothered by an assumption of homogeneity of capital goods implicit in most growth models, including, of course, the Solow-Swan model.

III. MOVING FROM AGGREGATIVE GROWTH PROBLEMS TO ISSUES OF SOCIAL CHOICE THEORY

Sen moved to examine the nature of social values and social choice and made himself the most innovative successor of Arrow (1951) in that field. While engaged in this endeavour, he also sought to bridge to distance between 'social values' and 'economic facts', a subject that had engaged his attention from the beginning of his career.

Sen his paper, 'Optimising the Rate of Saving' [Sen, 1961/1984], criticized the solutions based on individuals maximizing their utility on several grounds. First, they did not embody 'consumers' sovereignty': how can the present generation represent the 'sovereign' consumer of tomorrow whose fates were going to be decided by the savers of today? How can such a solution be democratic either, since again the future generation is not represented among today's decision-makers? The decision about saving necessarily involves a political choice because everybody's welfare is going to be affected by what everybody else does. For analysing the nature of this independence, Sen introduced the concept of the 'isolation paradox'. Person X may save more today if she knows that Y is also going to save more, but not if she has no such knowledge. For while X cares about the welfare of the future generation, she thinks that her saving alone is not going to make much difference to the welfare whereas other persons also saving more is going to make a big difference for her to give up a larger part of her current consumption. This phenomenon of two different kinds of behaviour in the two cases was described as 'isolation paradox' by Sen.

In extending his earlier paper he wrote another paper on 'Isolation, Assurance and the Social Rate of Discount', Sen (1967/1984) identified the purely individualistic resolution of the 'isolation paradox' with the non-co-operative solution in the Prisoner's Dilema game, and more generally with the solution of an n-person 'non-co-operative game'. He then formulated an alternative game, in which all individuals except all the others to do the 'right thing', that is, save more for the next generation, and accordingly do the right thing themselves. This situation was characterized by him as the 'assurance problem' (cr the 'assurance game'). In the absence of such assurance a market-based solution might easily produce a rate of saving which is considered too low from a political economy point of view. One way out of that difficulty would be for the legally constituted authorities to enforce a scheme of compulsory saving. But if the savers are knowledgeably playing an 'assurance game' then such outside enforcement is no longer necessary.

The general conclusion, we can draw from these papers is that issues such as the choice of the national rate of saving, the choice of the appropriate shadow prices for programme evaluation, or selection of 'appropriate' technologies are necessarily political economy in nature, and involve the recognition of informational and operational constraints. This way of approaching these ranges of problems was given a strong formal foundation in his masterpiece, *Collective Choice and Social Welfare,* finished by 1969 and published in 1970 [Sen, 1970b]. We know that even this approach was also reflected in the new introduction he wrote to the third edition of *Choice of Techniques* [Sen, 1968/1984], in his Kandy conference paper [Sen 1970d], the *UNIDO Guidelines for Project Evaluation,* he authored in 1970 jointly with Partha Dasgupta and Stephen Marglin [Dasgupta, Marglin and Sen, 1970], and the defence of those Guidelines against the alternative method of evaluation written for the OECD by IMD Little and James Mırrlees [Little and Mirrlees, 1969, Sen, 1972/1984].

Sen in his paper on 'Hume's Law and Hare's Rule' in the *Journal of Philosophy* (1966b), disputed the Humean proposition that facts and values are categorically different and that it is impossible to deduce value judgments from factual proposition alone. Sen had basically two sets of arguments for doubting the efficacy of Hume's Law. The first was that few value judgments are really as basic as 'thou shalt not kill'. Secondly, most value judgments are based on a combination of a preferred ranking of situations and believes about the facts of the world and the way those facts influence or connect with other relevant facts. These value judgments can be disputed if the two-fold believes about the facts of the case can themselves be disputed. Disputing the validity of the water tight fact-value compartmentalization is part of the grant conceptual strategy that allowed Sen to break out of the confines of old new welfare economics, and connect social welfare judgments with issues of human deprivation and capability, and of freedom in a world of necessity. Sen belived that the so called 'new welfare economics', in spite of interesting contributions by a number of authors, and it seemed to reach an impasse. On the one hand, there remained a group of 'individualists' who ruled out all interpersonal comparisons. Besides this, for them only the Pareto principle remained: all states of affair in which no person could be made better of without making some body else worse-off are equally good. Only a state of affairs in which at least one person is better-off while the others are at least as well off as before could be pronounced better than the other state of affairs. But these left the question of income distribution hanging in the air: no economist could recommend a change on 'objective ground' if it meant taking away one rupee from a billionaire in order to benefit a starving woman. Those who thought that interpersonal comparisons of utility or welfare could be made evolved so called compensation criteria. However, these criteria often produced inconsistent results. Moreover, supplementary propositions to strengthen the compensation criteria proved to be in adequate to produce a complete ordering of the range of choice.

There seemed to be another way out of the dilemma posed by the weakness of the Pareto principle in ordering the space of social states and the inconsistency and incompetence if the ordering produced by the compensation criteria advanced by Hicks, Kaldor and Scitovsky and later on further supplemented by Little. This is the formulation of a social welfare function along the lines proposed by Bergson (1938) and Samuelson (1947). However, the startling Possibility Theorem, which is better called the impossibility theorem, proved by Arrow (1951) showed that it is impossible to derive a consistent social ordering from reasonably behaved individual preference functions if that social choice function or ordering is to satisfy certain very reasonable-seeming conditions. One, for example, was the condition that no single persons choice alone should decide the social choice.

When Arrow begun working on voting theory, the subjects had a negligible history. This is not denied that it had attracted some colourful personalities. Almost 200 years before Arrow, the Marquis de Condorcet and Jean Charles de Borda had been intrigued by a strange feature of the majority decision rule, which allows it to generate cycles. The problem had latter attract the eccentric genius of Lewis Caroll who wrote mathematics using his real name, C.L. Dodgson, who had called it 'cyclical majorities'. The problem is easy enough to illustrate. Suppose three persons, 1, 2 and 3, have to choose between three candidates, X, Y and Z. suppose 1 prefers X to Y to Z, 2 prefers Y to Z to X and 3 prefers Z to X to Y. If they agree to use the majority decision rule , it is easy to see that between X and Y, X will win the election; between Y and Z, Y will win; and between Z and X, Z will win, thereby given rise to troubling cyclicity. Instead of starting from a specific voting rule, such as the majority decision, Arrow sought to get around the problem by writing down some normative axioms which a voting rule or to satisfied. To give an example, one axiom required that the voting rule must have the property that if every body preferred candidate X to Y, then Y must not be selected. This was called the Pareto axiom, after the Italian economist and sociologist of the turn of the country, Vilfredo Pareto. Arrow's shattering discovery was that if one wrote down a few more axioms, along with the Pareto axiom, no voting rule would be able to satisfy them all.

Now, this theorem set the agenda on which Amartya Sen's work on social choice was based. One set of papers that he wrote, alone, and with Prasanta Pattanaik, specified some limiting conditions on the domain of preferences, under which the majority rule 'works', that is, does not give rise to cycles. Another direction that he pursued was to introduce a new axiom into this frame-work, that of individual liberty, capturing the notion, which goes back to John Stuart Mill, that every individual should have some 'protected sphere' over which he or she has the right to decide, without being constrained by what others feel. This work turned out to be extremely influential, drawing the subjects of rights and liberty into the domain of social choice and Sen became a staunch defender of individual liberty, to the point of valuing it, in some situations, more than the Pareto axiom.

Sen's book, CCSW, played a very significant role in the coming together of welfare economics and moral philosophy. Like liberty, other concepts and ideas from philosophy, such as universalisability, fairness and justice came to be analysed using the tools of social choice theory.

During his stay at the London School of Economics (LSE) his interest moved on to something which had always, though somewhat subliminally, been there—the subject of poverty and inequality. Towards the end of his seven years at the LSE and after he moved to Oxford as professor in 1977. Amartya Sen worked on this subject. One branch of this interest was concerned with the technical problem of how best we measure poverty. The standard method in those days was to consider an income-level—the poverty line below which a person could be called poor, and then to find the percentage of a nation's population that lived below the poverty line. This was the so-called 'head-count measure'. Sen noted that this had an obvious restrictiveness. If you take away 10 dollars from a person way below the poverty line and give it to some one just below the poverty line. Clearly the head-count measure of poverty will fall, since the recipient will cease to be below the poverty line. But, surely, in an important sense, such a transfer (from someone poor to someone better-off) cannot be thought of as a poverty-reducing act. Hence, government that was using the head-count measure to design policy risked crafting faulty policy.

Sen drew on his expertise in choice theory and constructed a new measure of poverty, approaching the problem axiomatically, that is, by setting down a set of axioms of poverty that a good poverty measure should satisfy. The paper that resulted was published in *Econometrica* in 1976 and it immediately caused a groundswell of interest in the subject.

The other branch of Sen's work on poverty was related to more practical concerns: what causes famines and how best famines should be controlled or avoided. This resulted in the book, *Poverty and Famines,* which is arguably his most widely read book. This was an extremely important book, beautifully written, full of practical policy implications and insights (some of which he pursued further in his subsequent work with Jean Dreze), but it was not as intellectually significant as his earlier work. It was like some of Picasso's later works. The same book written by a less famous person would not have caused as much of a stir. This was an area where Amartya Sen was using his already established reknown to campaign for state action to eradicate poverty and to leaven the burden of the weaker sections of society. The incidence of poverty, famine, illiteracy and inequality influenced Sen to scrutinize Arrow's "impossibility theorem".

Impossibility results in social choice theory led by the pioneering work of Arrow (1951)—have often been interpreted as being thoroughly destructive of the possibility of reasoned and democratic social choice, including welfare economics. Sen has argued against that view. Indeed, he thought Arrow's powerful "impossibility theorem" invites engagement, rather than resignation. He also admitted that democratic decisions can sometimes lead to incongruities. In reality, to the extent that this is a feature of the real world, its existence and reach are matters for objective recognition. To him, inconsistencies arise more readily in some situations than in others, and it is possible to identify the situational differences and to characterize the processes through which consensual and compatible decisions can emerge.

But the impossibility results certainly deserve serious study. They often have wide—indeed sweeping—reach, not merely covering day-to-day politics, but also questioning the possibility of any assured framework for making social welfare judgments for the society as a whole. According to Sen, impossibilities thus identified also militate against the general possibility of an orderly and systematic framework for normatively assessing inequality, for evaluating poverty, or for identifying intolerable tyranny and violations of liberty. Not to be able to have a coherent framework for these appraisals or evaluations would indeed be most damaging for systematic political, social, and economic judgment. It would not be possible to talk about injustice and unfairness without having to face the accusation that such diagnoses must be inescapably arbitrary or intellectually despotic.

These bleak conclusions do not, Sen said, endure searching scrutiny, and fruitful procedures that militate against such pessimism can be clearly identified. This has indeed been largely an upbeat lecture—emphasizing the possibility of constructive social choice theory, and arguing for a productive interpretation of the impossibility results. Indeed, these apparently negative results can be seen to be helpful inputs in the development of an adequate framework for social choice, since the axiomatic derivation of a specific social choice procedure must lie in between—and close to—an impossibility, on one side, and an embarrassment of riches, on the other.

Sen argued that the possibility of constructive welfare economics and social choice (and their use in making social welfare judgments and in devising practical measures with normative significance) turns on the need for broadening the informational basis of such choice. We know that the different types of informational enrichment have been considered in the literature. A crucial element in this broadening is the use of interpersonal comparisons of well-being and individual advantage. Then it is not surprising that the rejection of interpersonal comparisons must cause difficulties for reasoned social decision, since the claims of different persons, who make up the society, have to be assessed against each other. We cannot even understand the force of public concerns about poverty, hunger, inequality, or tyranny, without bringing in interpersonal comparisons in one form or another. The information on which our informal judgments on these matters rely is precisely the kind of information that has to be—and can be—incorporated in the formal analysis of systematic social choice.

The pessimism about the possibility of interpersonal comparisons that fuelled the "obituary notices" for welfare economics (and substantially fed the fear of impossibility in social choice theory) was ultimately misleading for two distinct reasons. First, it confined attention to too narrow an informational base, overlooking the different ways in which interpersonally comparative statements can sensibly be made and can be used to enrich the analysis of welfare judgments and social choice. An over concentration on comparisons of mental states crowded out a plethora of information that can inform us about the real advantages and disadvantages of different persons, related to their substantive well-being, freedoms, or opportunities. Second, the pessimism was also based on demanding too much precision in such comparisons, overlooking the fact that even partial comparisons can serve to enlighten the reasoned basis of welfare economics, social ethics, and responsible politics.

According to Sen, addressing these problems fits well into a general program of strengthening social choice theory (and "non-obituarial" welfare economics). In general, informational broadening, in one form or another, is an effective way of overcoming social choice pessimism and of avoiding impossibilities, and it leads directly to constructive approaches with viability and reach. Formal reasoning about postulated axioms (including their compatibility and coherence), as well as informal understanding of values and norms (including their relevance and plausibility), both point in that productive direction. Indeed, the deep complementarity between formal and informal reasoning—so central to the social sciences—is well illustrated by developments in modern social choice theory.

IV. SEN'S THEORY OF JUSTICE

In his most recent, great book, Amartya Sen's life—long quest for justice is revealed with great clarity. The identification of redressable injustice is not only what animates us to think about justice and injustice, it is also central, Sen argued in his book, *The Idea of Justice*. He asked three major questions: What is the need to go beyond our sense of justice and injustice? Why must we have a theory of justice? What is the role of rationality and of reasonableness in understanding the demands of justice?

These closely related general questions are addressed by Sen, in the first ten chapters of his book, before he moved on to issues of application, involving critical assessment of the grounds on which judgments about justice are based (whether freedoms, capabilities, resources, happiness, well-being or something else), the special relevance of diverse considerations that figure under the general headings of equality and liberty, the evident connection between pursuing justice and seeking democracy seen as government by discussion, and the nature, viability and reach of claims of human rights. He has presented his theory of justice in a very broad sense. Its aim is to clarify how we can proceed to address questions of enhancing justice and removing injustice, rather than to offer resolutions of questions about the nature of perfect justice. He argued that there are clear differences with the pre-eminent theories of justice in contemporary moral and political philosophy. There are three differences in particular which demand specific attention.

First, a theory of justice that can serve as the basis of practical reasoning must include ways of judging how to reduce injustice and advance justice, rather than aiming only at the characterization of perfectly just societies—an exercise that is such a dominant feature of many theories of justice in political philosophy today.

Second, while many comparative questions of justice can be successfully resolved—and agreed upon in reasoned arguments—there could well be other comparisons in which conflicting considerations are not fully resolved. He agued that there can exist several distinct reasons of justice, each of which survives critical scrutiny, but yields divergent conclusions. Reasonable arguments in competing directions can emanate from people with diverse experiences and traditions, but they can also come from within a given society, or for that matter, even from the very same person. Therefore, Reasoning and impartial scrutiny are essential.

Third, the presence of remediable injustice may well be connected with behavioural transgressions rather than with institutional shortcomings. Then Justice is ultimately connected with the way people's lives go, and not merely with the nature of the institutions surrounding them. In contrast, many of the principal theories of justice concentrate overwhelmingly on how to establish 'just institutions', and give some derivative and subsidiary role in behavioural features. He explained with an example, John Rawls's rightly celebrated approach of 'justice as fairness' yields a unique set of 'principles of justice' that are exclusively concerned with setting up 'just institutions' (to constitute the basic structure of the society), while requiring that people's behaviour complies entirely with the demands of proper functioning of these institutions. In the approach to justice presented in his book, it is argued that there are some crucial inadequacies in this overpowering concentration on institutions (where behaviour is assumed to be appropriately compliant), rather than on the lives that people are able to lead. So, the focus on actual lives in the assessment of justice has many far-reaching implications for the nature and reach of the idea of justice. The recent investigation of what has come to be called 'capability perspective' fits directly into the understanding of justice in terms of human lives and the freedoms that the persons can respectively exercise.

Again, the use of a comparative perspective, going well beyond the limited—and limiting—framework of social contract, can make a useful contribution here. We are engaged in making comparisons in terms of the advancement of justice whether we fight oppression (like slavery, or the subjugation of women), or protest against systematic medical neglect (through the absence of medical facilities in parts of Africa or Asia, or a lack of universal health coverage in most countries in the world, including the United States), or repudiate the permissibility of torture (which continues to be used with remarkable frequency in the contemporary world—sometimes by pillars of the global establishment), or reject the quiet tolerance of chronic hunger (for example, in India, despite the successful abolition of famines). We may often enough agree that some changes contemplated (like the abolition of apartheid, to give an example of a different kind) will reduce injustice, but even if all such agreed changes are successfully implemented, we will not have anything that we can call perfect justice. In fact, practical concerns, no less than theoretical reasoning, seem to demand a fairly radical departure in the analysis of justice.

Even though in the approach presented by Sen in his book principles of justice will not be defined in terms of institutions, but rather in terms of the lives and freedoms of the people involved, institutions cannot but play a significant instrumental role in the pursuit of justice. Together with the determinants of individual and social behaviour, an appropriate choice of institutions has a critically important place in the enterprise of enhancing justice. Institutions come into the reckoning in many different ways. They can contribute directly to the lives that people are able to lead in accordance with what they have reason to value. Institutions can also be important in facilitating our ability to scrutinize the values and priorities that we can consider, especially through opportunities for public discussion (this will include considerations of freedom of speech and right to information as well as actual facilities for informed discussion).

In his book, democracy is assessed in terms of public reasoning, which leads to an understanding of democracy as 'government by discussion' (an idea that John Stuart Mill did much to advance). But he argued that democracy must also be seen more generally in terms of the capacity to enrich reasoned engagement through enhancing informational availability and the feasibility of interactive discussions. So, democracy has to be judged not just by the institutions that formally exist but by the extent to which different voices from diverse sections of the people can actually be heard.

He also thought that there are powerful traditions of reasoned argument, rather than reliance on faith and unreasoned convictions, in India's intellectual past, as there are in the thoughts flourishing in a number of other non-Western societies. In confining attention almost exclusively to Western literature, the contemporary—and largely Western—pursuit of political philosophy in general and of the demands of justice in particular has been limited and to some extent parochial. It is not, however, his claim that there is some radical dissonance between 'Western' and 'Eastern' (or generally, non-Western) thinking on these subjects.

However, despite the differences between the two traditions of the Enlightenment—the contractarian and the comparative—there are many—points of similarity as well. The common features include reliance on reasoning and the invoking of the demands of public discussion. Even though his book relates mainly to the second approach, rather than to contractarian reasoning developed by Immanuel Kant and others, much of the book is driven by the basic Kantian insight (as Christine Korsgaard puts it) : 'Bringing reason to the world becomes the enterprise of morality rather than metaphysics, and the work as well as the hope of humanity.' But, to what extent reasoning can provide a reliable basis for a theory of justice is, of course, itself an issue that has been subject to controversy. There is, however, a different kind of critique of the reliance on reasoning that points to the prevalence of unreason in the world and to the unrealism involved in assuming that the world will go in the way reason dictates. The prevalence and resilience of unreason may make reason-based answers to difficult questions far less effective. Reasoned discussion can accommodate conflicting positions that may appear to others to be 'unreasoned' prejudice, without this being quite the case. There is no compulsion, as is sometimes assumed, to eliminate every reasoned alternative except exactly one.

However, we argue that, the central point in dealing with this question is that prejudices typically ride on the back of some kind of reasoning—weak and arbitrary though it might be. Indeed, even very dogmatic persons tend to have some kinds of reasons, possibly very crude ones, in support of their dogmas (racist, sexist, classist and caste-based prejudices belong there, among varieties of other kinds of bigotry based on coarse reasoning). Unreason is mostly not the practice of doing without reasoning altogether, but of relying on very primitive and very defective reasoning. There is hope in this, since bad reasoning can be confronted by better reasoning. So the scope for reasoned engagement does exist, even though many people may refuse, at least initially, to enter that engagement, despite being challenged. Sen argued that reasoning is central to the understanding of justice even in a world which contains much 'unreason'; indeed, it may be particularly important in such a world.

V. CONCLUSION

We have examined in our preceding sections how Sen was breaching the ramparts of the narrowly confined space of traditional welfare economics and choice theory and allowing ethical considerations and interpersonal value judgments to enter that space. He was engaged, at the same time, in a closer examination of the nature and structure of inequality in existing human societies by providing us his latest valuable book, *The Idea of Justice*. What is more important is that Sen's contribution on Social Choice Theory in particular and normative economics in general have been influenced United Nations Development programme (UNDP) to a large extent in the construction of different development indicators.

References

Arrow, K.J. (1951). Social Choice and Individual Values, Second Edition. Wiley, 1963, New York.

———, (1963): 'Uncertainty and the Welfare Economics of Medical Care', *American Economic Review*, Vol. 53.

Atkinson, A.B. (1969) : 'Import Strategy and Growth under Conditions of Stagnant Export Earnings', Oxford Economic Papers, Vol. 21.

———, (1970): 'On the Measurement of Inequality', *Journal of Economic Theory*, 2(3), September.

Bagchi, A.K (1998): Amartya Kumar Sen and the Human Science of Development, *EPW*, Dec. 5.

Raj, K.N. and A.K. Sen (1959) : 'Sectoral Models for Development Planning', *Arthaniti*, Calcutta, 2(2), May, 173-82.

Sen, A.K. (1956a): 'On Choosing one's Technique', *The Economic Weekly* (EW), 8(29).

———, (1960): 'Choice of Techniques: An Aspect of the Theory of Planned Economic Development, Blackwell, Oxford.

———, (1961/1984): 'On optimizing the rate of saving', *Economic Journal*, Vol. 71, September : reprinted in Sen (1984 : 115-34).

———, (1965/1970): 'The money rate of interest in the pure theory of growth', in F.H.J. Hahn and F.P.R. Breching (eds), The Theory of Interest Rates, London, Macmillan, 268-80; excerpt reprinted as 'Interest, Investment and Growth' in Sen (1970 : 219-32).

———, (1966/1982): 'A possibility theorem on majority decisions', *Econometrica*, Vol. 34, April; reprinted in Sen (1982: 109-17).

———, (1966a/1984): 'Peasants and dualism with or without surplus labour', *Journal of Political Economy*, Vol. 74, October, reprinted in Sen (1984: 37-72).

———, (1966b): 'Hume's Law and Hare's Rule', *Philosophy*, Vol. 41.

———, (1967/1984) : 'Isolation, Assurance and the Social Rate of Discount', *Quarterly Journal of Economics*, 82(1), Fehruary; reprinted in Sen (1984,: 135-46).

———, (1968/1984): 'Optimum savings, technical choice and the shadow price of labour', Introduction to Sen, Choice of Techniques, third edition, Blackwell, Oxford; reprinted in Sen (1984: 207-23).

———, (Ed.) (1970): Growth Economics, Harmondsworth, Middlesex, Penguin Books.

Sen, A.K. (1970b): Collective Choice and Social Welfare, Oliver and Boyd, London.

———, (1970c/1971) : 'The aspects of Indian Education', Part 2 of the Lal Bahadur Shastri Memorial Lecture; reprinted in Pramit Chaudhuri (ed.), *Aspects of Indian Economic Development,* Allen and Unwin, London 144-59.

———, (1970d): 'Strategies of Economic Development: Feasibility Constraints and Planning' in E.A.G. Robinson and M. Kidron (eds.), *Economic Development in South Asia,* Macmillan, London, 369-78.

———, (1972/1984): 'Control Areas and Accounting Prices: An Approach to Economic Evaluation', *Economic Journal,* Vol. 82, March; reprinted in Sen (1984: 224-41).

———, (1973): On Economic Inequality, Clarendon Press, and Oxford.

———, (1973a): 'Poverty, Inequality and Unemployment: Some Conceptual Issues in Measurement', *EPW,* 8(31-33), Special Number, 1457-64.

———, (1976b): 'Famines as Failures of Exchange Entitlements'.

———, (2002): The Possibility of Social Choice, Rationality and Choice, Oxford University Press.

———, (2009): The Idea of Justice, Allen Lane, Published by Penguin Group.

CHAPTER

14

Amartya Sen's Contribution in Development Economics

SUSHAMA DESHMUKH

INTRODUCTION

Professor Amartya Sen is one of the worlds most important and influential intellectuals, one of its foremost thinkers. The award of the 1998 Nobel Prize for Economics to the great economist, master practitioner of the human sciences, was the best thing that happened to the Nobel Prize in his field. I have tried to put forth Amartya Sen's views about development economics and capability approach.

SEN'S CONTRIBUTION IN DEVELOPMENT ECONOMICS

Amartya Sen, has been writing about development issues a science mid-1950s' most notably, but far from exclusively in the 1960s. As a young man he was influenced by Tagore, by Nehru, and by his teacher's in Calcutta and Cambridge. He generally adopted an anti-market, anti-neoclassical stance. In the period 1957-76 Sen worked on choice of techniques, surplus labor in Indian agricultural and the rationale for import substitution in Indian planning, a group on issues relating to pervasive sub optimality to what can be termed "humane economics" which challenges conventional utility theory. It began with applied work on the Bengal famine leading to the concept of "entitlement" and branched outwards into intensive studies of poverty and deprivation, the end result is the creation of a new set of concept in economics and philosophy with human concerns at the centre. This by and passes many central preoccupations of economics and shifts work on development in to new ground.

He don't think development is softer that implies it's not sufficiently exacting . . . but certainly there was a sense for a while that development was a very hard process, ands that people had to sacrifice. There was a lot of blood, sweat and tears involved .That hadn't always been the case. If you look at the early, classical writings in development, you find that it was always assumed the economics development was a beginning process in the interest of the people. The view that you have to ignore any kind of social sympathies for the underdog, and that you can't have a democracy, didn't become the dominant thought until the beginning of modern development economics which is really in the 1940s. That lasted until quite recently, he think its fair to say that development these days is not quite as harsh as it used to be.

Standard indicators of economics success are crucial to the well-being and freedom of citizens. We have to examine critically the ends as well as the means involved in development strategies. The impact of public education, health care and social security have to be seen both in terms of their direct effects on human capabilities and their indirect consequences on people's light through raising productivity and earnings posers, and through helping to reduce the burden, especially on young women, of light fertility, the two aspects have to be considered together.

WHY THAT CHANGE DID CAME ABOUT?

Well, He think, may be because the previous view was mostly mistaken, there was a tension in it, the market economy succeeds not because some people's interests are suppressed and other people are kept out of the market, but because people gain individual advantage from it. So he don't really see that the proponents of the harsh model got the general idea at all right. It's a totally misleading analogy a pretty constantly one aesthetically, and also it's quite mistaken in terms of understanding the nature of man so he think the change came about because it was overdue.

But did something happen in a more practical sense? Why did the establishment suddenly wake up to the error of its views?

Asia's leader's kept on saying that such securities are not needed in Asia because of "Asian Values" that community values are such that people; will automatically take care of each other in a crisis well, the fact is they didn't, there is a need for a social mechanism and that social mechanism wasn't in place.

Development as Freedom is a popular summary of economist *Amartya Sen* work on development. In it he explores the relationship between freedom and development, the ways in which freedom is both a basic constituent of development in itself and enabling key to other aspects.

No knowledge of economics is assumed—there is no mathematics at all, not a single equation—and the more philosophically complex material is concentrated into a few places. And, while there's the occasional historical analysis, most of the examples are recent or even current. Sen's prose does have tendency to the wordy, lacking concisions, but the result is nevertheless broadly accessible. Covering a diverse range of topics, it should have something for anyone involved with development. Rather than common focus of income and wealth, or on mental satisfaction (by utilitarian) or processed (By libertarians), Sen suggests a focus on what he calls capabilities-substantive human freedoms. And he argues for a broad view of freedom, one that encompasses both processes and opportunities, and for recognition of "the heterogeneity of distinct components of freedom".

"An adequately broad view of development is sought in order to focus the evaluative scrutiny of things that really matter, and in particular to avoid the neglect of crucially important subjects". Though of course it is—and must be—a matter of debate as to what is important.

Freedom is both constitutive of development and instrumental to it: instrumental freedoms include political freedom, economic facilities, social opportunities, transparency, and security, which are all different but interconnected.

Sen himself suggesting some readers may want to skip sections. In it he explores different informational bases for evaluating justice—utilitarian, libertarian, and Rawlsian—and argues for a focus on the capabilities of people to do and be what they value. He stresses that this is not an "all or none" choice—that even if an approach has limited application, answers to some questions may be useful. He argues that capability deprivation is a better measure of poverty than low income, because it can capture aspects of poverty hidden by income measure. "Political rights, including freedom of expression and discussion, are not only pivotal in inducing social responses to economic needs, they are also central to the conceptualization of economic needs themselves." It is also important to support the effective functioning of democracy: formal rules are not enough without good democratic practice. Another focus of Sen's work has been the role of women in development. Here he argues that, while improving their well-being is important, enhancing their agency is just as critical, and one notable illustration: women's literacy and employment levels are the best predictors of both child survival and fertility rate reduction.

Sen surveys the relationships between justice, freedom, and responsibility. And he reiterates the advantages of capabilities over narrower measures of human development. The ides of "human capital" is a step forwards, but is still too narrow in its restriction to effects on production; it fails to capture the direct contribution of human capabilities to well-being and freedom land their indirect effects on social change.

SEN'S APPROACH

Sen explicitly considers and rejects the three ethical or philosophical perspectives provided by utilitarianism, libertarianism, and Rawlsianism. Implicitly, he also rejects Posner's wealth maximization argument as a fourth alternative. Before him, others to have contested utilitarianism as the putatively superior theoretical or ethical framework include John Rawls, E.F. Schumacher, Richard Posner and—in the development economics context—Gunnar Myrdal and Benjamin Higgins. Thus, the appropriate context in which to apprehend Sen's attempt to develop a superior decision-making framework is one which explicitly considers utilitarianism and available critiques of it. Sen endorses his own position as a composite of utilitarianism and libertarianism.

1. Utilitarianism

Sen's objection is more that destitute people make an accommodation to their poverty and distort their own apprehension of utility prospects. His concern is less with the qualitative difference between the pleasures than with the qualitative difference between the capability of fortunate and unfortunate people to enjoy those pleasures. Sen's concern is thus with something close to the opposite of the "utility monsters" who are of concern to Posner, i.e. his concern is with the deprived rather than the depraved. Sen, orthodoxy thus has a lot to answer for especially in the context of development economy. Sens stance on rights in quite different form Posners but is nonetheless not one of ancient natural right. Sen does not explicitly discuss Poseners throty, but implicitly dismisses it in rejecting libertarianism and utilitarianism as alternatives to his own capability approach.

2. Libertarianism

Sen rejects libertarianism as too limited in its approach. Whereas libertarians tend to stress negative freedoms. Sen is more focused on positive freedoms in his development work. Poverty is not a violation of negative freedom but rather of positive freedom because a "person in extreme poverty is not free to do many things".

Sen criticizes those libertarian theories (e.g. Nozick's) that place a high priority on freedoms, insofar as they advocate that a person has the right to pursue anything he likes provided he does not violate the constraints that restrain him from interfering in the legitimate activities of another. Sen objects that such libertarian arguments place too much stress on processes and not enough stress on actual results or consequences. A "consequent-independent theory of political priority" is unacceptable to Sen, and in his view giving such a priority to liberty may still lead to "the violation of substantive freedoms of individuals to achieve those things to which they have reason to attach great importance" such as avoidable mortality, being well nourished, healthy and educated. No one's rights may be violated in a famine, for example, but people still suffer severe deprivations.

Accordingly, for Sen, an understanding of justice needs a broader informational basis than that on matters of negative freedom. His concern therefore is with freedom in terms of both its positive and negative dimensions.

3. Rawls' "Correction of Utilitarianism" (1972)

The defect Sen sees in Rawls is that Rawls focuses on the distribution of resources rather than on the enhancement of a person's capabilities. Insofar as Sen's Development As Freedom is effectively a re-write of Rawls—with some modification of Rawls not for wanting to lift the floor, but for mis-specifying the "primary goods" which need to be lifted—Bloom's critique of Rawls remains potentially applicable to Sen (and indirectly to Sen's philosopher collaborator Nussbaum (1993), whose review of Bloom's *Closing of the American Mind* (1987) is as misconstructed as it is dismissive). Sen knows what he wants in the here and now. He wants improved living and opportunities for the worlds poorest. If utilitarianism, libertarianism and Rawlsianism don't themselves justify what Sen wants, what does? Given the humaneness of the goal, it might be expected that something must. Sen seeks—and purports to find—this desirable and necessary ethical underpinning in Smith and Aristotle, or at least in particular interpretations thereof.

4. Higgins on Economics and Ethics in the New Approach to Development (1978)

Higgins and Sen therefore argue that some conception of a "good society" is inevitably being pursued, and in their respective views this requires going well beyond a Paretian optimum.

5. Sen and his Capabilities Approach (2000)

Amartya Sen is the most recent entrant into this campaign to find an ethically superior maxim and, or conception of justice, within which to apprehend human development. He has pushed his capabilities approach for some time now, most recently in *Development as Freedom* (2000). In the context of development economics he therefore now advocates an "improvement" on the usual utilitarian normative approach—per medium of a recognition of what constitutes human capabilities and what accordingly constitutes an appropriate re-definition of poverty (with less emphasis on financial poverty and more emphasis on unfulfilled human capability). For him (1987: 35), the orthodox "criterion of Pareto optimality is an extremely limited way of assessing social achievement".

CONCLUSIONS

Sen has highlighted various limitations in the orthodox neoclassical approach to development, and directed attention to the need to develop human capabilities. In short, he has sought to again widen the philosophical and teleological focus of economics and to direct attention to the conscious articulation of human ends and to consideration of factors which constrain the free exercise of individual agency. He said that the importance of economic philosophy needs to be more generally recognized.

Sen's approach is pragmatic and well intentioned, and as such it derives support from those who want to intervene to help the worst-off.

In arguing for development as freedom, or freedom as development, Sen is effectively, if tacitly, positing a view of the nature of man and of teleology. He leaves us without a reason to accept that wealth is merely useful in the service of something else while freedom is axiomatically the ultimate end, rather than merely another means to that end.

His implicit claim is that he has provided the correct interpretations of such concepts as the nature of humankind, freedom, teleology, and human capability and development.

REFERENCES

Meghnand Desai, Amartya Sens' Contribution to Development Economics.

L.A. Duhs, (Real-world Economics Review Issues No. 47) Sen's Economics Philosophy.

Benicourt, Emmanuelle 2004. "Amartya Sen Again", *Post-autistic Economics Review*, Issue No. 24, March, http://www.btinternet.com/~pae_news/review/issue24.htm

Duhs, L.A., 1998. "Five Dimensions of the Interdependence of Philosophy and Economics: Integrating HET and the History of Political Philosophy", *International Journal of Social Economics*, Vol. 25/10.

Higgins, B., 1978. "Economics and Ethics in the New Approach to Development", *Philosophy in Context*, Vol. 7.

Pettit, P., 2001. "Symposium on Amartya Sen's Philosophy: Capability and Freedom: A Defence of Sen", *Economics and Philosophy*, 17(1).

Sen, A., 2000. *Development as Freedom*, Anchor Books, New York

Freedom as Progress Laurawallace Interviews Nobel Prize Winner Amartya Sen.

Amartya Sen, Development and Thinking a Beginning of the 21st Century Research Paper.

Development : Which Way Now Amartya Sen (*The Economics Journal*, 1983).

Dr. Sushama Deshmukh, Associate Professor, Mahila Mahavidyalay, Amravati, D.O.B. 4th April 1966.

CHAPTER

15

Some Thoughts of Amartya Sen : A Discussion on Social Choice and Individual Behaviour

M.B. Mistry and S. Ahmed

The idea of reason to identify and promote better and more acceptable societies has powerfully moved people in the past and continues to do so even now. However, in economic literature there is skepticism of the possibility of reasoned progress. Amartya Sen in this regard identifies three distinct lines of skepticism that demand particular attention which are as follows:

(i) Given the heterogeneity of preferences and values that different people have, even in a given society, it is not possible to have a coherent framework for reasoned soçial assessment, because there can be no such thing as rational and social assessment, because there can be no such thing as rational and social evaluation. Kenneth Arrow's famous "Impossibility Theorem" is often used to drive home this point. This theorem is interpreted as proving the impossibility of rationally deriving social choice from individual preferences, and it has been taken to be a deeply pessimistic result.

(ii) The second line of criticism takes a methodological form and draws on an argument that questions our ability to have what we intend to have, arguing that "unintended consequences" dominate actual history. If most of the important things that happen are not intended (i.e. they are not brought about by (purposive action) then reasoned attempts at pursuing what we want might appear to be rather pointless.

(iii) The third line of criticism relates to the possible range of human values and behavioural norms. In a market economy, we cannot have social arrangements that call for anything more "social" or "moral" or "committed". Thus the possibility of reasoned social change cannot go beyond the working of market mechanism. To ask for more would be hopelessly utopian.

Amartya Sen has countered the above three lines of criticism in the following manner and proved that it is possible to have social choice based on reason and reasoned progress for betterment of society can be achieved.

I. IMPOSSIBILITY AND INFORMATIONAL BASES

Amartya Sen reinterprets Arrow's impossibility theorem which is so often used to support the first criticism. In his view, the Arrow theorem in effect establishes not the impossibility of rational social choice but the impossibility that arises when we try to base social choice on a limited class of information, as is the case in the literature in welfare economics. The traditional informational base of which the majority decision procedure is a prominent example, is extremely limited and it is clearly quite inadequate for making informed judgments about welfare economic problems. This is not primarily because it leads to inconsistency as generalized in Arrow theorem but because we cannot really make social judgements with so little information. Indeed through informational broadening, it is possible to have a coherent and consistent criteria for social and economic assessment. Thus in Amartya Sen's view, the social choice literature, which has resulted from Arrow's pioneering move, is as much a world of possibility as of conditional impossibilities.

2. INTENDED CHANGES AND UNINTENDED CONSEQUENCES

The idea that unintended consequences of human action are responsible for many of the big changes in the world is not hard to appreciate. For example, discovery of penicillin from a left-over dish not intended for that purpose. There is nothing embarrassing in this for a rationalistic approach. What is required is that reasoned attempts to bring about social change should in the relevant circumstances, help us to get better results. There are plenty of examples of success in social and economic reforms guided by motivated programs. For example, universal literacy program and eradication of small pox. Sometimes things may go wrong while doing but they can be done better next time. Thus learning by doing is a great ally of the rationalist reformer.

Adam Smith is supposed to be the originator of the "theory of unintended consequences". For example, butcher-baker-brewer, all sell for money not for consumer's welfare, i.e. they are all guided by self-interest. Menger and Hayek are the later economists who contributed to this theory. A reinterpretation of the theory would show that it is not so much that some consequences are unintended but that causal analysis can make the unintended effects reasonably predictable. Indeed the butcher may predict that exchanging meat for money not only benefits him but also the consumer so that the relationship can be expected to work on both sides and is thus sustainable. Thus the idea of unintended consequences is in no way hostile to the possibility of rationalist reform. Economic and social reasoning can take note of consequences that may not be intended but which nevertheless result from institutional arrangements and the case for particular institutional arrangements can be better evaluated by noting the likelihood of various unintended consequences.

3. SOCIAL VALUES AND PUBLIC INTEREST

Can we really claim that human beings are uncompromisingly self-interested? Amartya Sen argues that such skepticism is quite unjustified, in spite of the fact that self-interest is an extremely important motive. And yet we see actions, day in and day out, that reflect values with clear social components that take us well beyond the narrow confines of purely selfish behavior. The emergence of social norms can be facilitated both by communicative reasoning and by evolutionary selection of behavioral modes.

The use of socially responsible reasoning and of ideas of justice relate closely to the centrality of individual freedom. Different persons may have very different ways of interpreting ethical ideas including those of social justice and they may even be far from certain about how to organize their thoughts about it. But the basic ideas of justice are not alien to social beings, who not only worry about their own interests but are also able to think about their family members, neighbors, fellow citizens, and about other people in the world. The thought experience involving the "impartial spectator" that Adam Smith analyzed is a formalization of an informal and pervasive idea that occurs to most of us. Space does not have to be artificially created in the human mind for the idea of justice or fairness. That space already exists, and it is a question of making systematic and effective use of the general concerns that people do have.

The role of values is extensive in human behavior and to deny this would amount not only to a departure from the tradition of democratic thought but also to the limiting of our rationality. It is the power of the reason that allows us to consider our obligations and ideals as well as interest and advantages. To deny this freedom of thought would amount to a severe constraint on the reach of our rationality.

Social values can play and have played an important part in the success of various forms of social organization, including the market mechanism, democratic politics, elementary civil and political rights, provision of basic public goods and institutions for public action and protest.

Capitalism though popularly perceived as an arrangement that works only on the basis of greed of every one, is in fact dependent on powerful systems of values and norms. Capitalism works effectively through a system of ethics that provides the vision and the trust needed for successful use of market mechanism and related institutions. Thus, successful operation of an exchange economy depends on mutual trust and the use of norms, explicit as well as implicit. The merits of selfless work and devotion to enterprise in raising productivity have been seen as important for economic achievements in many countries in the world and there are many variations in these behavioral codes even among the most developed industrial nations. However, in an economy when there is a limited emergence of business norms, it may lead to the hold of organized crime. For example, Mafia in Italy.

Norms and values in behavior pattern in a market economy play a crucial role in making of public policy. Special attention should be paid to create conditions for more informed understanding and enlightened public discussion. Thus, public policy has a role not only in attempting to implement the priorities that emerge from social values and affirmations but also in facilitating and guaranteeing fuller public discussion. The reach and quality of open discussion can be helped by a variety of public policies such as press freedom and media independence, expansion of basic education and schooling, enhancement of economic independence and other social and economic changes that help individuals to become participating citizens. Central to this approach is the idea of the public as an active participant in change rather than as a passive and docile recipient of instructions or of dispensed assistance.

References

Arrow, Kenneth (1999), "Amartya K. Sen's Contributions to the Study of Social Welfare", *The Scandinavian Journal of Economics*, Vol. 101, No. 2, pp. 163-72.

Atkinson, A.B. (1999), "The Contributions of Amartya Sen to Science to Welfare Economics", *The Scandinavian ...*, pp. 173-90.

Bagchi, Amiya Kumar (1998), "Amartya Kumar Sen and the Human Science of Development", *Economic and Political Weekly*, Vol. XXXII, No. 49, pp. 3139-50.

Mitra, Tapan (1999), "Amartya Sen's Contirbution to Social Choice and Measurement", *Science and Culture*, Vol. 65, Nos. 9-10, pp. 292-93

"Press Release from the Royal Swedish Academy of Sciences", *The Scandinavian*, pp. 157-62.

Sen, Amartya (1999), "The Possibility of Social Choice", *The American Economic Review*, Vol. 89, No. 3, pp. 349-78.

Sen, Amartya (1999), *Development as Freedom*, Oxford, Delhi.

CHAPTER

16

Amartya Sen and Many Faces of Gender Inequality and Development Economics

SHWETA AGRAWAL

EARLY LIFE OF AMARTYA SEN

Amartya Kumar Sen, an Indian economist and winner of the Nobel Prize was born on 3rd November 1933 in Santiniketan, West Bengal. His ancestral home was in Wari, Dhaka in modern-day in Bangladesh. His family migrated to India following partition in 1947. Rabindranath Tagore is said to have given Amartya Sen his name "Amartya" meaning "immortal". Sen's maternal grandfather Kistimohan Sen was a renowned scholar of medieval Indian literature. Amartya Sen was born to professor father Ashutosh Sen, who taught Chemistry at Dhaka University and mother Amita Sen, St. Gregory's school in Dhaka in modern-day Bangladesh was Amartya Sen's high-school. Before moving to Trinity College,

Cambridge. Sen studied in India at the school system of Visva Bharati University and Presidency College, Kolkata, where he earned a first class B.A. in 1953. At Trinity College he received B.A. in 1956 and then a Ph.D. in 1959. He was also allowed four years to immerse himself in philosophical issues during his stay at Trinity College.[1]

HONOURS AND AWARDS FOR AMARTYA SEN

- He received the Nobel Memorial Prize in Economics for his work in Welfare Economics in 1998.
- In 1999 he received Bharat Ratna 'the highest civilian award in India' by the President of India.
- In 1999 he was offered honorary citizenship of Bangladesh from Prime Minister Sheikh Hasina in recognition of his achievements in winning the Nobel Prize, and given that his family origins were in what has become the modern state of Bangladesh.
- He received the 2000 Leontief Prize for his outstanding contribution to economic theory from the Global Development and Environment Institute.
- He was the 351st Commencement Speaker of Harvard University.
- In 2002, he received the International Humanist Award from the International Humanist Ethical Union.
- Eisenhower Medal, for Leadership and Services USA, 2000.
- Companion of Honour, UK, 2000.
- In 2002, he received honorary degree from the University of Tokyo.
- In 2003, he was conferred the Lifetime Achievement Award by the Indian Chamber of Commerce.
- Lifetime Achievement award by Bangkok-based United Nations Economic and Social Commission for Asia and the Pacific (UNESCAP).

Amartya Sen has been writing about development issues since the mid-1950s, most notably, but far from exclusively, in the 1960s. As a young man he was influenced by Tagore, by

Nehru and by his teachers in Calcutta and Cambridge. He generally adopted an anti-market, anti-neoclassical stance. In the period 1957-76 Sen worked on choice of techniques, surplus labor in Indian agriculture and the rationale for import substitution in Indian planning; a group of issues relating to "pervasive sub-optimality", which led to development of the concept of shadow pricing. The second phase came from 1976 onwards when there was a shift from sub-optimality to what can be termed "humane economics", which challenges conventional utility theory. It began with applied work on the Bengal famine, leading to the concept of "entitlement", and branched outwards into intensive studies of poverty and deprivation. The end result is the creation of a new set of concepts in economics and philosophy with human concerns at the centre. This by-passes many central preoccupations of economists and shifts work on development on to new ground.

MAJOR WORKS OF AMARTYA K. SEN

- "On Optimizing the Rate of Saving", 1961, *EJ*.
- *Collective Choice and Social Welfare*, 1970.
- "Behavior and the Concept of Preference", 1973, *Economica*.
- *On Economic Inequality*, 1973.
- "Informational Bases of Alternative Welfare Approaches", 1974, *JPubE*.
- "Liberty, Unanimity and Rights", 1976, *Economica*.
- "Welfare Inequalities and Rawlsian Axiomatics", 1976, *Theory and Decision*.
- "Poverty: An ordinal approach to measurement", 1976, *Econometrica*.
- "Social Choice Theory: A re-examination", 1976, *Econometrica*.
- "Real National income", 1976, *RES*.
- "On Weights and Measures: Informational constraints in social welfare analysis", 1977, *Econometrica*.
- "Rational Fools: A critique of the Behavioral Foundations of Economic Theory", 1977, *Philosophy and Public Affairs*.

- "Interpersonal Comparisons of Utility", 1979, in Boskin, editor, *Economics and Human Welfare.*
- "Personal Utilities and Public Judgments: Or what's wrong with welfare economics", 1979, *EJ.*
- "Utilitarianism and Welfare", 1979, *J of Philosophy*
- "The Welfare Basis of Real Income Comparisons", 1979, *JEL.*
- "The Sexual Division of Labor and the Working Class Family", 1980, *RRPE.*
- *Poverty and Famines: An Essay on Entitlement and depression,* 1981.
- *Choice, Welfare and Measurement,* 1982.
- "Liberty and Social Choice", 1983, *Journal of Philosophy.*
- *Resources, Values and Development,* 1984.
- "Social Choice Theory", 1986, in Arrow and Intiligator, editors, *Handbook of Mathematical Economics,* Vol. III.—intro.
- *The Standard of Living,* 1987.
- *Inequality Re-examined,* 1995.
- "East and West: The Reach of Reason", 2000, *New York Review of Books.*

Nobel Laureate Amartya Sen's work on gender inequality is of seminal importance. His work on the theory of the household represents the household not as an undifferentiated unit, but as a unit of cooperation as well as of inequality and internal discrimination. He has worked on problems of discrimination against women in the development process, on survivorship differentials between men and women under conditions of social discrimination against women, and on women's agency in the process of social development. Along with his academic collaborator Jean Dreze, Professor Sen proposed and popularized the concept of "missing women"—estimated to exceed 100 million round the world—which has given us a new way of understanding and mapping the problem.[2]

Professor Sen takes a comprehensive and deeply concerned look at the "many faces of gender inequality." Focusing on South Asia, he discovers in the data thrown up by the Census of 2001 an interesting phenomenon—a split India, "something of a social and cultural divide across India, splitting the country into two nearly contiguous halves, in the extent of anti-female bias in nasality and post-nasality mortality." He concludes by identifying the principal issues, emphasising the need to "take a plural view of gender inequality," and calling for a new agenda of action to combat and put an end to gender inequality.

SEVEN TYPES OF INEQUALITY

IT was more than a century ago, in 1870 that Queen Victoria wrote to Sir Theodore Martin complaining about "this mad, wicked folly of 'Woman's Rights'." The formidable empress certainly did not herself need any protection that the acknowledgment of women's rights might offer. Even at the age of eighty, in 1899, she could write to A.J. Balfour, "We are not interested in the possibilities of defeat; they do not exist." That, however, is not the way most people's lives go—reduced and defeated as they frequently are by adversities. And within each community, nationality and class, the burden of hardship often falls disproportionately on women.

The afflicted world in which we live is characterized by deeply unequal sharing of the burden of adversities between women and men. Gender inequality exists in most parts of the world, from Japan to Morocco, from Uzbekistan to the United States of America. However, inequality between women and men can take very many different forms. Indeed, gender inequality is not one homogeneous phenomenon, but a collection of disparate and interlinked problems. Let me illustrate with examples of different kinds of disparity.

(1) Mortality Inequality

In some regions in the world, inequality between women and men directly involves matters of life and death, and takes the brutal form of unusually high mortality rates of women and a consequent preponderance of men in the total population, as opposed to the preponderance of women found in societies with little or no gender bias in health care and nutrition. Mortality inequality has been observed extensively in North Africa and in Asia, including China and South Asia.

(2) Nasality Inequality

Given a preference for boys over girls that many male-dominated societies have, gender inequality can manifest itself in the form of the parents wanting the newborn to be a boy rather than a girl. There was a time when this could be no more than a wish (a daydream or a nightmare, depending on one's perspective), but with the availability of modern techniques to determine the gender of the fetus, sex-selective abortion has become common in many countries. It is particularly prevalent in East Asia, in China and South Korea in particular, but also in Singapore and Taiwan, and it is beginning to emerge as a statistically significant phenomenon in India and South Asia as well. This is high-tech sexism.

(3) Basic Facility Inequality

Even when demographic characteristics do not show much or any anti-female bias, there are other ways in which women can have less than a square deal. Afghanistan may be the only country in the world the government of which is keen on actively excluding girls from schooling (it combines this with other features of massive gender inequality), but there are many countries in Asia and Africa, and also in Latin America, where girls have far less opportunity of schooling than boys do. There are other deficiencies in basic facilities available to women, varying from encouragement to cultivate one's natural talents to fair participation in rewarding social functions of the community.

(4) Special Opportunity Inequality

Even when there is relatively little difference in basic facilities including schooling, the opportunities of higher education may be far fewer for young women than for young men. Indeed, gender bias in higher education and professional training can be observed even in some of the richest countries in the world, in Europe and North America.

Sometimes this type of division has been based on the superficially innocuous idea that the respective "provinces" of men and women are just different. This thesis has been championed in different forms over the centuries, and has had much implicit as well as explicit following. It was presented with particular directness more than a hundred years before Queen Victoria's complaint about "women's rights" by the Revd James Fordyce in his Sermons to Young Women (1766), a book which, as Mary Wollstonecraft noted in her A Vindication of the Rights of Women (1792), had been "long made a part of woman's library." Fordyce warned the young women, to whom his sermons were addressed, against "those masculine women that would plead for your sharing any part of their province with us", identifying the province of men as including not only "war", but also "commerce, politics, exercises of strength and dexterity, abstract philosophy and all the abstruse sciences."[1] Even though such clear-cut beliefs about the provinces of men and women are now rather rare, nevertheless the presence of extensive gender asymmetry can be seen in many areas of education, training and professional work even in Europe and North America.

(5) Professional Inequality

In terms of employment as well as promotion in work and occupation, women often face greater handicap than men. A country like Japan may be quite egalitarian in matters of demography or basic facilities, and even, to a great extent, in higher education, and yet progress to elevated levels of employment and occupation seems to be much more problematic for women than for men.

In the English television series called "Yes, Minister," there is an episode where the Minister, full of reforming zeal, is trying to find out from the immovable permanent secretary, Sir Humphrey, how many women are in really senior positions in the British civil service. Sir Humphrey says that it is very difficult to give an exact number; it would require a lot of investigation. The Minister is still insistent, and wants to know approximately how many women are there in these senior positions. To which Sir Humphrey finally replies, "Approximately, none."

(6) Ownership Inequality

In many societies the ownership of property can also be very unequal. Even basic assets such as homes and land may be very asymmetrically shared. The absence of claims to property can not only reduce the voice of women, but also make it harder for women to enter and flourish in commercial, economic and even some social activities. This type of inequality has existed in most parts of the world, though there are also local variations. For example, even though traditional property rights have favored men in the bulk of India, in what is now the State of Kerala, there has been, for a long time, matrilineal inheritance for an influential part of the community, namely the Nairs.

(7) Household Inequality

There are often enough, basic inequalities in gender relations within the family or the household, which can take many different forms. Even in cases in which there are no overt signs of anti-female bias in, say, survival or son-preference or education, or even in promotion to higher executive positions, the family arrangements can be quite unequal in terms of sharing the burden of housework and child care. It is, for example, quite common in many societies to take it for granted that while men will naturally work outside the home, women could do it if and only if they could combine it with various inescapable and unequally shared household duties. This is sometimes called "division of labor," though women could be forgiven for seeing it as "accumulation of labor." The reach of this inequality includes not only unequal relations within the family, but also derivative inequalities in employment and recognition in the outside world. Also, the established fixity of this type of "division" or "accumulation" of labor can also have far-reaching effects on the knowledge and understanding of different types of work in professional circles. When I first started working on gender inequality, in the 1970s, I remember being struck by the fact that the Handbook of Human Nutrition Requirement of the World Health Organization (WHO), in presenting "calorie requirements" for different categories of people, chose to classify household work as "sedentary activity," requiring very little deployment of energy. I was, however, not able to determine precisely how this remarkable bit of information had been collected by the patrician leaders of society.[3]

I may end by trying briefly to identify some of the principal issues I have tried to discuss. First, I have argued for the need to take a plural view of gender inequality, which can have many different faces. The prominent faces of gender injustice can vary from one region to another, and also from one period to the next.

Second, the effects of gender inequality, which can impoverish the lives of men as well as women, can be more fully understood by taking detailed empirical note of specific forms of inequality that can be found in particular regions. Gender inequality hurts the interests not only of girls and grown-up women, but also of boys and men, through biological connections (such as childhood undernourishment and cardiovascular diseases at later ages) and also through societal connections (including in politics and in economic and social life).[4]

Development economics is a comparatively young area of inquiry. It was born just about a generation ago, as a sub-discipline of economics, with a number of other social sciences looking on both skeptically and jealously from a distance. So writes Albert Hirschman in this illuminating essay, aptly called 'The Rise and Decline of Development Economics', Hirschman puts his main thesis thus: our sub-discipline had achieved its considerable luster and excitement through the implicit idea that it could slay the dragon of backwardness virtually by itself or, at least, that its contribution to this task was central.

There is some plausibility in this diagnosis, but is it really true that development economics has no central role to play in the conquest of underdevelopment and economic backwardness? More specifically, were the original themes in terms of which the subject was launched really so far from being true or useful? I shall argue that the obituary may be premature, the original themes while severely incomplete in coverage—did not point entirely in the wrong direction, and the discipline of development economics does have a central role to play in the field of economic growth in developing countries. But I shall also argue that the problematique underlying the approach of traditional development economics is, in some important ways, quite limited, and has not—and could not have—brought us to an adequate understanding of economic development. Later on, I shall take up the question as to the direction in which we may try to go instead.[5]

There is a methodological problem in identifying a subject—or a sub-discipline as Hirschman calls it—with a given body of beliefs and themes rather than with a collection of subject matters and problems to be tackled. But Hirschman is certainly right in pointing towards the thematic similarities of the overwhelming majority of contributions in development economics.

It was argued by development economists that neoclassical economics did not apply terribly well to underdeveloped countries. This need not have caused great astonishment, since neoclassical economics did not apply terribly well anywhere else. However, the role of the state and the need for planning and deliberate public action seemed stronger in underdeveloped countries, and the departure from traditional neoclassical models was, in many ways, more radical.

The World Development Report, 1982 (henceforth (WDR)) presents comparative growth data for the period 1960-80 for 'low-income economies' and 'middle income economies', with a dividing line at US $ 410 in 1980. Leaving out small countries (using a cut-off line of 10 million people) and excluding the OPEC countries which have had rather special economic circumstances during the 'seventies, we have 14 countries in the low-income category for which data on economic growth (GNP or GDP) are given in WDR. Correspondingly, there are 18 such countries in the middle-income category. For three of the low-income countries, namely, China, Bangladesh and Afghanistan, the GNP growth figures are not given in WDR and they have been approximately identified with GDP growth. In interpreting the results, this has to be borne in mind, and only those conclusions can be safely drawn which would be unaffected by variations of these estimates within a wide range.

The fourteen low-income economies vary in terms of growth rate of GNP per capita during 1960-80 from minus 0.7% in Uganda to 3.7% in China. The top three countries in terms of economic growth are China (3.7%), Pakistan (2.8%) and Sri Lanka (2-4%). (Note that China's pre-eminent position would be unaffected even if the approximated growth figure is substantially cut.) In the middle-income group, the growth performance again varies a great deal, ranging from minus 1.0% for Ghana to 8.6% for Romania. The top three countries in terms of economic growth are Romania (8.6%), South Korea (7.0%) and Yugoslavia (5-4%).[6]

How do these high-performance countries compare with others in the respective groups in terms of the parameters associated with the main theses of traditional development economics? Take capital accumulation first. Of the three top growth-performers, two also have the highest share of gross domestic investment in GDP, namely, Sri Lanka with 36% and China with 31%. Pakistan comes lower, though it does fall in the top half of the class of fourteen countries.

Turning now to the middle-income countries, the top three countries in terms of growth are also the top three countries in terms of capital accumulation, namely, Yugoslavia with 35%, Romania with 34%, and South Korea with 31%. Thus, if there is anything to be learned from the experience of these successful growers regarding the importance of capital accumulation, it is certainly not a lesson that runs counter to the traditional wisdom of development economics.

I shall not try to summaries the main points of the paper, but I will make a few concluding remarks to put the discussion in perspective. First, traditional development economics has not been particularly unsuccessful in identifying the factors that lead to economic growth in developing countries. In the field of causation of growth, there is much life left in traditional analyses. Secondly, traditional development economics has been less successful in characterizing economic development, which involves expansion of people's capabilities. For this, economic growth is only a means and often not a very efficient means either because of close links between entitlements and capabilities, focusing on entitlements—what commodity bundles a person can command—provides a helpful format for characterizing economic development. Supplementing data on GNP per capita by income distributional information is quite inadequate to meet the challenge of development analysis.

NOTES AND REFERENCES

1. www.indianetzone.com › ... › Indian Scientists.
2. *Frontline*, Volume 18—Issue 22, Oct. 27 to Nov. 09, 2001.
3. *Ibid*.
4. Amartya Sen, "Development: Which Way Now?", *The Economic Journal*, Vol. 93, No. 372. (Dec., 1983), pp. 745-62.
5. Amartya Sen, "Inequality Reexamined", 1995.
6. Brahmananda, P.R. (1999): Amartya Sen and Welfare Economics.

CHAPTER

17

Amartya Sen's Concept and Contribution to Economics of Poverty

K. HARIHARAN

INTRODUCTION

Poverty is one of the main problems which has attracted the attention of sociologists and economists. It indicates a condition in which a person fails to maintain a living standard adequate for his physical and mental efficiency. It is a situation where people want to escape. It gives rise to a feeling of discrepancy between what one has and what one should have. The term poverty is a relative concept. It is very difficult to draw a demarcation line between affluence and poverty. According to Adam Smith, man is rich or poor according to the degree in which he can afford to enjoy the necessaries, conveniences and the amusements of human life.

CONCEPT OF POVERTY

Poverty can be defined as a social phenomenon in which a section of the society is unable to fulfil even its basic necessities of life. When a substantial segment of society is deprived of the minimum level of living and continues at a bare subsistence level, that society is said to be plagued with mass poverty. The countries of the third world exhibit invariably the existence of mass poverty although pockets of poverty exist even in the developed countries of Europe and America. According to the Planning Commission of India, poverty line is drawn with an intake of 2400 calories in rural areas and 2100 calories in urban areas, if a person is unable to get that much minimum level of calories then he/she is considered as being below poverty line.

MEASUREMENT OF POVERTY

Below poverty line is an economic benchmark and poverty threshold is used by the Government to indicate economic disadvantage and to identify individuals and households in need of Government assistance and aid. It is determined using various parameters which vary from State to State and within States.

INTERNATIONAL BENCHMARKS

Internationally an income of less than $ 1 per day per head of purchasing power parity is defined as extreme poverty. Income-based poverty lines consider the bare minimum income to provide basic food requirements, it does not account for other essentials such as health care and education. That is why some times the poverty lines have been described as starvation lines.

MEASUREMENT OF POVERTY IN UNITED STATES

The poverty line in United States is fixed in terms of annual family income. In 1969, the requirements of family in terms of food was worked out with reference to 1963 prices, and it was found that a family of four would require $ 1,033 annually to meet the food requirements. The study revealed that families in that income spent nearly one-third of their income on food and therefore the poverty line for a four person family was fixed at $ 3,099 annually. The poverty line is revised annually adjusting for inflation. The thresholds are updated annually for price charges and so are not charged in real terms. In other words, the 2008, that weighed average poverty threshold of $ 22,025 for a family of 4 represents the same purchasing power as 19 threshold of $ 3,099. In 1992, the National Academy of Sciences study panel recommended that the official U.S. poverty threshold should comprise a budget for 3 basic categories such as food, clothing and shelter and a small additional amount to allow for other needs.

MEASUREMENT OF POVERTY IN THE EUROPEAN UNION

Within the European Union, the issue of poverty is a subject of perennial, intrinsic interest but in recent years, it has received increasing political attention. Rowen tree's study in 1901—was the first to develop a poverty standard based on estimates of nutritional and other requirements. In the 1960s main focus was on the level of Y reflected in macro-economic indicators like GNP per head. In the 1970s, the emphasis was on relative deprivation. The concept of European Social Model has increasingly seen the quality of life as a complement or replacement for the central focus on economic wealth. Unfortunately, it is difficult to find a definition of quality of life that satisfies everyone.

An official definition was adopted by the European Council in 1984 which regards as poor those persons, families and groups of persons whose resources (material, cultural and social) are so limited as to exclude them from the minimum acceptable way of life in the Member-State to which they belong. A set of 18 indicators were adopted by the European Council in 2001 called Laeken indicators for the measurement of poverty. The focus of the Laeken indicators is on the ability to participate in one's own society, i.e. a relative measure which recognises that, behaviour patterns can and do change over time and space in response to circumstances.

MEASUREMENT OF POVERTY IN INDIA

Criteria are different for rural and urban areas. In the Ninth Five Year Plan, BPL for rural areas was set at an annual family income less than Rs. 20,000, less than two hectares of land and no television or refrigerator. The number of rural BPL families was 650,000 during the Ninth Plan.

In the Tenth Five Year Plan survey, BPL for rural areas was based on the degree of deprivation in respect of 13 parameters with scores from 0-4: landholding, type of house, clothing, food security, sanitation, consumer durables, literacy status, labour force, means of livelihood, status of children, type of indebtedness, reasons for migration, etc. The Planning Commission fixed an upper limit of 3.26 lakh for rural BPL families on the basis of simple survey. Accordingly, families having less than 15 marks out of maximum 52 marks have been classified as BPL and their number works out to 3.18 lakh. This survey formed the basis for benefits under Government of India schemes.

The State Governments are free to adopt any criteria/ survey for state-level schemes.

In its Tenth Five Year Plan BPL for urban areas was based on the degree of deprivation in respect of seven parameters namely, roof, floor water, sanitation, education level, type of employment and status of children in a house. A total of 1.25 lakh families were identified as BPL in urban areas in 2004.

The poverty line was originally fixed in terms of income/ food requirements in 1978. It was stipulated that the calorie standard for a typical individual in rural areas was 2400 calories and was 2100 calories in urban areas. Then the cost of grains (about 650 gms) that fulfil this normal standard was calculated. This cost was the poverty line. In 1978, it was Rs. 61.80 per person per month for rural areas and Rs. 71.30 for urban areas. Since then the Planning Commission calculates the poverty line every year adjusting for inflation.

STUDIES ON POVERTY IN INDIA

Several economists and organisations have conducted studies on the extent of poverty in India. Some of the important and eminent studies are the following:

(a) Ojha's Estimate of (a) (Ojha's Estimate of Poverty)

Mr. P.D. Ojha estimated the number of persons below the poverty line on the basis of an average calorie intake of 2,250 per capita per day. He stipulated a monthly per capita consumption expenditure of Rs. 15-18 in urban areas and Rs. 8-11 in rural areas. On this basis Ojha estimated that 184 million persons in the rural areas and 6 million persons in the urban areas lived below the poverty line in 1960-61.

(b) Dandekar and Rath's Study of Poverty in India

Dandekar and Rath estimated the value of the diet with 2250 calories as the desired minimum level of nutrition. They suggested Rs. 180 per capita per annum and Rs. 270 per capita per annum as the minimum required per capita expenditure. On this basis they estimated that about 40% of the rural population and a little more than 50% of the urban population lived below the poverty line in 1968-69.

(c) Minhas' Study of Rural Poor

Minhas' study on the basis of NSS data revealed that taking per capita annual consumption expenditure of Rs. 240 as the bare minimum, about 50.6% of the population lived below the poverty line in 1967-68.

(d) Bardhan's Study of Rural Poor

Bardhan considered Rs. 15 at 1960-61 prices to be the national mimimum and concluded that the percentage of rural people below the poverty line has gone up from 38% in 1960-61 to 54% in 1968-69.

(e) Montek Ahluwalia's Study of Rural Poverty

Montek Ahluwaiia studied the trends in the incidence of rural poverty in India for the period 1956-57 to 1973-74. He considered the expenditure level of Rs. 15 in 1960-61 prices in rural areas and Rs. 20 in urban areas. He found that the proportion of rural poverty declined initially from over 50% in the mid fifties to around 40% in 1960-61, rose sharply through the mid-sixties reaching a peak in 1967-68 and then declined again.

(f) Study by Gaurav Datt and Martin Ravallion

Gaurav Datt and Martin Ravallion in their paper 'Regional Disparities' Targeting and Poverty in India', developed the concept of poverty gap along the poverty line. The authors have used Rs. 89 as the poverty line. According to the study 40% of the urban population and 45% of the rural population were reckoned as poor in 1983. The paper measured the poverty gap as the distance from the poverty line of average consumtion expenditure of the poor in each state as a proportion of the national poverty line. The poverty gap was found to be greater in rural areas than in urban areas.

AMARTYA SEN'S CONTRIBUTION TO POVERTY

Sen's Early Life

Sen, was born on the 3rd November 1933 at 'Pratichi' in Santiniketan. He had his early education at St. Gregory's school at Dhaka. In 1947, he was matriculated from 'Patha Bhavan' an Open Air School in Shantiniketan. The Bengal famine of 1943 left an indelible impression on his young mind. He studied B.A. Economics in Presidency College, Calcutta. He passed B.A. (Honours) from Trinity College, Cambridge. He completed his Ph.D. under Dr. Joan Robinson. He has worked as Professor in Jadhavpur University, Delhi School of Economics, London School of Economics and Lamert Professor for Economics and Philosphy at Havard. He won the Nobel Prize in Economics in 1998 for his work on welfare economics.

Prof. Amartya Sen is an eminent economist of modern India. Amartya Sen is a philosopher, economist and a social thinker. At a time when the world was talking of globalisation, liberalisation and free market economy, Prof. Sen dared to differ, instead of the growth-oriented path to prosperity, Amartya Sen has emphasized the need for giving a human face to development. Sen's best known works are Poverty and

Famines, Choice of Techniques, Collective Choices and Social Welfare.

Sen is the first Asian and the first Indian to achieve this distinction of Nobel Award in economics securing him a permanent place in the Hall of Fame. He is the second economist after Arthur Lewis to have won the Nobel award from a developing country. It is difficult to label his ideas as belonging to any particular school of political economy. He should be credited for having established his own special paradigm in welfare economics particularly in the analysis of the relation between poverty and human development. He has successfully put forth a number of new measures like poverty index and the capability index which have been attempted to be empirically estimated.

Sen's Concept of Entitlement and Ownership

According to Sen starvation is the characteristic of some people not having enough food to eat. It is not the characteristic of there being not enough food to eat. Ownership relations are one kind of entitlement relations. It is necessary to understand the entitlement systems within which the problem of starvation is to be analysed. This applies more generally to poverty.

Exchange Entitlement

In a market economy a person can exchange what he owns for another collection of commodities. The exchange entitlements faced by a person depend on his position in the economic class structure as well as the modes of production is the economy. For e.g. a peasant differs from a landless labourer in terms of ownership but the landless share cropper differs from the labourer with respect to the resources they own, namely labour power. If the labourer is paid in terms of food output, he has some security advantage while a fixed money wage may not offer any security at all.

Requirements of Concept of Poverty

The first requirement of the concept of poverty is of a criterion as to who should be the focus of our concern.

According to Sen, the concept of poverty should be related to the interests of both the poor and the non-poor.

Poverty is a matter of deprivation. The recent shift in focus especially in the sociological literature from absolute to relative deprivation has provided a useful framework of analysis. But relative deprivation is essentially incomplete as an approach to poverty and supplements the earlier approach of absolute dispossession. The much maligned biological approach which deserves substantial reformulation but not rejection relates to the irreducible core of absolute deprivation keeping issues of starvation and hunger at the centre of the concept of poverty.

To view poverty as an issue in inequality as if often recommended seems to do little justice to either concept. Poverty and inequality relate closely to each other but they are distinct concepts and neither subsumes the other.

The measurement of poverty is an ethical exercise but primarily a descriptive one. The exercise of describing the predicament of the poor in terms of the prevailing standards of necessities involves ambiguities. Ambiguous description isn't the same thing as prescription. Instead, the arbitrariness that is inescapable in choosing between permissible procedures and possible interpretations of prevailing standards requires recognition and appropriate treatment.

POVERTY : IDENTIFICATION AND AGGREGATION

Identification of Poverty

The measurement of poverty involves first the identification of the poor. The identification exercise is prior to aggregation. The most common route to identification is through specifying a set of basic or minimum needs and regarding the inability to fulfil the needs as the test of poverty. The problem is to identify the basic needs in terms of commodities or characteristics. While wheat, rice, potatoes, etc. are commodities-proteins, vitamins, calories, etc. are characteristics. If each characteristic could be obtained from only one commodity then it would be easy to translate the characteristic needs into commodity needs. But this is very often not the case. It is for this reason that basic or minimum needs are often specified in terms of a hybrid vector, e.g. amounts of calories, proteins, housing, schools, etc., some of the components being pure characteristics which others are commodities.

Aggregation of Poverty

In identifying and aggregating the poor for a given set of basic needs, it is possible to use atleast two alternative methods. One is simply to check the set of people whose actual consumption basket happens to leave some basic need unsatisfied. This is called the direct method and it does not involve the use of any income notion. The second method which is called the income method is to calculate the minimum income at which all the specified minimum needs are satisfied. The next step is to identify those whose actual incomes fall below that poverty line.

The direct method is superior to the income method since it is not based on particular assumptions of consumption behaviour which may or may not be accurate.

Family Size and Equivalent Adults

In calculating the income necessary for meeting the minimum needs of families of different size, some method of correspondence of family income with individual income is needed. The simplest method of doing this is to divide the family income by the number of family members. However, this overlooks the economies of large scale. Therefore, the common practice for poverty estimation is to convert each family into a certain number of equivalent adults by the use of some equivalent scale or convert the families into equivalent households.

Poverty Gap

The income shortfall of a person whose income is less than the poverty line income can be called his income gap. In the aggregate assessment of poverty these income gaps must be taken into account. It seems reasonable to argue that any person's poverty cannot really be independent of how poor the others are.

If 'Q' is the number of people who are identified as being poor and 'n' is the total number of people in the community, then the head-count measure H is q/n.

Axiomatic Derivation of a Poverty Measure

The poverty measure P may be considered to be the weighed sum of the short-falls of all people who are judged to be poor. The concentration can be on aspects of relative deprivation. Let r (i) be the rank of person (i) in the ordering of all the poor in the decreasing order of income. If more than one person has the same income they can be ranked in any arbitrary order. The poorest poor has the largest rank value q when there are q people altogether on this side of the poverty line while the least poor has the rank value of 1. The greater the rank value, the more the person is deprived in terms of relative deprivation.

The axion of Ranked Relative Deprivation focuses on the distribution of income among the poor. H represents the proportion of people who are deprived in relation to the poverty line and I reflects the proportionate amount of absolute income deprivation. A simple representation leading to a convenient normalization is the product HI. This may be called the axiom of Normalized Absolute Deprivation.

If these two axions are imposed on a general format of the poverty measure being a weighed sum of income gaps then a precise measure of poverty emerges. When G is the Gini coefficient of the distribution of income among the poor, this measure is given by P = H {I + (l–l) G.) When all the poor have the same income then the Gini co-efficient of income distribution equals zero and P-HI. Given the same average poverty gap and the same proportion of poor population the poverty measure P increases with greater inequality of incomes below the poverty line as measured by the Gini coefficient. Then the measure P is a function of H (the number of poor), I (the aggregate poverty gap) and G (the Inequality of income distribution below the poverty line).

Measures to Eradicate Poverty

The Indian Government has made poverty reduction a priority in its development planning. Policies have focussed on improving the poor standard of living by ensuring food security, promoting self-employment through greater access to assets, increasing wage employment and improving access to basic social services.

- India's Public distribution system launched in 1965 has helped meet people's needs by providing rations at subsidized prices.
- Integrated Rural Development Programme launched in 1979 provides rural households below the poverty line with credit to purchase income generating assets.
- TRYSEM (Training Rural Youth for Self-employment) provides technical skills to the rural youth to help them to get self-employment in fields such as agriculture, industry, services and business activities.
- With these programmes formulated by the Government Sen is of the opinion that poverty eradication has to take into account the distribution parameters below the poverty line. The measure of poverty is lower, the higher the ratio of the mean consumption of people below the poverty line to the poverty line and the less skewed the distribution of consumption below the poverty line.

CONCLUSION

Since Independence, the only issue which baffles, our Government is the terrible consequences of the painful poverty. The aim and expectation of forming an egalitarian society could be achieved by the constant efforts and prudent planning of our economists, planners and thoughtful policy-makers. Let us hope that our Bharat keeps its head high in pronouncing "All are equal and are provided with all needed".

Bharathiar, the Tamil Board made a clarion call and said, "If one individual starves without food, there is no meaning in the existence of this World. Let us destroy the deplorable system". Thus, we could sum up the contribution and concept of our Nobel Laurate Amarthya Sen.

References

Abdullah, A., Land Reforms and Agrarian Change in Bangladesh.

Adelman, I. and Morris, C.T., Economic Growth and Social Equity in Developing Countries.

Ady, P., Inflation in India.

Ahluwalia, M., Rural Poverty and Agricultural Performance in India.

Bardhan, P.K., On the Minimum Level of Living and the Rural Poor.

Beckerman, W., Some Reflections on Redistribution with Growth.

Bhatia, B.M., Famines in India.

Chaudhuri Pramit, The Indian Economy: Poverty and Development.

Dasgupta, BIP Lab—Agrarian Change and the New Technology in India.

Dutt, R.C., Famines and Land Assessment in India.

Friedman, M., A Method of Comparing Income of Families Differing in Composition.

Jackson, Poverty.

Kaldor Icholas, Inflation and Recession in the World Economy.

Kuznets, Modern Economic Growth.

Miller, H.P., Rich Man, Poor Man.

Gunnar Myrdal, Asian Drama.

Radhakrishna, R. and Sarma, A., Distributional Effects of the Current Inflation.

Rodgers, A Conceptualisation of Poverty in Rural India.

Sen, A.K., Choice of Techniques.

Sen, A.K., Poverty, Inequality and Unemployment : Some Conceptual Issues in Measurement.

CHAPTER

18

An Analysis of Poverty and Inequality : With Special Reference to Sen's Capability Approach

K. SURESH AND S.N. SUKUMAR

INTRODUCTION

The view that the traditional utilitarian notion of welfare can render only a partial picture of human well-being is now-a-days quite widely accepted by the community of economists. In fact this conception relies only on the welfarist criteria of utility (in theory) and income (in application). The consequent measurements of welfare are generally derived through the observation of preferences revealed by actual choices, and interpreted in terms of the numerical representation of these choices.[1] Therefore, the notion of welfare reflects only the class of differences captured by money metric, under the economic rationality of self-interested utility maximization. Moreover, the income approach to well-being doesn't account for the diversity in human beings and for the heterogeneities of contingent circumstances. Thus, income can be intended only as a mean to reach an acceptable standard of living, and in no way as an end in itself, since there are other important dimensions to the flourishing of human well-being that income doesn't account for: health, education, social relationships, longevity, employment, environmental conditions, housing conditions.

The need to move towards such a broader notion of well-being has been strongly advocated, among others, by Amartya Sen, whose major contributions all stress the centrality of individual entitlements, opportunities, and rights as conceptual foundations of economics and social choice. Sen has in fact gradually developed an approach[2] focused on the freedom of individuals to pursue their own project of life, in which well-being is seen (in terms of a person's ability to do valuable acts or reach valuable states of being) (Sen, 1993:30). This is the core of the so-called capability approach.

The Capability Approach developed and pioneered by the economist Amartya Sen, provides a conceptual framework for analyzing well-being and a strong critique of existing traditions in welfare economics. Much of Amartya Sen's work has focused on inequality and poverty. In his earlier writings, Sen (1973) criticized the existing literature on inequality measurement in welfare economics for being too concerned with complete rankings of different social states. Sen argued that we should not assume away complexities or ambiguities, and that often we can only make partial comparisons. For example, we might be able to say that person 1 (or country 1) is definitely better off than persons 2 and 3, but we might not be able to rank the well-being of 2 and 3. Sen has also criticized the inequality literature in economics for being exclusively focused on income (Amartya Sen, 1985, 1987, 1992, 1993, 1995, 1998). Instead, Sen argues, we should focus on the real freedoms that people have for leading a valuable life, that is, on their capabilities to undertake activities such as reading, working or being politically active, or of enjoying positive states of being, such as being healthy or literate. This line of Sen's work, known as the capability approach, postulates that when making normative evaluations, the focus should be on what people are able to be and to do, and not on what they can consume, or on their incomes. The latter are only the means of well-being, whereas evaluations and judgments should focus on those things that matter intrinsically, that are on a person's capabilities.

It is immediately clear that the capability approach has enormous potential for addressing feminist concerns and questions. Ever since its inception, the women's movement has focused on many issues that are not reducible to financial welfare, such as reproductive health, voting rights, political power, domestic violence, education, and women's social status. In this paper I want to explain the merits and demerits of the Sen's capability approach. More precisely, I will outline how poverty and inequality can be conceptualized and assessed from a capability perspective. Ordinary income measures of inequality are not enough to explain the poverty and inequality. So there is a need for going beyond income inequality to find the reality.

THE NEED FOR GOING BEYOND INCOME INEQUALITY

A convenient point of departure is A.B. Atkinson's (1970) pioneering move in the measurement of inequality.[3] He assessed inequality of incomes by bringing in an overall social objective function and measured inequality of an income distribution through the social loss (in terms of equivalent income) from that distribution in comparison with a corresponding equal distribution. However, he took the individuals to be symmetrical and also did not explicitly consider what the individuals respectively get out of their incomes and other circumstances.

There is a case for going beyond this structure and for examining the nature of individual advantages themselves as the constituent elements of social welfare (or, more generally, of social objectives). In this context, we have to take note of the heterogeneities of the individuals and of their respective non-income circumstances.

The important point to note is that the valuation of income is entirely as a means to other ends and also that it is one means among others. A more inclusive list of means has been used by John Rawls in his theory of justice through his concentration on primary goods, which include rights, liberties and opportunities, income and wealth, and the social bases of self-respect (Rawls 1971, pp. 60-65). Income is, of course, a crucially important means, but its importance lies in the fact that it helps the person to do things that she values doing and to achieve states of being that she has reasons to desire. The worth of incomes cannot stand separated from these deeper concerns, and a society that respects individual well-being and freedom must take note of these concerns in making interpersonal comparisons as well as social evaluations.

The relationship between income (and other resources) on the one hand and individual achievements and freedoms on the other is not constant. Different types of contingencies lead to systematic variations in the conversion of incomes into the distinct functioning's we can achieve (i.e., the various things we can do or be), and that affects the lifestyles we can enjoy. There are at least five important sources of parametric variation.

(1) *Personal heterogeneities*: People have disparate physical characteristics connected with disability, illness, age, or gender, making their needs diverse. For example, an ill person may need more income to fight her illness than a person without such an illness would need. While the compensation needed for disadvantages will vary, some disadvantages may not be correct—able even with more expenditure on treatment or care.

(2) *Environmental diversities*: Variations in environmental conditions, such as climatic circumstances (temperature ranges, rainfall, flooding, and so on), can influence what a person gets out of a given level of income.

(3) *Variations in social climate*: The conversion of personal incomes and resources into functionings is influenced

also by social conditions, including public health care and epidemiology, public educational arrangements, and the prevalence or absence of crime and violence in the particular location. Aside from public facilities, the nature of community relationships can be very important, as the recent literature on social capital has tended to emphasize.

(4) *Differences in relational perspectives*: The commodity requirements of established patterns of behavior may vary between communities, depending on conventions and customs. For example, being relatively poor in a rich community can prevent a person from achieving some elementary functionings (such as taking part in the life of the community) even though her income, in absolute terms, may be much higher than the level of income at which members of poorer communities can function with great ease and success. For example, to be able to "appear in public without shame" may require higher standards of clothing and other visible consumption in a richer society than in a poorer one (as Adam Smith [1776] had noted more than two centuries ago). The same parametric variability may apply to the personal resources needed for the fulfilment of self-respect. This is primarily an inter-societal variation rather than an inter-individual variation within a given society, but the two issues are frequently interlinked.

(5) *Distribution within the family*: Incomes earned by one or more members of a family are shared by all, non-earners as well as earners. The family is, thus, the basic unit for consideration of incomes from the point of view of their use. The well-being or freedom of individuals in a family will depend on how the family income is used in furtherance of the interests and objectives of different members of the family. Thus, intra-family distribution of incomes is quite a crucial parametric variable in linking individual achievements and opportunities with the overall level of family income. Distributional rules followed

within the family (e.g., related to gender or age or perceived needs) can make a major difference to the attainments and predicaments of individual members.[4]

A BRIEF DESCRIPTION OF SEN'S CAPABILITY APPROACH

The capability approach advocates that we focus on people's capabilities when making normative evaluations, such as those involved in poverty measurement, cost-benefit analysis, efficiency evaluations, social justice issues, development ethics, and inequality analysis. What are these capabilities? Capabilities are people's potential functionings. Functionings are beings and doings. Examples are being well fed, taking part in the community, being sheltered, relating to other people, and working on the labor market, caring for others, and being healthy. The difference between a functioning and a capability is similar to the difference between an achievement and the freedom to achieve something, or between an outcome and an opportunity. All capabilities together correspond to the overall freedom to lead the life that a person has reason to value. Sen stresses the importance of "reason to value" because we need to scrutinize our motivations for valuing specific lifestyles, and not simply value a certain life without reflecting upon it.

By advocating that normative evaluations should look at people's capabilities, Sen criticizes evaluations that focus exclusively on utilities, resources or income. He argues against a utility-based evaluation of individual well-being because such an evaluation might hide important dimensions and lead to misleading inter-personal or inter-temporal comparisons. A person may be in a desperate situation and still be contented with life if she has never known differently. A utilitarian evaluation will only assess her satisfaction and will not differentiate between a happy, healthy, well-sheltered person, and an equally happy, but unhealthy and badly sheltered person who has mentally adapted to her situation. This is especially important from a gender perspective because utility seems to have a gendered dimension. For example, Andrew

Clark (1997) has shown that British women have a higher job satisfaction or utility from doing paid work than men, even after controlling for personal and job characteristics. Women who are worse-off than men in objective terms might still have the same utility level. Clark examined several possible explanations for this gender differential and concluded that women's higher job-related utilities were caused by their lower expectations.

The capability approach also rejects normative evaluations based exclusively on commodities, income, or material resources. Resources are only the means to enhance people's well-being and advantage, whereas the concern should be with what matters intrinsically, namely people's functionings and capabilities. Resource-based theories do not acknowledge that people differ in their abilities to convert these resources into capabilities, due to personal, social or environmental factors, such as physical and mental handicaps, talents, traditions, social norms and customs, legal rules, a country's public infrastructure, public goods, climate, and so on. In traditional welfare economics, income (and sometimes expenditure) is the most widely used variable, and there is little discussion on whether other variables should be used (Frank Cowell, 1995; Alissa Goodman, Paul Johnson, and Steven Webb, 1997; D.G. Champernowne and Frank Cowell, 1998). Economic historians have long looked at other dimensions, such as height, mortality, and political freedoms. Welfare economists who measure individual well-being have also begun to pay more attention to other indicators, but income remains the dominant focus.

One important aspect of Sen's capability approach is its underspecified character. The capability approach is a framework of thought, a normative tool, but it is not a fully specified theory that gives us complete answers to all our normative questions. It is not a mathematical algorithm that prescribes how to measure inequality or poverty, nor is it a complete theory of justice. The capability approach, strictly speaking, only advocates that the evaluative space should be that of capabilities. However, it does not stipulate which capabilities should be taken into account, or how different capabilities should be aggregated in an overall assessment.

Applying the capability approach implies that we choose the relevant capabilities and indicate how important each will be in an overall judgment. In addition, normative frameworks always depend on explanatory or ontological views of human nature and society, and Sen's capability approach does not defend one particular worldview. If we interpret all of Sen's work as being one integrated body of thought, as Sabina Alkire (2002: 87) does, then many theories of human nature and society would be excluded (e.g. strong libertarian or communitarian theories), but there will still remain a range of theories (e.g. most strands of liberal theories) that are compatible with the capability approach.[5]

Initially Sen argued for:

- the importance of real freedoms in the assessment of a person's advantage,
- individual differences in the ability to transform resources into valuable activities,
- the centrality of the *distribution* of welfare within society,
- the multi-vitiate nature of activities that give rise to happiness, and
- against excessive materialism in the evaluation of human welfare.

Subsequently, and in collaboration particularly with political philosopher Martha Nussbaum, development economist Sudhir Anand and economic theorist James Foster, Sen has helped to make the capabilities approach predominant as a paradigm for policy debate in human development where it inspired the creation of the UN's Human Development Index (HDI). The HDI is a popular measure for capturing the multidimensionality of human development, as it also accounts for health and education. Furthermore, since the creation of the Human Development and Capability Association in the early 2000s, the approach has been much discussed by political theorists, philosophers and a range of social sciences, including those with a particular interest in human health.

The approach emphasizes functional capabilities ("substantive freedoms", such as the ability to live to old age, engage in economic transactions, or participate in political activities); these are construed in terms of the substantive freedoms people have reason to value, instead of utility (happiness, desire—fulfilment or choice) or access to resources (income, commodities, and assets). Poverty is understood as capability-deprivation. It is noteworthy that the emphasis is not only on how human beings actually function but on their having the capability, which is a practical choice, to function in important ways if they so wish. Someone could be deprived of such capabilities in many ways, e.g. by ignorance, government oppression, lack of financial resources, or false consciousness.

This approach to human well-being emphasizes the importance of freedom of choice, individual heterogeneity and the multi-dimensional nature of welfare. In significant respects, the approach is consistent with the handling of choice within conventional microeconomics consumer theory although its conceptual foundations enable it to acknowledge the existence of claims, like rights, which normatively dominate utility-based claims.

WHAT CAPABILITIES MATTER?

Nussbaum (2000) frames these basic principles in terms of ten capabilities, i.e. real opportunities based on personal and social circumstance. This approach contrasts with a common view that sees development purely in terms of GNP growth, and poverty purely as income-deprivation. It has been highly influential in development policy where it has shaped the evolution of the human development index, (HDI) has been much discussed in philosophy and is increasingly influential in a range of social sciences.

The ten capabilities Nussbaum argues should be supported by all democracies are:

1. *Life*. Being able to live to the end of a human life of normal length; not dying prematurely, or before one's life is so reduced as to be not worth living.
2. *Bodily Health*. Being able to have good health, including reproductive health; to be adequately nourished; to have adequate shelter.

3. *Bodily Integrity*. Being able to move freely from place to place; to be secure against violent assault, including sexual assault and domestic violence; having opportunities for sexual satisfaction and for choice in matters of reproduction.
4. *Senses, Imagination, and Thought*. Being able to use the senses, to imagine, think, and reason—and to do these things in a "truly human" way, a way informed and cultivated by an adequate education, including, but by no means limited to, literacy and basic mathematical and scientific training. Being able to use imagination and thought in connection with experiencing and producing works and events of one's own choice, religious, literary, musical, and so forth. Being able to use one's mind in ways protected by guarantees of freedom of expression with respect to both political and artistic speech, and freedom of religious exercise. Being able to have pleasurable experiences and to avoid non-beneficial pain.
5. *Emotions*. Being able to have attachments to things and people outside ourselves; to love those who love and care for us, to grieve at their absence; in general, to love, to grieve, to experience longing, gratitude, and justified anger. Not having one's emotional development blighted by fear and anxiety. (Supporting this capability means supporting forms of human association that can be shown to be crucial in their development.)
6. *Practical Reason*. Being able to form a conception of the good and to engage in critical reflection about the planning of one's life. (This entails protection for the liberty of conscience and religious observance.)
7. *Affiliation*.
    1. Being able to live with and toward others, to recognize and show concern for other humans, to engage in various forms of social interaction; to be able to imagine the situation of another. (Protecting this capability means protecting institutions that constitute and nourish such

forms of affiliation, and also protecting the freedom of assembly and political speech.)

2. Having the social bases of self-respect and non-humiliation; being able to be treated as a dignified being whose worth is equal to that of others. This entails provisions of non-discrimination on the basis of race, sex, sexual orientation, ethnicity, caste, religion, national origin and species.

8. *Other Species.* Being able to live with concern for and in relation to animals, plants, and the world of nature.
9. *Play.* Being able to laugh, to play, to enjoy recreational activities.
10. *Control over one's Environment :*
    1. *Political.* Being able to participate effectively in political choices that govern one's life; having the right of political participation, protections of free speech and association.
    2. *Material.* Being able to hold property (both land and movable goods), and having property rights on an equal basis with others; having the right to seek employment on an equal basis with others; having the freedom from unwarranted search and seizure. In work, being able to work as a human, exercising practical reason and entering into meaningful relationships of mutual recognition with other workers.

The approach was first fully articulated in Sen (1985) and discussed in Sen and Nussbaum (1993). Applications to development are discussed in Sen (1999), Nussbaum (2000), and Clark (2002, 2005) and are now numerous to the point where the capabilities approach is widely accepted as a paradigm in development.

CAN CAPABILITIES BE MEASURED?

Applications to welfare economics and health in high income countries are now also beginning to emerge, Anand,

Hunter and Smith (2005). A key dilemma for the capabilities approach has been how to measure what people could do, as opposed to what they actually do, and this has been the subject of a large international research project. Bringing together researchers from economics, philosophy and psychology, their work demonstrates that capability indicators can be found in standard data-sets and more significantly that it is possible to develop new survey instruments which operationalise Nussbaum's list above. The project solves an important problem for the approach and will be of use to any researchers interested in measuring multi-dimensional aspects of poverty or quality of life. The main capabilities measurement instrument has over 60 indicators, is being used by a number of research groups and is discussed further in Anand *et. al.* (2009) and Anand, Santos and Smith (2009).

SOME STRENGTHS AND WEAKNESSES OF THE CAPABILITY APPROACH

Why make normative assessments in the space of capabilities, and why would this framework be attractive for an analysis of gender inequality? In this section, I will discuss three strengths and one weakness of the capability approach for normative assessments in general and for gender inequality analysis in particular.

The first advantage is that functionings and capabilities are properties of individuals. Hence the capability approach is an ethically (or normatively) individualistic theory. This means that each person will be taken into account in our normative judgments. Ethical individualism implies that the units of normative judgment are individuals, and not households or communities. At the same time, the capability approach is not ontologically individualistic. It does not assume atomistic individuals, nor that our functionings and capabilities are independent of our concern for others or of the actions of others. The social and environmental conversion factors also allow us to take into account a number of societal features, such as social norms and discriminatory practices. In sum, the ethically individualistic and ontologically non-individualistic nature of the capability approach is a desirable characteristic for well-being and inequality analysis (Ingrid Robeyns, 2001b). This is also attractive for feminist research, because ethical individualism rejects the idea that women's well-being can be subsumed under wider entities such as the household or the community, while not denying the impact of Mcare, social relations, and interdependence between family or community members.

The capability approach is therefore a major improvement over standard well-being approaches in welfare economics or political philosophy. In the latter, accounts of inequality and well-being often use implicit assumptions about gender relations within the family which are unrealistic and deny or ignore intra-household inequalities (Susan Okin, 1989, Diemut Bubeck, 1995). In welfare economics generally, inequality theories are ethically individualistic, but this principle gets lost in applied work. Individuals and families are often sloppily equated as in assumptions that partners pool their incomes, or that they receive equal shares of the benefits. There is by now a substantial literature on intra-household allocations, but this literature has had little significant impact on inequality measurement in welfare economics. As Frances Woolley and Judith Marshall (1994: 420) have argued: "standard approaches to inequality measurement presume that there is no inequality within the household." But this standard assumption turns out to be unrealistic, as not all partners share the total household income equally (Shelly Lundberg, Robert Pollak, and Terrence Wales, 1997; Jan Pahl 1989; Shelley Phipps and Peter Burton, 1995). Moreover, Woolley and Marshall (1994) and Phipps and Burton (1995) have shown that assumptions about the degree of sharing within the household significantly affect inequality and poverty measurement. And even if household income were shared completely, it is problematic to assume that it does not matter in a well-being assessment whether a person has earned this money herself, or obtained it from her partner. Conceptualizing and measuring gender inequality in functionings and capabilities helps avoid these problems, since it focuses on the lives that individuals can and do choose to live, and not on their average household income.

The second advantage of the capability approach is that it is not limited to the market, but looks at people's beings and doings in both market and non-market settings. The inclusion of non-market dimensions of well-being in our normative analysis will reveal complexities and ambiguities in the distribution of well-being that an analysis of income or wealth alone cannot capture. This is especially important for gender inequality research. Feminist economists have long been arguing that economics needs to pay attention to processes and outcomes in both the market economy and the no market economy (e.g. Nancy Folbre, 1994, 2001; Susan Himmelweit, 2000). Inequality comparisons based only on the market economy, such as comparisons of income, earnings, and job-holdings, exclude some important aspects of well-being such as care labor, household work, freedom from domestic violence, or the availability of supportive social networks. They also miss the fact that women spend much more time outside the market than men. These aspects matter particularly in gender-related assessments of well-being and disadvantage.

The third strength of the capability approach is that it explicitly acknowledges human diversity, such as race, age, ethnicity, gender, sexuality, and geographical location as well as whether people are handicapped, pregnant, or have caring responsibilities. Sen has criticized inequality approaches that assume that all people have the same utility social and environmental characteristics: "Investigations of equality—theoretical as well as practical—that proceed with the assumption of antecedent uniformity . . . thus miss out on a major aspect of the problem. Human diversity is not a secondary complication (to be ignored or to be introduced 'later on'); it is a fundamental aspect of our interest in equality" (Sen, 1992: xi). Again, this characteristic of the capability approach is important for gender inequality analysis. Sen's concern with human diversity contrasts strikingly with the tendency in standard welfare economics to neglect intra-household inequalities in non market labor and total work-loads. Equality is ultimately measured in "male terms" with an exclusive focus on the market dimensions. Feminist scholars have argued that many theories of justice claim to address the lives of men and women, but closer scrutiny reveals that men's lives form the standard and gender inequalities and injustices are assumed away or remain hidden, and are thereby indirectly justified. For example, many theories of justice simply assume that families are just social institutions where love, justice, and solidarity are the rule. This assumption renders these theories inadequate in their very design for understanding or analyzing intra-household inequalities. Susan Okin (1989: 10-13) has called this "false gender neutrality". As these theories use gender neutral language, we might be tempted to see them as including the concerns of both men and women. But they ignore the biological differences between the sexes, and the impact that gender has on our lives through gendered social institutions, gender roles, power differences, and ideologies: "Thus gender-neutral terms frequently obscure the fact that so much of the real experiences of 'persons', so long as they live in gender-structured societies, does in fact depend on what sex they are" (Okin, 1989: 11). By conceptualizing gender inequality in the space of functionings and capabilities, there is more scope to account for human diversity, including the diversity stemming from people's gender.

However, these positive features notwithstanding, the capability approach also has one major drawback, which stems from its underspecified character. Capability egalitarianism, strictly speaking, only advocates that when making inequality assessments we should focus on capabilities. But every evaluative assessment, implicitly or explicitly, endorses additional social theories, including accounts of the individual, social and environmental conversion factors, and a normative theory of choice. We get quite divergent normative results, depending on which social theories we add to the capability framework. If the social theories are racist, homophobic, sexist, ageist, Eurocentric, or biased in any other way, the capability evaluation will be accordingly affected. For example, gender discrimination in the market can reduce a person's capability set. Or mechanisms that form gendered preferences, such as socialization, can have an impact on the different choices that women and men make from their capability sets. If someone denies the existence of gender discrimination and gendered preference formation, or claims that they have no normative significance, then she will come to different conclusions about gender inequality in capabilities. Thus, a major concern for feminists is that the capability approach is vulnerable to andocentric interpretations and applications. In the remainder of this paper, I present a feminist capability perspective on gender inequality. This implies that the view of social and human nature that I endorse is one that does not assume away people's interconnectedness, or the importance of care and interpersonal interdependencies, or the gendered nature of society.

However, viewing social and human nature from a feminist perspective is not sufficient for applying the capability approach to gender inequality. Because of its underspecified nature, Sen's capability approach needs at least three additional specifications before we can apply it. First, we have to select which capabilities are important for evaluating gender inequality and should therefore be included in a list of relevant capabilities. Second, we have to take a stand on whether to look at gender inequality in functionings or in capabilities. Third, to make an overall evaluation, we need to decide how to weight the different functionings or capabilities. In this paper I am concerned mainly with the selection of capabilities, and will discuss the other two issues only briefly.

CONCLUSION

In this paper I have investigated how we can use the capability approach to study poverty and inequality. After arguing against the view that Sen's capability approach needs one definite list of capabilities, I proposed a methodology to select relevant capabilities. It is obvious that this is not a completed research project. There is much work to be done on furthering the capability approach to poverty and inequality analysis. On the empirical side we need carefully collected micro-data on all these capabilities. On the theoretical side, we need to further our understanding of the income nature of preference formation and the constraints on choice. Once we have a deeper analytical understanding of these phenomena, we can ask how we should deal with them in a normative framework.

Notes and References

1. In the traditional utilitarian framework (from Bentham, to Edgeworth, Marshall, Pigou), the concept of utility is simply a matter of pleasure, happiness, desire fulfilment. The main limit of this view is that utility is seen in terms of mental metric, highly subjective and therefore possibly misguiding.
2. See, for instance, Sen (1980, 1985, 1987(b), 1992, 1999).
3. See also Dalton (1920) and Kolm (1969).
4. See Sen (1990) and the literature cited therein.
5. A good introduction to these theories can be found in Will Kymlicka (2002).

References

Alkire, S. (2002), *Valuing Freedoms: Sen's Capability Approach and Poverty Reduction*. (Oxford: Oxford University Press).

Anand, P., Hunter, G., Carter, I., Dowding, K., van Hees M., (2009), The Development of Capability Indicators, *Journal of Human Development and Capabilities*, 10, 125-52.

Anand, P., Santos, C. and Smith, R., (2009), *The Measurement of Capabilities* in Arguments for a Better World: Essays in Honor of Amartya Sen, Basu, K. and Kanbur, R. (eds.) (Oxford, Oxford University Press).

Clark, David A. (2002), Visions of Development: A Study of Human Values (Edward Elgar, Cheltenham).

Clark, David A. (2005), 'Capability Approach' in D.A. Clark (ed.) forthcoming (2006). The Elgar Companion to Development Studies (Edward Elgar, Cheltenham). Draft available online athttp://www.gprg.org/pubs/workingpapers/pdfs/gprg-wps-032.pdf

Dalton, H. (1920), The Measurement of the Inequality of Incomes. *Economic Journal*, 30:348-61.

Kuklys, Wiebke (2005), Amartya Sen's Capability Approach: Theoretical Insights and Empirical Applications (Springer, Berlin).

Otto, H-U and Schneider, K. (2009), From Employability Towards Capability: Luxembourg.

Nussbaum, Martha C. (2000), Women and Human Development: The Capabilities Approach (Cambridge University Press, Cambridge).

Nussbaum, Martha C. and Amartya Sen, eds. (1993), "The Quality of Life", Oxford: Clarendon Press. (Google book preview).

Rawls, J. (1971), A theory of justice. Cambridge, MA: Harvard University Press.

Sen, Amartya K. (1979), 'Utilitarianism and Welfarism', *The Journal of Philosophy*, LXXVI (1979), 463-89.

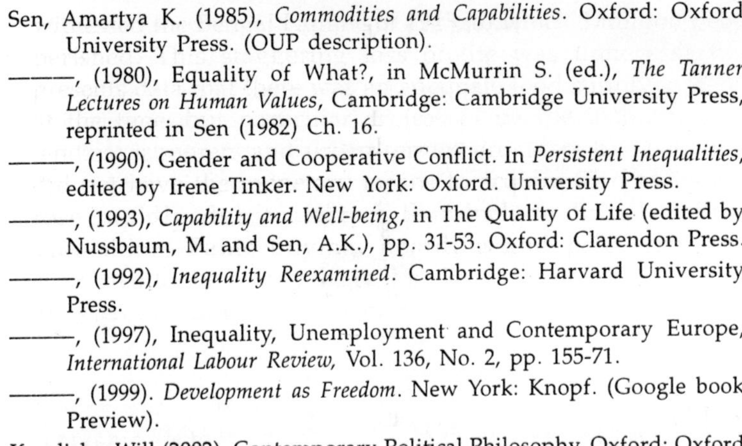

Sen, Amartya K. (1985), *Commodities and Capabilities*. Oxford: Oxford University Press. (OUP description).

———, (1980), Equality of What?, in McMurrin S. (ed.), *The Tanner Lectures on Human Values*, Cambridge: Cambridge University Press, reprinted in Sen (1982) Ch. 16.

———, (1990). Gender and Cooperative Conflict. In *Persistent Inequalities*, edited by Irene Tinker. New York: Oxford. University Press.

———, (1993), *Capability and Well-being*, in The Quality of Life (edited by Nussbaum, M. and Sen, A.K.), pp. 31-53. Oxford: Clarendon Press.

———, (1992), *Inequality Reexamined*. Cambridge: Harvard University Press.

———, (1997), Inequality, Unemployment and Contemporary Europe, *International Labour Review*, Vol. 136, No. 2, pp. 155-71.

———, (1999). *Development as Freedom*. New York: Knopf. (Google book Preview).

Kymlicka, Will (2002). Contemporary Political Philosophy. Oxford: Oxford University Press.

CHAPTER

19

Economic Theory, Freedom and Human Rights : The Work of Amartya Sen

VISHAL PAWASE AND KEDAR KARAMUNGE

This Briefing Paper reviews the ways in which the Nobel Prize winning economist Professor Amartya Sen has focused international attention on the significance of fundamental human freedoms and human rights for development theory and practice. In the past, dominant approaches have often characterized development in terms of GDP per capita; food security in terms of food availability; and poverty in terms of income deprivation. Emphasis was placed on economic efficiency—with no explicit role being given to fundamental freedoms, individual agency and human rights. In contrast, Sen's research has highlighted the central idea that, in the final analysis, market outcomes and government actions should be judged in terms of valuable human ends. His work has contributed to important paradigm shifts in economics and development—away from approaches that focus exclusively on income, growth and utility, with an increased emphasis on individual entitlements, capabilities, freedoms and rights. It has increased awareness of the importance of respect for human rights for socio-economic outcomes—challenging the proposition that growth should take priority over civil and political rights, while highlighting the role of human rights in promoting economic security, and the limitations of development without human rights guarantees.

MOVING THEORETICAL AND EMPIRICAL ECONOMICS FORWARD : THE BUILDING BLOCKS OF SEN'S APPROACH

The Limitations of Traditional Welfare Economics

Formal frameworks in economics have traditionally been dominated by 'welfarist' criteria such as 'utility'. This concept is generally interpreted in terms of individual 'pleasures and pains', 'happiness' and 'desire-fulfilment', while it is commonly operationalised in economics in terms of 'revealed preference' and the observation of actual choices. Sen has elaborated a far-reaching critique of utility as an informational base—for ethical and social judgment, as well as for the ability of economics to address real world phenomena such as poverty and famine, and for its explanatory and predictive power. This critique has challenged the equation of rational behavior with self-interested utility maximization; the use of self-interested utility maximization as a predictor of individual behavior; and the use of choice information as an indicator of individual preference and value. It has highlighted the limitations of utility information as a basis for evaluating and comparing human interests, and of utility-based interpretations of economic efficiency and social optimality—as reflected in standard approaches to 'Pareto Efficiency' and the 'Fundamental Theorems of Welfare Economics'.

Economics Beyond 'Welfarism'

Given the limitations of traditional approaches, Sen has elaborated a series of formal proposals for moving the economics agenda forward—beyond 'welfarism'—and for expanding the types of variables and influences that are accommodated in theoretical and empirical economics. His contributions include far-reaching proposals for incorporating individual entitlements, functionings, opportunities, capabilities, freedoms and rights into the conceptual foundations and technical apparatus of economics and social choice. These proposals reflect a number of central recurring themes including:

- The importance of pluralist informational frameworks that take account of both the well-being aspect of a person (relating to his or her own personal physical and mental well-being) and the agency aspect (relating to the goals that a person values, desires and has reasons to pursue; and being sensitive to processes as well as to outcomes—reflecting the intrinsic value of individual choice and participation).
- The need to go beyond the assessment of utility and income, taking account of entitlements, capabilities and functionings, and adopting a broad view of preferences, incorporating the capability to achieve what is valued and counterfactual choice (what people would choose, given the choice).
- The importance of approaches giving a central role to freedoms and rights. In Sen's view, this importance cannot be captured in terms of the utility metric. Welfarist informational bases are too narrow to reflect the intrinsic value of freedom and rights, which should be brought directly into social-economic evaluation.

Individual Entitlements

Sen's 'entitlement approach' provides a framework for analyzing the relationship between rights, interpersonal obligations and individual entitlement to things. A person's entitlement set is a way of characterizing his or her 'overall command over things' taking note of all relevant rights and obligations. Whereas rights are generally characterized as relationships that hold between distinct agents (e.g. between one person and another person, or one person and the state), a person's entitlements 'are the totality of things he can have by virtue of his rights'. Sen has hypothesized that 'most cases of starvation and famines across the world arise not from people being deprived of things to which they are entitled, but from people not being entitled, in the prevailing legal system of institutional rights, to adequate means for survival'. His empirical work suggests that in many famines in which millions of people have died, there was no overall decline in food availability, and starvation occurred as a consequence of shifts in entitlements resulting from exercising rights that were legitimate in legal terms. It establishes that a range of variables other than agricultural productivity and aggregate food supply can undermine a person's entitlement to food, and that there is a possibility of an asymmetry in the incidence of starvation deaths among different population groups, with entitlement failures arising not only because of overall food shortages, but because people are unable to trade their labour power or skills. These findings highlight the possibility of insecure food entitlements that do not result from market failure as traditionally understood—challenging approaches to general equilibrium analysis that rule out the possibility of starvation death due to inability to acquire sufficient food through production or exchange.

INDIVIDUAL FOOD ENTITLEMENTS AND FOOD SECURITY POLICY

The entitlement approach has helped to shift the focus of international attention away from statistics describing per capita calories and food supplies, and towards statistics describing the differential ability of individuals, groups and classes to command food in practice. New approaches to food security policy place an increased emphasis on identifying the precise causes of the food vulnerability of population groups. The UN Special Reporters on the Human Right to Food has recommended that the first step in a national food security strategy is to map the situation for different groups taking into account a range of variables including occupation, gender, ethnicity, race and rural/urban location.

FUNCTIONING AND CAPABILITY

Sen's concept of functioning relates to the things a person may value doing or being. Functionings are features of a person's state of existence ranging from relatively elementary states (e.g. being adequately nourished), to complex personal states and activities (e.g. participation and appearing without shame). The concept of capability relates to the ability of a person to achieve different combinations of functionings—the various combinations of valuable beings and doings that are within a person's reach, reflecting the opportunity or freedom to choose a life that a person values. Sen's empirical research has highlighted the possibility of divergences between the expansion of economic growth and income on the one hand, and the expansion of valuable human capabilities on the other. His findings establish that economic growth and income can be poor predictors of the capability to live to a mature age, without succumbing to premature mortality, in different countries (e.g. India, China, Sri Lanka, Costa Rica, Jamaica), and for different population groups (e.g. women *versus* men; black men *versus* other groups in the US; the population in the Indian state of Kerala in relation to other states). For these reasons, Sen has proposed that capabilities and functionings may be the most appropriate focal variables for many evaluative exercises concerning human interests. Equality and inequality may be best assessed in terms of capabilities—rather than in terms of GDP, consumption or utility—while poverty may be best characterized in terms of the absence or deprivation of certain basic capabilities to do this or to be that.

MULTIDIMENSIONAL CONCEPTS OF POVERTY AND DEVELOPMENT

The UNDP's Human Development Reports are based on Sen's approach and characterize human development in terms of the expansion of valuable human capabilities. The Human

Development Index captures the importance of three critical human capabilities—achieving knowledge, longevity and a decent standard of living. The Gender-Related Development Index captures gender-based inequalities in the achievement of these capabilities, while the Human Poverty Index captures deprivations (where 'living standard' is characterized in terms of access to safe water, health services and birth-weight). The World Bank's World Development Report, 2000-01, also adopts a multidimensional concept of poverty. It attempts to go beyond the analysis of achieved functioning's and to accommodate the ideas of individual agency and rights by emphasizing that poverty is more than inadequate income and human development—it is also vulnerability and lack of voice, power and representation.

Sen has advocated new approaches to thinking about fundamental freedoms and human rights. In the past, poverty and hunger were often excluded from dominant discourses on fundamental freedoms and human rights. Sen has challenged this approach, arguing that: 'When we assess inequalities across the world in being able to avoid preventable morbidity, or escapable hunger, or premature mortality, we are not merely examining differences in well-being. . . . The available data regarding the realization of disease, hunger, and early mortality tell us a great deal about the presence or absence of certain central basic freedoms'.

This analysis contrasts sharply with that of the philosopher and economist Friedrich A. Hayek and the philosopher Robert Nozick. Sen has rejected the 'outcome-independent' position (which suggests that socio-economic outcomes are generally irrelevant to ethical evaluation), and has called for the development of 'consequence-sensitive' approaches to the characterization of freedoms and rights. In Sen's view, the idea that consequences such as life, death, starvation and nourishment are intrinsically matters of moral indifference—or have only very weak intrinsic moral relevance—is 'implausible' and fails to reflect 'complex interdependences' that arise in relation to the exercise and valuation of freedoms and rights in a society.

In addition, Sen has rejected exclusively negative characterizations of freedoms and rights, focusing attention away from the absence of intentional coercion as an exclusive condition of individual freedom, and towards the constituent elements of what a person can actually do or be. In this conceptual framework, the absence or deprivation of certain capabilities or real opportunities—as well as the denial of political and civil liberties—are relevant to the characterization of freedoms and rights, and 'poverty as well as tyranny, poor economic opportunities as well as systematic social deprivation, and neglect of public facilities as well as intolerance or over activity of repressive states' can all represent major sources of unfreedom. Sen has defended the validity of expressions such as 'freedom from hunger,' 'freedom from malaria' and 'freedom from epidemics' in this context. Against the view that these expressions represent a rhetorical 'misuse' of the term freedom, he has suggested that if freedom is characterized in terms of counterfactual desires and choices—rather than purely in terms of the number of options available—then the elimination of hunger, malaria and epidemics may be directly relevant to freedom. If people have reasons to value a life without hunger, malaria or epidemics—if they desire and would choose such a life—then the absence of these maladies enhances their 'liberty to choose to live as they desire'.

THE IDEA OF SUBSTANTIVE FREEDOM

'Lack of substantive freedoms [some times] relates directly to economic poverty, which robs people of the freedom to satisfy hunger, to achieve sufficient nutrition, or to obtain remedies for treatable illnesses, or the opportunity to be adequately clothed or sheltered, or to enjoy clean water or sanitary facilities. In other cases, the unfreedom links closely to the lack of public facilities and social care, such as the absence of epidemiological programs, or of organized arrangements for health care or educational facilities, or of effective institutions for the maintenance of local peace and order. In still other cases, the violation of freedom results precisely from a denial of political and civil liberties by authoritarian regimes and from imposed restrictions on the freedom to participate in the social, political and economic life of the community'.

THE NATURE OF OBLIGATIONS (OR DUTIES)

Individual rights are often characterized in terms of correlative obligations or duties on other parties—individuals, groups or governments. Sen has built on this idea, characterizing human rights in terms of claims on individuals, collectivities and the design of social arrangements. 'Human rights are moral claims on ... individual and collective agents, and on the design of social arrangements. Human rights are fulfilled when the persons involved enjoy secure access to the freedom or resource (adequate health protection, freedom of speech) covered by the right'.

Whereas some authors have suggested that rights such as the 'human right to adequate food' are of rhetorical value only when they are not located in some specified institutional structure, Sen (2000) has challenged the view that rights must be rigidly matched-up with correlative duties, and that the articulation of rights-based claims in the absence of the precise specification of duties is 'loose talk'. In Sen's view, an 'inflexible' can militate against the principles of 'solidarity and fairness in social living' embodied in the Universal Declaration of Human Rights, which suggests that 'people have some claims on others and on the design of social arrangements regardless of what laws happen to be enforced'. Sen has invoked the Kantian distinction between 'perfect' and 'imperfect' duties in this context, arguing that whereas the former entail prespecified exact duties of particular agents, the latter entail more general duties of those who can help. He has argued that even when there is no clear right-duty link, the neglect of an 'imperfect duty' can amount to serious moral or political failure, citing the example of gender discrimination. 'Women's human rights give them a claim that male only suffrage and many other practices be ended through social, legal and institutional reforms. The duties correlated with this right cannot easily be allocated to particular duty bearers because the task of reforming these unjust practices falls on the group as a whole. Yet individual surely have imperfect duties correlative to this right, and speaking of this right clearly expresses something of great normative importance'. Defending the idea of universal human rights Sen has also developed a framework for defending the idea of universalism against relativist and culture-based critiques. He has challenged the proposition that the historical origins of the idea of human rights are uniquely rooted in Western traditions of natural law and natural rights, arguing that the broad traditions from which the idea of human rights has emerged—traditions of universalism, tolerance, freedom, respect for human dignity, concern for the poor, needy and exploited, and of interpersonal obligation and government responsibility—have not emerged exclusively in or from any single cultural tradition, and have deep historical roots in non-Western societies. He has highlighted the ideas of Confucius, Ashoka, Kautilya and Akbar in this context.

DO CIVIL AND POLITICAL RIGHTS HAMPER ECONOMIC GROWTH?

The idea that civil and political rights hamper economic growth was articulated by certain governments at the World Conference on Human Rights (in Vienna in 1993), while high growth rates in parts of East Asia during the 1980s and 1990s, together with China's recent record of economic growth and poverty reduction, are sometimes cited in support of the proposition that economic development should take priority over civil and political liberties. Sen has rejected the view that a core of so-called 'Asian values' have played a crucial role in economic successes in East Asia and that these values are in some way opposed to civil and political rights. In addition, he has questioned the empirical basis of the claim that authoritarianism plays a positive role in securing high rates of economic growth

'Some relatively authoritarian states [e.g. South Korea ... and recently China] have had faster rates of economic growth than some less authoritarian ones [e.g. India, Costa Rica, Jamaica]. But the overall picture is ...[more complex. Systematic] statistical studies give no real support to the claim that there is a general conflict between political rights and economic performance. That relationship seems conditional on ... [other variables. It is hard to reject] the hypothesis that there is no relation between them in either direction . . . .

Furthermore, Sen has argued that the selective and anecdotal evidence of the positive impact of authoritarianism on economic growth from East Asia is contradicted by the African evidence. Even when Singapore and South Korea were growing faster than other Asian countries, Botswana—a major defender of democracy—was the fastest growing economy in Africa. He concludes that the selective and anecdotal evidence goes in contrary directions—while the limits of growth without guarantees of a full range of civil and political rights were underlined by calls for greater democracy following the crash of the Asian financial markets in 1997.

THE ROLE OF CIVIL AND POLITICAL RIGHTS IN PROMOTING ECONOMIC SECURITY

Finally, Sen has focused international attention on the role of human rights in promoting human development and economic security. He has argued that civil and political rights can reduce the risk of major social and economic disasters by empowering individuals to complain, ensuring that these views are disseminated, keeping government informed and precipitating a policy response. 'Civil and political rights ... give people the opportunity to draw attention forcefully to general needs and to demand appropriate public action. Whether and how a government responds to needs and sufferings may well depend on how much pressure is put on it, and the exercise of political rights (such as voting, criticizing, protesting, and so on) can make a real difference'.

Sen's empirical research illustrates the ways in which the denial of civil and political rights can function as an obstacle to human development. His analysis of the phenomenon of excess mortality and artificially lower survival rates of women in many parts of the world (the 'Missing Women') demonstrates that although excess mortality in women of a childbearing age may be partly the result of maternal mortality, no such explanation is possible for female disadvantage in survival in infancy and childhood. The lower female-male ratios in countries in Asia and North Africa indicate the influence of social factors resulting in gender inequality, discrimination and the comparative neglect of female health and nutrition.

Conversely, empirical research illustrates the positive ways that civil and political rights can function to promote economic security. Sen has articulated the view that no major famine has occurred in any country with a democratic form of government and a relatively free press. He has suggested that this statement applies not only to the affluent countries of Europe and America, but also to the poor but broadly democratic countries such as India and Botswana; while the incidence of famines in India until independence in 1947 (for example, the Bengal famine in 1943 killed between 2 and 3 million people) contrasts with the post-independence experience following establishment of a multiparty democratic system—providing inter-temporal evidence of the positive impact of democracy in reducing the risk of famine. Furthermore, this evidence contrasts sharply with the experience of famine in China. When the 'Great Leap Forward' proved mistaken, policies were not corrected for three years (1958 to 1961)—while 23 to 30 million people died. In Sen's view, 'no democratic country with opposition parties and a free press would have allowed this to happen'.

CONCLUSION

In the past, human rights issues have typically been analyzed from the perspectives of separate academic disciplines. Philosophers have focused on foundational issues in ethics, and lawyers on questions of international legal obligation, while both disciplinary perspectives have tended to neglect the institutional, economic and structural processes that impact on individual freedoms and human rights. Meanwhile, in traditional economics, welfarist frameworks—that are unsuitable for thinking about human freedom and human rights—have dominated the landscape, and economists have often failed to incorporate the ideas of freedom and rights

Emerging International Agendas on Poverty, Freedom and Human Rights

The UNDP's Human Development Report, 2000 focuses on the inter-relationships between human development and human rights. It analyses the impact of economic structures, growth and development on human rights, and the impact of respect for human rights on social and economic outcomes, and conveys the central message that poverty is a limit on freedom, and that the elimination of poverty should be addressed as a basic entitlement and a human right—not merely as an act of charity. It calls for a framework for trade and investment that respects, protects and promotes human rights, encouraging greater commitment by donor governments to adequate funding of human rights priorities in developing countries, and suggesting that debt and economic and development policies, including structural adjustment, should be assessed in terms of their impact on human rights. Although the World Development Report, 2000-01 does not adopt a human rights approach to development, it nevertheless recognizes that 'poor people live without fundamental freedoms of action and choice' into their theoretical and empirical work. Sen's research agenda challenges past thinking and provides a basis for moving forward.

References

Sen, A.K. (1981) Poverty and Famines: An Essay on Entitlement and Deprivation. Oxford: Clarendon.

———, (1984) 'Rights and Capabilities'. Resources, Values and Development. A.K. Sen. Oxford: Blackwell.

———, (1992) Inequality Reexamined. Oxford: Clarendon.

———, (1999a) Development as Freedom. Oxford: OUP.

———, (1999b) 'Human Rights and Economic Achievements'. The East Asian Challenge for Human Rights. J.R. Bauer and D.A. Bell. Cambridge: CUP.

UNDP (2000) Human Development Report, 2000: Human Rights and Human Development, New York: OUP.

World Bank (2000) World Development Report, 2000-01: Attacking Poverty. Oxford: OUP.

CHAPTER

20

"Missing Women" in the Developing Countries and Amartya Sen

DHIRENDRA NATH KONAR

INTRODUCTION

The economist-*cum*-philosopher, the great humane, philanthropist and the Nobel-Laureate in Economics (in 1998), Professor Amartya Sen's one of the major concerns is the term coined (about three decades earlier) by himself as "Missing Women" which is still now found especially in the developing countries like the SAARC Countries each of which suffers from the problem of explosive population.

It is a fact that biologically the number of girls born per one hundred boys is relatively less, say, 97 or 98 so that the number of women born per 1000 men (this is commonly known as the sex ratio) should vary between 970 and 980. In practice, however, the picture is highly bewildering. Table 1 with two parts (A) and (B) demonstrates such an astonishing scenario.

Table 1(A)
Female-Male Ratio (Unfavorable to Women) in Some Countries of the World

Countries	*Sex Ratio*
Iran	970
Cuba	970
SriLanka	990
China	940
Iraq	960
Egypt	970
Hongkong	940
Singapore	970
Fizi	990
Pakistan	938
Bangladesh	953
Nepal	950
India	927
Bhutan	930
Peru	990
Mongolia	990
Thailand	990
Zordan	950

Source : Collected from Relevant Issues of the World Development Report.

The general scenario of the female-male ratio across the world is discerned in Table 1. Though there is no uniformity in this ratio, it can be said that this ratio is highly congenial to women in the highly developed countries like France, Japan, USA, Germany, Finland, and Portugal and so on. On the other hand, this ratio is highly unfavorable to women in the

TABLE 1(B)
Female-Male Ratio (Favorable to Women) in Some Countries of the World

Countries	*Sex-Ratio*
Canada	1020
Switzerland	1050
Japan	1030
France	1050
USA	1050
Germany	1080
Austria	1090
Belgium	1050
Finland	1060
Hungary	1070
Portugal	1070
Denmark	1030
Chili	1020
Mexico	1000
Australia	1000

Source : Collected from Relevant Issues of the World Development Report.

relatively less developed countries, especially in India, Bhutan, Pakistan, China and the like.

THE SCENARIO OF FEMALE-MALE RATIO IN INDIA

Even in case of India this ratio has continuously been declining from 972 in 1901 to 927 in 1991. However, in 2001 there has been an arrest to this trend and there has been a marginal improvement in it. We are to wait for about one year or so to know the exact figure in the coming census of 2011.

Among the states of India only Kerala has been divulging a ratio very much congenial to the women. Finally, the Union Territory of Pondicherry alone has revealed this ratio favorable to the women.

Let us now bring out the State-wise decomposition of the inter-temporal male-female ratio in India over the last hundred years between 1901 and 2001. This has been presented in Table 2.

The annual trend growth rate of the sex ratio in India between 1901 and 2001 has been found to be -0.43 percentage and the exponential curve fitting this ratio has been

$$St = 965.7(0.9957)^{t - 1901}$$

Let us now bring out the pattern of sex ratio as revealed by each of the thirty-five states and Union Territories of our great country in 1991 and 2001. The idea can be guessed from Table 2 itself. However, to examine if there is any change in the pattern of sex ratio in the last two censuses we have attached ranks to all the states and Union Territories in the usual manner (the case of a tie has also been taken into account). It may be mentioned that in 1991 Kerala alone had a sex ratio (1036) really favorable to the women whereas in 2001 besides Kerala, Pondicherry had shown such a favorable ratio (1000). In one decade both Kerala and Pondicherry had gained 22 points in this ratio. Other states gaining substantial improvement in this ratio are Arunachal Pradesh (from 859 to 901), Andaman and Nicobar Islands (from 818 to 846), Uttaranchal (from 936 to 964), Nagaland (from 886 to 909), Jharkhand (from 922 to 941) and Mizoram (from 921 to 811). But for Daman and Diu there has been an unexpected deterioration in this ratio (from 969 to 709). An almost similar situation (from 952 to 811) has been faced by Dadra and Nagar Haveli.

Compared to 1991 there are 24 states where this ratio had improved in 2001 while there are 11 states where this ratio had deteriorated. All the 35 states and Union Territories of India have been classified according to the nature of female-male ratio in 1991 and 2001 and this has been expressed in Table 3.

Table 2
Intertemporal Trend in Female-Male Ratio in India During the Last 100 Years between 1901 and 2001

States and UT	*1901*	*1911*	*1921*	*1931*	*1941*	*1951*	*1961*	*1971*	*1981*	*1991*	*2001*
(1)	*(2)*	*(3)*	*(4)*	*(5)*	*(6)*	*(7)*	*(8)*	*(9)*	*(10)*	*(11)*	*(12)*
Andhra Pradesh	985	992	993	987	980	986	981	977	975	972	978
Arunachal Pradesh	NA	NA	NA	NA	NA	NA	894	861	862	859	901
Assam	919	915	896	874	875	868	869	896	910	923	932
Bihar	1061	1051	1020	995	1002	1000	1005	957	948	907	921
Chhattisgarh	1046	1039	1041	1043	1032	1024	1008	998	996	985	990
Goa	1091	1108	1120	1088	1084	1128	1066	981	975	967	960
Gujarat	954	946	944	945	941	952	940	934	942	934	921
Haryana	867	835	844	844	869	871	868	867	870	865	861
Himachal Pradesh	884	889	890	897	890	912	938	958	973	976	970
J & K	882	876	870	865	869	873	878	878	892	896	900
Jharkhand	1032	1021	1002	989	978	961	960	945	940	922	941
Karnataka	983	981	969	965	960	966	959	957	963	960	964
Kerala	1004	1008	1011	1022	1027	1028	1022	1016	1032	1036	1058
Madhya Pradesh	972	967	949	947	946	945	932	920	921	912	920
Maharashtra	978	966	950	947	949	941	936	930	937	934	922

Manipur	1037	1029	1041	1065	1055	1036	1015	980	971	958	978
Meghalaya	1036	1013	1000	971	966	949	937	942	954	955	975
Mizoram	1113	1120	1109	1102	1069	1041	1009	946	919	921	938
Nagaland	973	993	992	997	1021	999	933	871	863	886	909
Orissa	1037	1056	1086	1067	1053	1022	1001	988	981	971	972
Punjab	832	780	799	815	836	844	854	865	879	882	874
Rajasthan	905	908	896	907	906	921	908	911	919	910	922
Sikkim	916	951	970	967	920	907	904	863	835	878	875
Tamil Nadu	1044	1042	1029	1027	1012	1007	992	978	977	974	986
Tripura	874	885	885	885	886	904	932	943	946	945	950
Uttar Pradesh	938	916	908	903	907	998	907	876	882	876	898
Uttaranchal	918	907	916	913	907	940	947	940	936	936	964
West Bengal	945	925	905	890	852	865	878	891	911	917	934
Andaman & Nikobar	313	352	303	495	574	625	617	644	760	818	846
Chandigarh	771	720	743	751	763	781	652	749	769	790	773
Dadra & Nagar Haveli	960	967	940	911	925	946	963	1007	974	952	811
Daman & Diu	995	1040	1143	1088	1080	1125	1169	1099	1062	969	709
Delhi	862	793	733	722	715	768	785	801	808	827	821
Lakshadweep	1063	983	1027	994	1018	1043	1020	978	975	943	947
Pondicherry	NA	1058	1053	NA	NA	1030	1013	989	985	979	1001
India	972	964	955	950	945	946	941	930	934	927	933

Source : Economic Survey, Government of India, 2001-02.

TABLE 3

Classification of States and Union Territories of India in 1991 and 2001 According to the Nature of Female-Male Ratio

Nature of Sex Ratio (in favor of women)	*States and Union Territories of India*	
	1991	*2001*
(1)	*(2)*	*(3)*
(a) Favorable: More than 1000	Kerala=1	Kerala and Pondicherry=2
(b) Good: More than 950 but less than 1000	Chhattisgarh, Pondicherry, Himachal Pradesh, Tamil Nadu, Andhra Pradesh, Orissa, Daman and Diu, Goa, Karnataka, Manipur, Meghalaya, Dadra & Nagar and Haveli=13	Chhastigarh, Tamil Nadu, Andhra Pradesh, Manipur, Meghalaya, Orissa, Himachal Pradesh, Karnataka, Uttaranchal, Goa and Tripura=11
(c) Unfavorable: More than 900 but less than 950.	Tripura, Lakshadweep, Uttaranchal, Maharashtra, Gujarat, Assam, Jharkhand, Mizoram, West Bengal, Madhya Pradesh, Rajasthan and Bihar=12	Tripura, Lakshadweep, Jharkhand, Mizoram, West Bengal, Assam, Sikkim, Manipur, Bihar, Gujarat, Maharashtra, Nagaland, Arunachal Pradesh and Jammu and Kashmir=15
(d) Highly Unfavorable: Less than 900.	Jammu & Kashmir, Nagaland, Punjab, Sikkim, Uttar Pradesh, Haryana, Arunachal Pradesh, Delhi and Andaman and Nicobar Islands=9.	Uttar Pradesh, Sikkim, Punjab, Haryana, Andaman and Nicobar islands, Delhi, Dadra & Nagar and Haveli=7

THE SCENARIO OF FEMALE-MALE RATIO IN WEST BENGAL

Let us now display the pattern of female-male ratio in West Bengal, as has been portrayed in Table 4.

TABLE 4
Female-Male Ratio in West Bengal in the Census Years Between 1901 and 2001

Year	*Total*	*Urban Area*	*Rural Area*
1901	945	652	994
1911	925	614	982
1921	905	591	971
1931	890	578	961
1941	852	559	945
1951	865	660	939
1961	878	701	943
1971	891	751	942
1981	911	819	947
1991	917	858	940
2001	934	893	950

Source : Relevant Censuses of India.

A clear analysis of Table 4 will make it clear that in the State of West Bengal the sex-ratio had always been unfavorable to women. There were 945 women against 1000 men in 1901 but in 1941 there became 852 women per 1000 men. So this ratio had become peak in 1901 while it reached at the lowest level in 1941. From 1951 it started improving and it became 934 in the latest census when it had just crossed the All-India figure of 933. Looking at the urban trend we observe that it was always highly adverse to the women, more so in the pre-independence period when it had fallen from 652 in 1901 to 559 in 1941. In 1951 there was a big jump and from then it had started increasing from 660 in 1951 to 893 in 2001. The rural scenario, in West Bengal, was also very unkindful to women. In

1901, it was really favorable to women, though in the subsequent censuses it turned unfavorable and this unfavorable situation persisted till 1991 and it is only the latest census when there was an advancement of 10 points, from 940 to 950, though it failed to touch the figure of the earlier century.

Let us now present the district-wise sex-ratio of West Bengal in 1991 and 2001, as has been portrayed in Table 5. This Table demonstrates that in the district-level the ratio does not favor the ladies who had become the worst sufferers in the very capital of the state. Next to Kolkata comes Howrah, so close to the capital itself. To display the nature of the female-

TABLE 5
Female-Male Ratio and Ranks Across Districts of West Bengal in 1991 and 2001

Years, Sex-Ratios and Districts	*1991*		*2001*	
	Sex Ratio	*Rank*	*Sex Ratio*	*Rank*
Darjeeling	914	14	943	11
Jalpaiguri	927	11	941	12
Cooch Behar	935	9	949	6.5
North Dinajpur	921	12	937	14
South Dinajpur	944	4.5	950	5
Maldah	938	7	948	8
Murshidabad	943	6	952	4
Nadia	936	8	947	9.5
North 24-Parganas	907	15	927	15
South 24-Parganas	929	10	938	13
Kolkata	799	18	828	18
Howrah	881	17	906	17
Hooghly	917	13	947	9.5
Burdwan	899	16	921	16
Birbhum	946	3	949	6.5
Bankura	951	1	953	2.5
Midnapore	944	4.5	955	1
Purulia	947	2	953	2.5

Source : Census of India, 2001, Series 20, West Bengal.
Spearman's rank correlation coefficient has been calculated to be +0.92.

male ratios across the districts of West Bengal in 1991 and 2001 we have displayed Table 6 which will amply reveal that in comparison to 1991 the ratio in 2001 had, in general, become congenial to the females. For example, in 1991 Bankura was the solitary district to have the ratio more than 950 while in 2001 besides Bankura, Midnapore, Purulia, Murshidabad and south Dinajpur had shown such a trend. In 1991 there were three districts showing adverse ratio while in 2001 the number of such districts got reduced to only one. In the last two censuses we have given ranks to each of eighteen districts of West Bengal in the usual manner and computed Spearman's rank correlation co-efficient which has been found to be +0.92, a very high value.

Let us now classify the districts of West Bengal on the basis of the nature of sex ratio over the last two censuses. This has been presented in Table 6.

TABLE 6

Districts of West Bengal Classified According to the Nature of the Female-Male Ratio in 1991 and 2001

Districts and Years	*Districts*	*Districts*
Nature of sex ratio	*1991*	*2001*
(a) Good: More than 950	Bankura=1	Midnapore, Bankura, Purulia, Murshidabad and South Dinajpur=5
(b) Unfavorable: More than 900 but Less than 950	Purulia, Birbhum, Midnapore, South Dinajpur, Murshidabad, Maldah, Nadia, Cooch Behar, South 24-Parganas, Jalpaiguri, North Dinajpur, Hooghly, Darjeeling and North 24-Parganas =14	Cooch Behar, Birbhum, Maldah, Nadia, Hooghly, Darjeeling, Jalpaiguri, South 24-Parganas, North Dinajpur, North 24-Parganas, Burdwan and Howrah=12
(c) Adverse: Less than 900	Burdwan, Howrah and Kolkata =3	

Source : Arranged from Table 5.

THE SCENARIO OF THE GIRL-BOY RATIO IN SOME STATES IN INDIA

An alarming situation that has come out from the census of India in 2001 is a sharply declining gender ratio in the age-group 0-6: it had reduced to 927 per 1000 male children in 2001 from 945 attained in 1991. We may display here such statistics of some of the states in India in Table 7.

TABLE 7
Girl-Boy Ratio in the Age-Group 0-6 in Some States of India

States	*Years*	
	1991	*2001*
Chandigarh	899	845
Delhi	915	865
Gujarat	928	878
Haryana	879	820
Himachal Pradesh	951	897
Punjab	875	793
West Bengal	967	963
India	945	927

Source: Collected from relevant issues of the Census of India.

It is revealed from Table 7 what a situation we are going to face! The decline in the gender ratio is so sharp that even the Provisional Census Report of 2001 questions whether the "sharp decline in the child sex ratios is indicative of any underlying trend of sex selective abortions."

From the above picture we may rightly state here that not much has changed since the 1980's when the Noble Laureate Professor Amartya Sen had coined the term "Missing Women", just to describe those literally not alive because of neglect and discrimination. He had estimated that world-wide there were 100 million missing women. Many believe 50 million, probably more, are in India. After Professor Sen's thesis experts have asserted that women go missing not only because of infanticide and foeticide. One estimate puts the number of abortions of female fetuses at 3 million to 5 million a year.

GIRL-BOY RATIO ACROSS DISTRICTS OF WEST BENGAL

Let us now present the scenario of the girl-boy ratio in the districts of West Bengal in the last two censuses. This has been presented in Table 8.

TABLE 8
Girl-Boy Ratios in the Age-Group 0-6 Across the Districts of West Bengal in 1901 and 2001

Districts	*1991*		*2001*		*Change*
	Ratio	*Rank*	*Ratio*	*Rank*	*Increase (+) or Decrease (–) Districts*
Darjeeling	976	3.5	971	5	-5
Jalpaiguri	973	7.5	973	3.5	0
Cooch Behar	967	11	968	8.5	+1
North Dinajpur	974	5.5	973	3.5	-1
South Dinajpur	974	5.5	968	8.5	-6
Maldah	960	14.5	967	10.5	+7
Murshidabad	977	2	975	1.5	-2
Nadia	983	1	975	1.5	-8
North 24-Parganas	969	9.5	961	12	-8
South 24-Parganas	973	7.5	969	6.5	-4
Kolkata	955	17	923	18	-32
Howrah	962	12.5	959	14	-3
Hooghly	960	14.5	952	16.5	-8
Burdwan	959	16	960	13	+1
Birbhum	976	3.5	969	6.5	-7
Bankura	962	12.5	955	15	-7
Midnapore	953	18	952	16.5	-1
Purulia	969	9.5	967	10.5	-2
West Bengal	967	—	963	—	-4
All-India	945	—	927	—	-18

Source : Census of India, 2001, Series 20, West Bengal.
Spearman's Rank Coefficient of Correlation has been calculated to be +0.90.

Mean and standard Deviations of the child sex ratio across the districts of West Bengal have been calculated and shown in the following form:

	1991	*2001*
Mean	967.9	963.2
Standard Deviation	8.3	12.1

We have already said that a very peculiar aspect of the census of India, 2001 is the highly declining gender ratio in the age-group 0-6 years. We now intend to demonstrate how far the districts of West Bengal are responsive in this aspect. Such responsiveness has appeared in Table 8 where we have presented the girl-boy ratios in the age-group across the districts of West Bengal in 1991 and 2001. We have also given the ranks to the districts in the usual manner. We have found that the Spearman's rank correlation coefficient has been +0.90, quite a high value. This suggests that the pattern of the child sex ratio across districts of West Bengal in the last two censuses has remained unaltered.

From Table 8 we notice that at the All-Bengal Level this ratio in 2001 had reduced to 963.2 from 967.9 attained a decade earlier. Besides, the standard deviation of the said ratio in 2001 had increased to 12.1 from 8.3 attained a decade earlier. These results are really a matter of grave concern.

In keeping with the above scenario as revealed by some States and Union Territories of India let us give some more information as has been revealed by a Bengali Daily. This has been presented in Table 9.

The number of girls born per 1000 boys in as many as 13 wards out of 141 wards in Kolkata in West Bengal as portrayed in Table 9 is highly disturbing. This is more so for the Ward number 75 where this ratio is the least. For the remaining wards the range of this ratio is 860-808=52. This ratio in each ward has been far less than what the census of 2001 had portrayed.

Together with the above picture let us display another startling picture of Jammu province of Jammu and Kashmir that had been published in the *Statesman*, Kolkata on 26th May, 2010: "About 7800 girls are being eliminated in the womb of

TABLE 9
Number of Girls per 1000 Boys in some Wards of Kolkata (*)

Ward Number	*Number of Girls*
1	860
4	851
6	823
7	843
10	860
11	844
21	839
25	826
52	832
65	853
75	520
76	825
133	808

(*Among the children of age-group 0-6)

Source : Information Portrayed in a Bengali Daily (*The Ananda Bazar Patrika*, Kolkata, dated 19th July, 2010).

mothers every year in Jammu province of Jammu and Kashmir and this illegal practice earns Rs. 5 crore per annum business to the illegal practitioners in the region".

Perhaps the impact of the content of Tables 7, 8 and 9 is now clear to all of us. However, this is not at all a happy state of affair. It is really a matter of great shame that the girl-boy ratio has gradually been declining as we are progressing and developing more and more. What is the difference between our attitude in the twenty-first century and that in the fifteenth century? Are we not destroying ourselves?

CONCLUSION

From the census data it is vividly clear that there has been an improvement in the number of females per one thousand of males which heralds an increase in the sex ratio in favor of the females. The increase in the sex ratio is really significant in that it is an indicative of the high status of women in the society. It also signifies dynamism among the female population in the community. The female-male ratio is, to a great extent, an index of the stability of the urban population. So an increasing urban sex ratio as it has been happening in (say West Bengal) indicates that the urban people of Bengal are becoming much more stabilized so far as their family life is considered. But together with such optimism we should not forget a pessimistic picture that has cropped up and about which we have given some vital statistics all over India and some states and even in Bengal and in Kolkata. This has been happening with the discovery of the amniocentesis tests which were actually conceived as a means of discovering whether the child in the womb suffers from any genetic defects so grave as to warrant an abortion. But these tests are now becoming much popular in India and many other developing countries only as an instrument for identifying the sex of the child in the womb. In case the child is detected to be a female one, there is a general tendency among the mothers to go in for an abortion. So amniocentesis tests followed by abortion of female fetuses will, far from strengthening the sex ratio, weaken it and the demographic gap between males and females will widen. This has really been happening in the nook and corner of India. All of us should be very cautious about it and should boldly protest it, otherwise the situation would be very precarious.

It is heartening to state that from January 1996 the Government of India had legally forbidden the determination of the sex of an unborn (foetus) by pre-natal diagnostic technique. But in spite of the legal ban abortion of the female foetus is going on and it has been increasing day-by-day. We have, in the previous paragraphs, given some such information. To get rid of such a sorry state of affair what we need is mass awareness which alone can prevent the said abortions. We may rightly say, "Legislation will mean nothing without mass awareness."

REFERNECES

Agarwalla, S.N. (1977): "India's Population Problems" 2nd Edition, Tata McGraw-Hill Publishing Co. Ltd., New Delhi.

Bose, Ashish (1974): "Studies on India's Urbanization", 1901-71, Tata McGraw-Hill Publishing Co. Ltd., New Delhi.

Census of India, Relevant Issues, Government of India.

Chatterjee, Shoma, A. (1987): "Foetal Guillotine", *Sunday Magazine*, Amrita Bazar Patrika, March 8.

Hicks, Mukherjee and Ghosh (1984): "The Framework of the Indian Economy", Oxford University Press.

Konar, D.N. (1988): "Changing Scenario of Indian Population: A Projection to 2000 A.D.", *Arthashastra*, Vol. 7, No. 1.

———, (2004): The Scenario of Population Growth in India, Akansha Publishing House, New Delhi.

———, (2009): Contemporary Issues of Indian Economy, Akansha Publishing House, New Delhi.

———, (1988): "An Attempt to Analyze the Trend of Sex Ratio in West Bengal", *Economic Studies*, Kolkata.

———, (2006): The Behavior of Infant Mortality Across the Districts of West Bengal", *Business Insight, Journal of the Department of Commerce*, Burdwan University, West Bengal, Vol. 1, No. 1.

———, (2007): "Women and the Present High Rate of Population Growth in India", *Artha Beekshan*, Vol. 16, No. 1, June.

Mukherjee, S. (1982): "Under-Enumeration in Indian Censuses—Impact on Intra-Censual Population Growth: 1901-81", *Economic and Political Weekly*, November, 13, 20.

Sen, A.K. (1983): "India: The Doing and the Undoing", *Economic and Political Weekly*, February 12.

———, (1988): A Lecture on "Economics, Culture and Sex Differential in Mortality" at the 71st Annual Conference of the Indian Economic Association held at Jadavpur University, West Bengal, 29-31 December

The World Development Report: The Relevant Issues.

The Ananda Bazar Patrika, Kolkata (2010), Dt. 19th July.

The Statesman (2010), Kolkata, Dt. 26th May.

Dutt and Konar (2000), (Ed.): Social Choice and Development, Deep and Deep Publications Pvt. Ltd.

CHAPTER

21

Amartya Sen's Economic Ideas on Welfare Economics

A. SHANMUGASUNDARAM, K. RAMEELA AND SASIKALA

INTRODUCTION

Amartya Sen has made a number of key contributions to the research on fundamental problems in welfare economics. His contribution range from axiomatic theory of the social choice, over-definition of welfare and poverty index, to empirical study of famine. In empirical studies, Sen's application of his theoretical approach have enhanced our understanding of the economic mechanism underlying famines. By combining tools from economics and philosophy, he has restored on ethical dimension to the discussion vital economic problems.

INDIVIDUAL VALUES AND COLLECTIVE DECISION

When there is general agreement, the choices made by

society are uncontroversial when opinion differ the problem is find methods for bringing together different opinions, in decision which concerned every one. The theory of social choice is pre-occupied precisely with this link between individual, values and collective choice. Sen's seminal work, collective choice and social welfare published in 1970, offered an answer to the US economist Kenneth Arrow's impossibility Theorem. Arrow argued that it is impossible to devise a voting system with an outcome which is both rational and egalitarian. If it is rational allowing full harmonization of individual preference it may well be dictatorial and therefore non-egalitarian.

Arrow's says in a democratic set-up there are five axioms like (i) complete ordering, (ii) non-dictatorship, (iii) non-imposition, (iv) irrelevant alternatives, and (v) voting paradox or majority rule. These axioms leads to impossibility of social welfare function. But Sen's has alleviated this pessimism. These are caused by inadequate basic education, a low level of health services, poor ownership pattern skewed social stratification and rising gender inequalities. He also argues that these variations in social opportunities can be reduced by political protests and opposition.

Sen treated problems such as : majority rule, individual rights and the availability of information about individual welfare.

INDIVIDUAL RIGHTS

A self-evident pre-requisite for a collective decision-making rule is that it should be "non-dictorial", that is it should not reflect the values of any single individual. A minimum requirement for protecting individual rights is that the rule should respect the individual preferences of atleast some people in atleast some dimension for instance regarding their personal sphere. Sen pointed to a fundamental dilemma by showing that no collective decision rule can fulfil such a mined requirement on individual rights and the other axioms in Arrow's impossibility theorem. This finding initiated an extensive, scientific discussion about the extent to which a collective decision rule can be made consistent with a sphere of individual rights.

INDEX WELFARE AND POVERTY

A common measure of poverty in a society is the share of the population, H with incomes below a certain pre-determined, poverty line. But the theoretical foundation for this kind of measure was unclear. It also ignored the degree of poverty among the poor, even a significant boost in the income of the poorest groups in society does not affect H as long as their income do not affect H as long as their incomes do not cross the poverty line. To remedy these deficiencies, Sen postulated five reasonable axioms from which he derived a poverty index: P=H (I + (1–I) G). Here, G is the Gini co-efficient and I is a measure (between 0 and 1) of the distribution of income, both computed only for the individuals below the poverty line. Relying on his earlier analysis of information about the welfare of single individuals. Sen clarified when the index can and should be applied; comparisons can, for example, be made even when data are problematic, which is often the case in poor countries where poverty indexes have their most intrinsic application. Sen's poverty index has subsequently been applied extensively by others. Three of the axioms he postulated have been used by those researchers who have proposed alternative indexes.

WELFARE OF THE POOREST

Sen analysed the choice of production technology in developing countries. Indeed almost all of Sen's works deal with development economics, as they are often devoted to the welfare of the poorest people in society. He has also studied actual famines, in a way quite in line with his theoretical approach to welfare measurement.

ANALYSIS OF FAMINE

He challenges the common view that a shortage of food is the most important explanation of famine. He argues that several observed phenomena cannot in fact be explained by a shortage of food alone. Example that famines have occurred even, when the supply of food was not significantly lower than during previous years (without famines) or that famine-stricken areas have some times exported food.

Sen showed that a profound understanding of famine requires a thorough analysis of how various social and economic factors influences different groups in society and determine their actual opportunities.

DEVELOPMENT ECONOMICS

In the realm of development economics, the fundamental stated objective has been to improve, if not maximize the welfare of the people at large and the disadvantaged in particular. Sen's contribution of economic development mentioned the following classification: (a) planning and growth, (b) poverty and famine, (c) deprivations and human development, (d) institution and role of the state, and (e) philosophy of progress. Sen's paradigm of development of economics is spread across these five spectra, and it would be interesting to identify the core that links these elements. In what follows, we attempt a revaluation of development economics in the contemporary world on the basis of Amartya Sen's contribution to the subject.

For a period in the history of post-second world war, when development planning was viewed as the essential tool for state sponsored economic development in may third world countries, Sen's methodology of evaluation of projects on the basis of their social costs and benefits have greatly helped in assessing impact of development projects in terms of the benefits reaped by the target group in particular, and the economy in general, and highlighting the conflict and trade-offs across social groups that these schemes have generated. His suggested methodology was widely used by development planners in devising the development policies in an otherwise non-market economic system as well as in mixed economies like India.

CONCLUSION

Amartya Sen has focused on the poor, viewing them not as objects of pity requiring charitable hand-outs, but as disempowered fold needing empowerment. Amartya Sen described so far on some specific grounds like poverty, inequality, standard of living and famine belong to the realm of purely axiomatic theory as well as empirical study of famine. In this paper Sen discuss how to prevent famine, or how to limit the effects of famine once it has occurred.

References

Yojana, Republic Day Special Issue, Vol. 43, No. 1, New Delhi, January 1999.

Brahmananda, P.R. (1999): Amartya Sen and Welfare-economics, Sudha Publications, Bangalore, 1999.

Brahmananda, P.R. (1998-99): "Amartya Sen and the Transformation of the Agenda of Welfare Economics", *The Indian Economic Journal*, Vol. 46, Oct.-Dec., No. 2, pp. 2-3.

Sen, Amartya Kumar (1970): Collective Choice and Social Welfare, San Francisco.

Sen, Amartya Kumar (1981): Poverty and Famine, Oxford.

Desai, Megnad (1993): Poverty, Famine and Economic Development—The Selected Essays of Megnand Desai, Vol. II, Edwar, Elgar, England.

CHAPTER

22

Amartya Sen on Employment Technology and Development : In a Policy Perspective

MAHESHWAR PRASAD YADAV AND
SHAKEEL AHMAD SIDDIQUI

The choice of technology is one of the key instruments of a development strategy. The employment implications of technological choice in development strategy can usefully be examined in terms of either spread of knowledge (innovations) or putting to use existing knowledge through an adequate institutional and incentives structure and pricing policies regarding factor inputs and products. Professor Amartya Sen falls into this second category. He lays emphasis to institutional factors and to economic and political feasibility considerations connected with appropriate technological choices. Two sets of general guidelines emerge from professor Sen's study. First, the household production modes which are prevalent in agriculture and services in less-developed countries have important implications for the utilization of technologies with domestic non-wage labour which may not be available for factory work. Second, too much emphasis should to be placed on the development of new intermediate technologies through research and development. If any point in the time the existing technology shelf is relevant frame for making current policy choices and decisions. The distinction made by Professor Sen on various aspects of employment problem helps in identifying the magnitude of the problem and formulating polices. Professor Sen is of the view that choice of technology should be considered with relevance of modes of production such as non-wage means of employment generation offers some advantage over wage modes of employment for utilization of labour-intensive techniques. If schemes can be designed in such a way that work can be done outside the wage system, the institutional wage rigidities need not conflict with the expansion of employment co-operative work projects are a useful method of overcoming the disadvantages of small scale operations in non-wage family system. Poor project planning and design, administrative rigidities, inadequate analysis of the nature of the employment problem and lack of criteria for the selection of projects have often resulted in public employment schemes failing to meet their objective of helping working poor below the poverty line. Some knowledge of size and distribution of different income groups below the poverty line is necessary if the public employment schemes[1] purpose of catching the really poor is not to be threaded. For example, functioning the Small Former Development Agency did not benefited to the poorest for whom it was meant to. Another issue of employment policy brought out by Sen is that price as signals for decision taking. In market-oriented economics the prices of factor and products are often out of line with their real scarcity and abundance, with the result that managerial decisions are not conductive to the achievements of socio-economic goals of employment in India. This provides justification for the use of shadow prices as tools for decision-making. Thus, economic policies, of formulated in isolation from the specific, political, social and institutional context are almost bound to flounder. These non-economic aspects and constraints are of fundamental importance for employment policy.

THE CONCEPT OF EMPLOYMENT

The concept of employment is notoriously vague in any economy in which the wage system is weak and in which self-employment unpaid family labours are common. The criteria of being paid a wage does not apply, and that of productivity is different to use since it is not easy to separate out the productive contribution of any particular member of the family in the total family enterprise.

At the risk of over-simplification employment can be distinguished between three different aspects. The income aspect employment gives an income to the employed. The production aspect employment yields an output. The recognition aspect—employment gives a person the recognition of being engaged in something worth his while.

TECHNOLOGY AND EFFICIENCY

Major problems of the technological advance in the developing countries seem to arise from difficulties in the translation of science into technology. In the context of employment policy this contrast between science and technology is relevant. Actual use of technology is production depends on a whole host of problems partly economic, partly social and partly one of pure organization.

Technical efficiency implies impossibility to move to an alterative such that change yields somethings for nothing. Controversies on employment policy and technological choice have frequently been geared to the notion of technical efficiency but it is empty of practical purpose. The concept of economic efficiency is notion of pareto optimality familiar in welfare economics. It is closer to the policy prescription. Though the problem of income distribution are completely left out of the discussion of economic efficiency and as a criterion of policy-making it is of very limited help.

EMPLOYMENT MODES AND THE WAGE SECTOR

Wage labour as a dominant form of employment, is of comparatively recent origin. Even today the vast majority of the labour force of the world works outside the wage system. Unpaid family work as a category of employment is an important one for many countries it is the dominant form of employment. Indeed, the growing importance of wage labour is recognized to be significant aspect of the process of economic development. In the less developed countries non-wage sector is dominant. The policy implication for the technological and employment expansion can be recommended with reference to relevant modes of production. If z is required compensation for additional unit of work by labour, a is the share going to the labour from additional unit of output production and the valuation of output going to others by the labourer. Economic development opens up technological possibilities exploitation of large scale.

CAPITAL INTENSITY AND TECHNOLOGY

For discussion on employment policy tend to be much concerned with concepts like capital intensity and problems of aggregation of capital are of obvious relevance for defining capital intensity and capital intensity has bearing with employment policy. But ranking of investment projects in terms of capital intensity may change substantially if human capital is introduced into the sums capital intensity has to be connected with specific values of specific resources.

INSTITUTIONS, TECHNOLOGY AND LABOUR

There exists multiple labour market in developing countries, wage gaps are readily noticeable for the same kind of labour in different labour markets. It may sometimes be the case that identical labour may be sold at different prices because of artificial distinctions. A typical example of this is the Indian phenomenon of using highly educated labour in jobs that do not require that type of education. Heterogeneous labour becomes homogeneous.

The economic decision processes that determine the technology and the level of employment in a given economy depend on the ownership of the means of production and the relations between the different economic classes. The financial arrangements are important and the contract between dependence on monopolistic money lenders and the availability of cheap institutional credit may be very significant for decisions affecting technology and employment.

THE EMPLOYMENT OBJECTIVE

Production and income considerations should be the dominant issues in the employment policy. In view of the policy the recognition aspect must also figure. In view of the policy-maker there are other positive consequences of employment. Worklessness induces vagrancy and crime. Expansion of female employment may be a greater force for change in a traditional society. Employment does indeed, involve more than production and income. But the policy-maker must take care that total wage employment creation should not exceed the available supply of wage goods. A reduction in output would tend to reduce wage goods so that even if direct employment is larger its overall impact on total employment can be negative.

EMPLOYMENT IN THE LONG-RUN

Under the wage system the volume of employment would be closely related to the output of consumer goods consumed by the wage earners. But the future output of consumer goods will depend on the growth of productive capacity and that in turn, will depend on the level of investment that in its turn, will depend on the level of investment today. There we have a conflict between employment today and employment tomorrow as well as between consumption today and consumption tomorrow. The conflict between present and future employment has come into the choice of labour intensity. In deed choice of techniques seems to be an integral part of this conflict.

CONCLUDING REMARKS

Any work of employment policy must begin with a sorting out of things that are within the control of the planners. Attitudes to work can certainly be influenced in the long-run. Four sets of structural factors that will constrain employment policy : (i) technological possibilities (ii) institutional features (iii) political feasibilities, and (iv) behavioural characteristics.

These factors are interlinked with each other. Valuation of labour will depend on the totality of all these features. Appropriate employment policies must be based on an assessment of the extent to which these structural relations can be deliberately influenced.

Technology institutions and politics are all variable over time. Given the particular problems of utilization of labour in developing countries, the case for aiming technical progress in certain specific direction scan be easily argued. Directions may vary from the general the development of techniques fielding a different seasonal pattern of production so as to redistribute the demand for labour more evenly over different months. Technical progress aimed at improving the output quality in the informal sector is also an important pursuit. Institutions come into employment in two different ways. Fast optimal technological choices depend substantially on the precise institutional framework within which choice has to be made and the alternatives has to be made and alternatives have to be evaluated with explicit reference to the mode of employment, methods of organization, pattern of ownership and such features. Second employment policy may also be geared towards institutional restricting which would bring about better utilization of labour force. While the first range of policies would be institution specific. The second would go beyond that into the dynamic of institutional change. Different types of political constraints is a matter of fundamental importance for employment policy. Economic policies can be discussed only in a specific political and social contest. The behavioral characteristics is also crucial to labour use. In considering the attitude to work one must look not only at cultural pattern but also at the institutional structure since behavior of people will be a reflection of both. Employment policy is a matter of interest not only for the government but also for the citizen. Policy-making ultimately is a social process. But the difficulties may be overcome using the structure of shadow prices.

References

Amartya Sen, Employment Technology and Development, Oxford University Press, India.

Bhalla, A.S. (1964), Investment Allocaton and Technological Choice, *Economic Journal*, Vol. 74.

Chaudhari, A.V. (1971), Aspects of Indian Economic Development, Alter and Unwin, London.

CHAPTER

23

Amartya Sen on Globalisation

M. Vijaya Bhaskar Reddy and S.E.V. Subrahmanyam

INTRODUCTION

Amartya Sen, in his article "How to Judge Globalisation", said that globalisation is often seen as global westernization. On this point, there is substantial agreement among many proponents and opponents. Those who take an upbeat view of globalization see it as a marvelous contribution of Western civilization to the world. There is a nicely stylized history in which the great developments happened in Europe: First came the Renaissance, then the Enlightenment and the Industrial Revolution, and these led to a massive increase in living in the West. And now the great achievements of the West are spreading to the world. In this view, globalization is not only good, it is also a gift from the West to the world. The champions of this reading of history tend to feel upset not just because this great benefaction is seen as a curse but also because it is undervalued and castigated by an ungrateful world.

Is globalization really a new Western curse? It is, in fact, neither new nor necessarily Western; and it is not a curse. Over thousands of years, globalization has contributed to the progress of the world through travel, trade, migration, spread of cultural influences, and dissemination of knowledge and understanding (including that of science and technology). These global interrelations have often been very productive in the advancement of different countries. They have not necessarily taken the form of increased Western influence. Indeed, the active agents of globalization have often been located far from the West.

INTERDEPENDENCE AND GLOBAL JUSTICE

According to Sen, Justice, it has been argued, should not only be done, it must also be 'seen to be done' or more explicitly. It is useful to think of this requirement of justice when assessing the pros and cons of globalization in general, and the particular role of interdependence in making globalization a success. There are good reasons to argue that economic globalization is an excellent overall good and that it is making a very positive contribution in the contemporary world. At the same time, it is hard to deny that there is some difficulty in persuading a great many people making them 'see' that globalization is a manifest blessing for all, including the poorest. The existence of this conformation does not make globalization a bad goal, but it requires us to examine the reasons for which there is difficulty in making everyone see that globalization is 'manifestly and undoubtedly' good.

The critical assessment of globalisation has to go hand in hand with trying to understand why so many critics, who are not moved just by contrariness, find it hard to accept that globalisation is a great boon for the deprived people of the world. If many people, especially in the less prosperous countries in the world, have genuine difficulty in seeing that globalisation is in their interest, then there is something seriously challenging in that non-meeting of minds. The underlying challenge involves the role of public reasoning and the need for what John Rawls, the philosopher, calls 'a public framework of thought', which provides 'an account of agreement in judgment among reasonable agents'. The goal of globalisation cannot be concerned only with commodity relations, while shunning the relations of minds.

INEQUALITY AND INSTITUTIONS

Amartya Sen says that the issue of inequality relates to globalisation in two distinct ways. There is, first, the crucial question of the sharing of the merging gains from globalisation, between rich and poor countries, and between different groups within a country. It is not adequate to understand that the poor of the world need globalisation as much as the rich do, it is also important to make sure that they actually get what they need. This may require extensive institutional reform, and that task has to be faced at the same time as globalisation is defended. Second, aside from the distribution of new benefits to come, the demands of justice cannot ignore the overwhelming presence of antecedent inequality that characterizes the contemporary world—the post-colonial present that has emerged from history.

This issue of inequality must, therefore, be addressed at different levels even as we give wholesome acknowledgement to the importance of international economic relations and its mutually beneficial potentialities. Perhaps the most important thing on which to focus is the far-reaching role of non-market institutions in determining the nature and extent of inequalities. Indeed, political, social, legal and other institutions can be critically significant in making good use even of the market mechanism itself—in extending its reach and in facilitating its equitable use. Their overwhelming importance are relevant both for disparities between nations and for inequalities within nations.

A second issue concerns the process through which income is earned as economic growth occurs. The ability of the poor to participate in economic growth depends on a variety of enabling social conditions. It is hard to participate in the expansionary process of the market mechanism if one is illiterate and unschooled, or if one is bothered by undernourishment and ill-health, or if social barriers excludes substantial parts of humanity from fair economic participation.

Similarly, if one has no capital, and no access to micro-credit, it is not easy for a person to show much economic enterprise in the market economy.

A third issue concerns the recognition that the fruits of economic growth may not automatically expand the important social services; there is an inescapable political process involved here. Decisions have to emerge at the social and political level about the uses to which the newly generated resources can be put. The route of "growth-mediated" advancement may be full of promise and favourable prospects for living conditions and freedoms of human beings, but political and social steps have to be taken to realise that promise and to secure those prospects.

INTERNATIONAL ASYMMETRIES AND INSTITUTIONS

As per Amartya Sen, the impact of asymmetries in global economic power, the distribution of the benefits of international interactions depends also on a variety of global social arrangements, including trade agreements, patent laws, medical initiatives, educational exchanges, facilities for technological dissemination, ecological and environmental restraints and fair treatment of accumulated debts. The issues urgently need global attention. So does the issue of the management of conflicts, local wars and global spending on armament, often encouraged by arms-selling rich countries.

DISTRIBUTION OF BENEFITS

The General Assembly of the United Nations requested the secretary general to prepare a report on 'globalisation and interdependence to forge greater coherence', they were opening the door not only to conventional questions of ways and means, but also to questions that deal with the transparency of assessments and the discernability of benefits. The achievements of globalisation are visibly impressive in many parts of the world. We can hardly fail to see that the global economy has brought prosperity to quite a few different areas on the globe. Pervasive poverty and 'nasty, brutish and short' lives dominated the world a few centuries ago, with only a few pockets of rare affluence. In overcoming that penury, extensive economic interrelations as well as the deployment of modern technology have been extremely influential and productive. It is also not difficult to see that the economic predicament of the poor across the world cannot be reserved by withholding from them the great advantages of contemporary technology, the well-established efficiency of international trade and exchange, and the social as well as economic merits of living in open rather than closed societies.

FEARS ABOUT GLOBALISATION

Amartya Sen says, make it sound like an animal- analogous to the big shark in Jaws—that gobbles up unsuspecting innocents in a dark and mysterious way. Globalization is neither new, nor in general a folly. Through persistent movement of goods, people, techniques and ideas, it has shaped the history of the world. India has been an integral part of the world in the most interactive sense. The forces of ideological separatism may be strong in India at present, as they are elsewhere, but they militate not just against the global history of the world, but also against India's own heritage.

Amartya Sen warns us against the temptation to see globalization as a "one-sided movement that simply reflects an asymmetry of power which needs to be resisted." Throughout history, "different regions of the world have benefited from progress and development occurring in other regions". Sen acknowledges that economic globalization poses risks to the vulnerable and the disadvantaged and his prescriptions appear close to the neo-liberal line. India should get behind it and, through smart public policies, tackle specific ills that arise from it, as well as invest in education, health care, micro-credit, land reforms, women's education, and infrastructure. He favors safety nets and well conceived social welfare programs that do less harm than good. He has persuasively argued that development should be measured not by GDP but in terms of "real freedoms people can enjoy".

But Sen's analysis is not without its flaws. According to Sen, "Global economic interactions bring general benefits, but they can also create problems for many, because of inadequacies of global arrangements as well as limitations of appropriate domestic policies." Sen seems to suggest economic globalization should create few problems. This is simplistic at best. Problems can also come from a culture's unpredictable response to it. This recognition, far from turning us against globalization, makes us more realistic about its effects.

GLOBALISATION AND WELFARE

Amartya Sen supports globalization. Does globalization increase welfare? Critics said that the problem of the evicted farmers exists not only in West Bengal but also all over India today. The cause is not promotion of industry as opposed to agriculture but a false economic idea imported from the United States, which disregard a planned and balanced economic development but promote a capitalistic development of the reformed economy that automatically invites evictions and exploitations of the poor. China is the best example of the success story of globalization, but what welfare the China people are enjoying now.

The so-called experts say India needs to get rid of its prohibitive labour polices, which are designed to protect the weakest members of the society against unrestricted exploitations by the private sector employers. Special Economic Zones where Indian labour laws and tax laws are not applicable in the answer, according to their proponents of "economic reforms". Economic reforms through the creation of Special Economic Zones by evicting farmers, when the majority has not benefited from the "economic reforms"during the last fifteen years of reforms. This policy will create mass unemployment in a country where employment opportunities are scarce. A country cannot be considered a great economic power if the people are unemployed and destitute and children are without education

CONCLUSION

Globalization is often seen as global westernization. Over thousands of years, globalization has contributed to the progress of the world through travel, trade, migration, and spread of cultural influences. There are good reasons to argue that economic globalization is an excellent overall good and that it is making a very positive contribution in the contemporary world. The issue of inequality therefore is addressed at different level even as we give wholesome acknowledgement to an importance of international economic relations and its mutually beneficial potentialities. Sen suggest economic globalization should create few problems. This is simplistic at best. Problems can also come from a culture's unpredictable response to it. This reorganization, far from turning us against globalization makes us more realistic about its effects.

References

Amartya Sen, "How to Judge Globalisation", *The American Prospect*, Jan. 1, 2002, Vol. 13, p. 2(5).

Amartya Sen, "Sharing the World", Globalisation and its Contents, Vol. V, Issues 4 and 5.

Amartya Sen, "Global Doubts as Global Solutions", The Alfred Dekin Lectures, 2001, May 15, 2001.

Namita Arora, "Amartya Sen on Globalisation", Nov. 2006.

Amartya Sen, "The Argumentative Indian: Writings on Indian History, Culture and Identity", Farrar and Giroux, New York.

Autumn, Winter, "Review Published on the Reach of Reason", *International Journal on Humanistic Idegology*", Vol. 2, No. 2, 2009.

www.amnestyusa.org/business/chinaprincipals.html.

CHAPTER

24

Amartya Sen's Idea of Justice

S.D. CHAMOLA

Amarteya Sen's book "The Idea of Justice" published in 2009, is the most important contribution on the subject of justice among the contemporary theorists. After reviewing the various theories, Sen has proposed his own ideas in which he has suggested steps both in theory and practice as how to reduce injustice and enhance justice in the world to make it a happier place to live in. The main objective of this article is to review the contemporary theories of justice and how an improvement has been made on these theories by Amartya Sen. It also highlights the main contents of his theory.

A REVIEW OF THEORIES OF JUSTICE

There are vast disparties in wealth and lifestyle in the same society and even in the same neighbourhood. There are people who berely make two meals a day and live hand to mouth whereas there are people who spend huge amount in clubs, social gatherings, luxuries, etc. There has always been two streams of thinking. One who never question the legitimacy of disparities and second who consider it as the worst state of affairs in any system. These disparties constitute the worst type of economic injustice in any social and political philosophy. In fact this is the core of debate as how to eliminate it and bring in a just economic distribution system.

Many answers have been given to this question of just economic distribution. Those answers and explanations are put mainly in three categories. These are also called philosophies of economic justice. These three schools of thought are named as (1) Libertarians, (2) Utilitarians and (3) Desertarians. Libertarians believe that the operation of a free market guarantees justice. Utilitarian, on the other hand, hold that the needs and interests of the people should be primary concern and the Desertarians are of the view that one's contribution in terms of labour and effort should be the main criterion of payment for economic justice.

Philosophers right from the ancient times have been concerned about the question as what is justice? For Greek philosophers like Plato and others "justice" is related to righteousness. In other words, a just action is always right and *vice-versa*. Similar relationship is also established between justice and morality. Thus justice and injustice, right and wrong, moral and immoral are the terms explained simultaneously in any discussion or writing on a just economic distributive philosophies in social and political fields. Recently, fairness, desert and equality are the new terms used in justice. Justice as fairness involves equality of opportunities and desert.

Philosophers have proposed three criteria to resolve the problem of just economic distribution. These criteria are : (1) effort, (2) need, and (3) equality. All the theories of just economic distribution have been put into two categories by the philosophers. First view is called "Consequentialism". According to this view consequences of distribution should be the main consideration of policy actions. The second view is called "Deontological" which says that duty or a right of a person should be taken into consideration while initiating steps to bring about a just economic distribution system.

A human society has both common interests and conflicts. Cooperation makes life easier whereas conflict arises due to distirbutive shares of social gains. The conception of justice relates to the proper distribution of this share which meets consensus. Thus a conception of justice is a set of principles for choosing between the social arrangements which determine this division and underwriting a consensus as to the proper distributive shares.

RAWLS AND BEYOND

Amartya Sen's Idea of Justice is mainly bed on Critical review of J. Rawls' Thoery of Justice. According to Rawls justice has to be seen in terms of the demands of fairness, i.e. "justice as fairness". Fairness involves taking note of the interests and concerns of others and avoid our vested interests, personal priorities or prejudicies. It is a demand for impartiality. Original position is the central idea in Rawls exposition. The original position is a situation when the parties invovled have no knowledge of their personal identies and vested interests in their original grouping on contract. There is viel of ignorance. The principles of justice are chosen in that original position unanimously. These principles of justice determine the basis of social institutions that should govern the society. The agreement reached in original position is fair. People differ in their religious, social, political and economic beliefs. But fairness of justice demands that one set of principles of justice can be arrived at through reasoning by the entire group. On the basis of these principles right institutions are selected to run the society. The working of these institutions further lead to social decisions and appropriate legislations. All these processes lead to the establishment of a just social arrangments.

In the original position of unanimous agreement the following principles of justice will emerge:

(a) Each person has equal right to a fully adequate scheme of equal basic liberties which is compatible with a similar of liberties for all.

(b) Social and economic inequalities are to satisfy two conditions. First, they must be attached to office and positions open to all under conditions of fair equality of opportunity and second, they must be to the greatest benefit of the least advantaged members of society.

Liberties that all can enjoy cannot be violated on grounds of furtherance of income and wealth or for a better distribution of economic resources among the people. For equity of distribution of resources Rawls invokes an index what he calls "primary goods". Primary goods include rights, liberties and opportunities, income and wealth and the social bases of self-respect. The demand of incentives is wrong ir the case of original position as all will play their role sincerely.

A SUMMARY OF SEN'S IDEA OF JUSTICE

Amartya Sen has critically reviewed all these approaches. His idea of justice is summarised under sub-heads to articulate and emphasize his point of view.

Reasoning and Objectivity

According to the Rational Choice Theory promotion of self-interest is the only rational choice and even doing good to others for ones own self will be rational choice. Reasoning is the basis of arriving at justice. It is also an instrument to find out rational choice. The example of Akbar, the medieval Mughal king is shining example of running the administration by reasoning in political and religious spheres.

Ethical decisions should also be based on sound reasoning because it is the only way at reaching the truth. However, the reasoning should be objective rather than subjective. What is ethical objectivity ? According to Rawls there are people in every society who are impartial and reasonable. Their reasoning can be helpful in arriving at justice. Adam Smith invoked the idea of impartial spectator in his book Theory of Moral Sentiments. An impartial spectator is away from the self-interest and other biases of parties under disputation. He is also away from local parochialism of values prevailing in a particular culture. In both the approaches one thing is common that objectivity should be linked to the ability to surve challenges from informed scrutiny coming from diverse quarters. Reasoning is helpful in democracy. It can also help in eliminating famines and prevent environmental degradation.

Social Choice Theory

The basic objective of the social choice theory is to arrive at aggregate assessments based on individual priorities. It seeks to establish aggregation over individual judgements of a group of different persons. A paradox known Condorcet Paradox, after the name of famous phiolosopher Condorcet, arises due to this theory of social choice. In elections A defeating B and B defeating C and C in turn defeating A by the majority of votes is a paradox. Professor Kenneth Arrow in 1950 was also concerned with the difficulties of group decisions and the inconsistencies with social choice theory. He put social choice theory on firm mathematical ground and commented that with explicitly stated and examined axioms, social decisions can be arrived at which satisfy certain minimal conditions of reasonableness. From these, the appropriate social ranking and choices of social states would emerge. Professor Arrow proposed the Impossibility of Social Choice Theorem which states that even with some small conditions of variations among the members of society, social choice is not possible. Hence, it is not rational and democratic decision. Whatever pessimistic the Theorem may be it opened new gates of further research and debates. Amartya Sen and others stated that these inconsistencies and paradoxes can be resolved by making the social decision procedures more informationally sensitive. Information on interpersonal comparisons of well-being and relative advantages, turns out to be particularly crucial in the resolution.

It is generally belived that there is no connection between social choice theory and mainstream theories of justice. But it is not so. With the help of social choice theory we can select social alternatives of social judgements. Different states of rankings are possible from social point of view. It is different from mainstream Contractarian Theory of an absolute and supreme state.

The Contractarian Theory of justice is termed as transcendental whereas the social choice theory shows the alternatives and hence called the comparative approach. Both transcedental and comparative approaches are interrelated. One can reach the supreme state of judgement only through ranking the various other alternatives of social decision-making choices.

CLOSED AND OPEN IMPARTIALITY

According to Adam Smith's "The Theory of Moral Sentiments" while judging one's own conduct one should judge it like an impartial spectator. This idea of impartial spectator is a pioneering idea for justice as fairness. The impartial spectator is a disinterested man from other societies as well far as well as near. This open impartiality is necessary to survey own sentiments and motives which we ourselves cannot do.

In contrast Rawls contractarian approach to justice is based on parochial or closed impartiality within the focal group. This approach is not sufficient and comprehensive for open scrutiny of our own principles and objectives, biases and prejudices common to a focal group objectively and impartially. Closed impartiality is not suitable even for a focal group. The focal group undergoes a change with the change in the composition and structure of its population over a period of time. Here again the open impartiality of an impartial spectator will be helpful in formulating the principles of justice.

POSITION, RELEVANCE AND ILLUSION

For the theory of justice position has great relevance. Persons from the same position confirm the same observations and same person in different positions will have different observations. Thus, positionality creates illusion. The position dependent observation does not lead to objectivity. The positional illusion may be due to variety of reasons. It may be physical when a rope in the dim light is mistaken for a snake. It may be cultural when sufficient facilities are not provided to women education, due to which they cannot excel in science and mathematics. There are fewer women scientists than men.

There arises an illusion that women are mentally inferior to men. Thus women remained negleted for centuries in some cultures. This illusion can be removed with the help of impartial sepectator from other societies and cultures where women have done better than men or equal opportunities in education were provided for men and women.

Karl Marx also stated that there is a great illusion that there is fair exchange between the producers and workers in the market. This illusion is the crux of capitalist exploitation of labour by the capitalists. There is similar illusion about health and morbidity as well as gender discrimination. People of Kerala have longer life expectation because of education and health services. The people of Uttar Pradesh and Bihar have lower life expectation for the same reason. However, the illusion is that people of Kerala have higher morbidity feelings as compared to those of U.P. and Bihar. Similarly, women have higher survival rate than men but here again women have higher morbidity feeling than men. The demand of justice is the reach of public reasoning to enlighten people about these facts of reality and persue scientific reasoning. It is the only way to dispel these illusions as these are based on pre-existing concepts.

RATIONALITY AND OTHER PEOPLE

Assumption of rationality is the basis of mainstream economic theory. Rationality demands maximisation of gains and minimisation of losses. This is the reasoning behind rationality of choice by producers, consumers and firms. Utility maximisation by consumers, cost minimisation by producers, profit maximisation by firms and so on. Further, the rational choice is the actual choice is the basic assumption. This assumption has been challenged now on the basis of critical scrutiny of reasoning.

Rationality of choice depends on complete information available with the decision-maker. However, empirical works have demonstrated that the actual behaviour of people may be different from complete maximisation of their goals and objectives. This departure may be either lack of complete information or weakeness of will. What one sees as irrational or stupid behaviour of others may not be actually so. It is the reasoning by an individual which is important for taking decisions.

An important hypothesis in economics is that people choose rationally if and only if they intelligently peruse their self-interest and nothing else. This is the crux of Rational Choice Theory. Rational choice implies its sustainability. If one's goal is to act beyond one's own self-interest and if an individual imposes self-restraint in public activities then these activities may be rational for him though he is not acting to fulfil his self-interest. This behaviour is rational for him. An altruistic activity may come under rational choice.

A stream of economic throughts right from ancient and medieval periods emphasised the role of eithics in human behaviour. The ethical behaviour goes against the assumption of pure self-interest behaviour of indiviudals. Adam Smith gave three behavioural patterns which go against selfish interest. There are : (1) Sympathy, (2) Generosity, and (3) Public Spirit. However, economists have projected Adam Smith as the main supporter of the assumption of rationality based on selfish interest based on his other writings which were highlighted by the overwhelming majority of economists that followed him.

Lives, Freedoms and Capabilities

The most important is to have the freedom of lifestyle that we want to choose and lead. We must have freedom not only to lead a lifestyle but also enhance our capabilities for the time to come also. Freedom is valuable for two reasons. One, it gives us more opportunity to persue our objectives that we value the most and two we are free in process of choice as we are not being forced to make a particular choice. Thus, opportunities and processes are the two aspects of freedom.

The capability approach implies to do things he or she has reason to value. A person may be rich but he is ill or disabled. He cannot make free choice of using his wealth in the manner he wants to do. His capability cannot be translated in actual choice thus, the capability approach is not just on what a person actually does but also on what he is in fact able to do. Capability approach to development is better than that of income or resource centred concentration of income and wealth. A disabled person may be rich but has severe limitations of capability as compared to his poorer neighbour. Thus the focus should be from means of living to the actual apportunities a person has.

Happiness, Well-being and Capabilities

Economics has been called a dismal science by Thomas Carlyle and economists are often seen as terrible kill-jyos. Poverty, unemployment, famines, etc. the subject matter of economics are painful aspects the society in which we live. These are the issues where description does not spread cheerfulness and hapiness. But it is not always so. Economics also involves the study of the topics which give happiness. The basic objectives of economics is to solve the economic problems of the nation and its people. These problems are at the root of cause of unhappiness and their solutions automatically will spread happiness and cheerfulness.

Welfare economics which is a part of economics which deals with policies and issues of human happiness and well-being Utilitarianism initiated by Jermy Bentham and championed by many distinguished economists like J.S. Mill, Alfred Marshall, A.C. Pigou, etc. gave happiness and human well-being the main thrust of their theories. Even the contemporary economists are trying to establish that economic prosperity and human well-being are closely related. The basic philosophy of economic development is to eradicate poverty from the world and make it a happier place to live in.

However, empirical findings have thrown a paradox that the increase in income and wealth has not made people happier. The western nations which have recorded higher real income and higher standard of living are not as happier. The relationship between income and happiness is a complex one and not so simple as development theoriests thoughts it to be. Tibor Scitovesky's analysis of "Joyless Economy" and Richard Layard's "Happiness : Lesson from a New Science" are the books which have raised the issues of relationship between income and wealth on the one side and happiness and well-being on the other side.

Happiness is the ultimate goal and it is self-evidently good. Society needs critical reasoning the way people are living the prevailing norms and standards of society must be reasoned. Spread of education and health facilities will help in such a reasoning. Happiness depends on the achievement and failure of our objectives which we value. Achieving the goal increases happiness and failure leads to unhappiness and disappointment. Thus happiness is closely related to our success or failures in life.

How capability is linked to happiness or well-being? Capability is concerned with substantive opportunities for well-being. The state may provide for the well-being of different deprived sections of society a number of opportunities or facilities. For example, old age, pension for senior citizens, poverty alleviation programmes, health and education facilities for all etc. It is upto individual to avail that opportunity. It is individual's own judgement how he perceives these opportunities for his well-being. A person's persuit of values he likes most will decide his well-being. Great men like Mahatma Gandhi, Bhagat Singh and others suffered personal deprivations and hardships for greater causes of national interest and freedom from slavery. They gave, priorities to national and social well-being rather than personal well-being.

Democracy, Equality and Liberty

A normative theory of justice demands equality of liberty or equal income or equal treatment of everyone's rights or utilities. It is an instrument of distributive justice. Equality is demanded for impartiality and objectivity. Participatory governance and public reasoning has the central role in understanding justice. In other words, democracy and justice are deeply connected since democracy is defined as "government by discussion". Democracy is not only elections and ballots, rather than in broader perspective of government by discussion and public reasoning. These features are essential for the theory of justice. Ballots and elections are narrow institutional version of democracy. The real version is free speech, access to information and freedom of dissent, independence of media, civil rights and political liberties. In the absence of these, dictators have won elections.

A free and independent press is essential for democracy. An unrestrained and healthy media has many advantages.

First, it improvs quality of our lives. We can communicate better with the outside world second, it has a major informational role in disseminating knowledge and allowing critical scrutiny of various subjects and aspects of life. Third, it has protective functioning in the sense that it highlights disasters such as famine, draught and other natural disasters. No democratic government can afford to face public without telling them that what it has done to alleviate the sufferings of the people. Fourth, a free press helps in fostering values in the society as it can highlight the social evils and initiate public discussion on these issues. Fifth, media helps in giving quick justice by making valueable comments on the issues under debate.

Authoritarianism, censorship, regulation of press, suppression of dissent, banning of opposition parties and penalising the dissidents are the practices enemical to democracy and public reasoning.

Globalisation and Human Rights and Justice

Justice in the present globalisation era has many ramifications. Action and decision of one country may not be in the interest of other countries or the world. For example, use of atomic power, developing weapons of mass destruction may be justified by the country or group of countries for their defence yet the entire humanity is at the risk. There are many other examples of this type. Therefore, impartial, reasoning by reputed people is essential for justice. Human rights have assumed global proportions. Many institutions have come upto deal with these issues Sen's basic concepts of reasoning, critical secrutiny and impartiality of decision are equally applicable at global level. Human rights form the core of justice. Every citizen has some basic rights irrespective of citizenship, residence, race, class, caste or community. The major human rights violations are torture, incarceration, social discrimination, hunger, starvation, medical neglect and soon.

Resistance to injustice can help motivate people to effective reasoning and critical scrutiny of the cause of injustice. History shows that protests against injustice such as famines and gender bias have succeeded in compelling the governments to think and implement remedial measures as it led to the reasoning and critical scrutiny. It is to be ensured that not only justice is done but also justice being seen to be done. Justice seen to be done helps in giving judges a boost in other cases. It also helps in easy and speedier impelementation of the decision of the judgement. It sends right message of justice to the public.

A problem can be seen from different angles. There is plurality of reasons to uphold or reject a value system. There are schools of thought which say that distinct values must be reduced, ultimately to a single source of importance. A theory of justice relates to accomodate the diversity of objectives of value. Values to be adopted can be prioratised in which all alternatives are made clear. It is possible only when reasoned conclusions are drawn.

A theory of justice has to depend on partial orderings taking different reasons of justice that came into light during discussion. Reasoning and critical scrutiny of the issue involved it gives us sufficient alternative to choose from. A perfect just state may not always be possible. These orderings can also help in arriving at a just state and if it is not possible then what can be next alternative to be adopted. A comparative framework is practical and plausible solution of achieving justice in a society having multiple objectives and values.

It has also been suggested that for impartiality of decision an outside evaluation is required to avoid parochialism and long shared values of a close community and region.

CONCLUSION

The idea of justice is an important contribution by Amartya Sen. He has successfully integrated the economic theory with the theory of justice. It is an innovation both in the fields of justice and economics.

REFERENCES

Sen, Amartya (2009), The Idea of Justice, Allen Lane, England.

Arthur John and William, H. Shaw edited (1978), Justice and Economic Distribution, Prentice Hall, U.S.A.

Rawls, J. (1973), Distributive Justice in helps edited. Economic Justice, Penguin Education.

Rawls, J. (1971), Theory of Justice, Harvard University Press.

CHAPTER

25

The Contributions of Amartya Kumar Sen to Development Economics

SRINIVASULU BAYINENI

"Ours is also a world of extra-ordinary deprivation and of astonishing inequality. Millions perish every week from diseases that can be completely eliminated, or at least prevented from killing people with abandon".

—Amartya Sen

BACKGROUND

Amartya Kumar Sen (AKS) born 3rd November, 1933 is a Bengali economist. Sen is known as 'the Conscience and the Mother Teresa of Economics' for his work on famine, human development theory, welfare economics and the underlying mechanisms of poverty, gender inequality and political liberalism. In 1998, Sen won the Nobel Prize in Economic Sciences for his contributions to work on welfare economics. A.K. Sen is currently the Thomas, W. Lamont University Professor and Professor of Economics and Philosophy at Harvard University. Sen has taught at a dozen of the world's most prestigious universities, including Cambridge, Oxford and Harvard and the London School of Economics. He is also a senior fellow at the Harvard Society of Fellows and a fellow of Trinity College, London and previously served as the Master from year 1998 to 2004. He is the first Indian academic to head an Oxbridge College. Sen's books have been translated into more than 30 languages. He is a trustee of Economists for Peace and Security. He has received over 80 honorary doctorates. In the year 2010, *Time* magazine listed him among the 100 most influential persons in the world.

Among the awards he has received are the "Bharat Ratna" (the highest honour awarded by the President of India); the Senator Giovanni Agnelli International Prize in Ethics; the Alan Shawn Feinstein World Hunger Award; the Edinburgh Medal; the Brazilian Ordem do Merito Cientifico (Grã-Cruz); the Presidency of the Italian Republic Medal; the Eisenhower Medal; and Honorary Companion of Honour (UK). In 1999, he was offered honorary citizenship of Bangladesh from Prime Minister Sheikh Hasina in recognition of his achievements in winning the Nobel Prize, and given that his family origins were in what has become the modern state of Bangladesh. A.K. Sen received the 2000 Leontief Prize for his outstanding contribution to economic theory from the Global Development and Environment Institute. In 2002 he received the International Humanist Award from the International Humanist and Ethical Union. In 2003, he was conferred the Lifetime Achievement Award by the Indian Chamber of Commerce. Life Time Achievement award by Bangkok-based United Nations Economic and Social Commission for Asia and the Pacific (UNESCAP). A.K. Sen has served as President of the Econometric Society, the Indian Economic Association, the American Economic Association and the International Economic Association. He was formerly Honorary President of OXFAM and is now its Honorary Advisor. He is a Fellow of the British Academy, Foreign Honorary Member of the American

Academy of Arts and Sciences, and a Member of the American Philosophical Society. This paper analyses the contributions of the Nobel Laureate Professor Amartya Sen in the field of development economics.

DEVELOPMENT

Development represents the growth of humans throughout the lifespan, from conception to death. The scientific study of human development seeks to understand and explain how and why people change throughout life. This includes all aspects of human growth, including physical, emotional, intellectual, social, perceptual, and personality development. The scientific study of development is important not only to psychology, but also to sociology, education, and health care. Development does not just involve the biological and physical aspects of growth, but also the cognitive and social aspects associated with development throughout life. The study of human development is important in a number of subjects, including biology, anthropology, sociology, education, history, and psychology. Most important, however, are the practical applications of studying human development. By better understanding how and why people change and grow, we can then apply this knowledge to helping people live up to their full potential. In this context, Sen describes five requirements that should ideally work together in order to bring true development, viz., *political freedoms, economic facilities, social opportunities, transparency guarantees* and *protective security*. Each of these distinct types of requirements and opportunities helps to advance the general capability of a person. The requirements for development can be described as an individual's ability to participate freely in the political process, the mechanisms and capacity to seek economic well-being, the networks and connections which make social integration possible, free access to reliable information sources, and structures which allow personal safety. Amartya Sen puts it well:

> "The improvement of human freedom is both the main object and the primary means of development. The

> objective of development relates to the valuation of the actual freedoms enjoyed by the people involved. Individual capabilities crucially depend on, among other things, economic, social, and political arrangements. In making appropriate institutional arrangements, the instrumental roles of distinct types of freedom have to be considered, going well beyond the foundational importance of the overall freedom of individuals. The instrumental roles of freedom include several distinct but interrelated components, such as economic facilities, political freedoms, social opportunities, transparency guarantees and protective security. These instrumental rights, opportunities and entitlements have strong inter-linkages, which can go in different directions. The process of development is crucially influenced by these interconnections. Corresponding to multiple interconnected freedoms, there is a need to develop and support a plurality of institutions, including democratic systems, legal mechanisms, market structures, educational and health provisions, media and other communication facilities and so on."

A.K. Sen's uniqueness as an economist rests on the fact that he has ranged far and wide over the vast terrain covered under the rubric of economics. His diversity not only embraced different areas of economics but also bridged what, for most practitioners of the science, is an unbridgeable chasm—that between the theoretical and the practical, combining empirical work with policy orientation. His contribution has been substantive to all the areas he has touched upon: social choice, definitions of poverty and welfare indices, causes of famine, and most importantly, the restatement of what indeed is development. Sen concentrated on grassroots issues right from the start. He wrote on the choice of techniques within agriculture in a populous economy. Later, he brought a much higher normative content to welfare economics. Sen engagement with welfare economics dates back to his years as a doctoral student in Cambridge, where his mentors were Joan Robinson and Maurice Dobb, both of whom had a deep distrust of 'received' economic mainstream (neo-classical) theory with its exclusive focus on the market mechanisms. However, Sen was not totally swayed by any anti-market philosophy. He acknowledged the information processing role of the market, but also started looking deeply into issues wherever he felt that people were being bypassed by the market. Such bypassing was inevitable under conditions where people lacked education, suffered from ill-health, or were discriminated against.

FREEDOM AND HUMAN RIGHTS

In the past, the idea of fundamental freedoms and human rights has often been neglected in theoretical and empirical economics. Dominant approaches have assessed the adequacy of economic processes and arrangements in terms of income expansion, at the same time as standard frameworks in welfare economics have evaluated interpersonal advantage and the efficiency and fairness of competitive market outcomes in terms of utility—with no explicit recognition of instrumental and intrinsic value of fundamental freedoms and human rights. The failure of standard frameworks in economics to take adequate account of the instrumental and basic value of fundamental freedoms and human rights is a central and re-occurring theme in Amartya Sen's work. A.K. Sen Research agenda over more than 40 years has highlighted the limitations of dominant income focused and utility-focused paradigms in theoretical and empirical economics from the perspective of fundamental freedoms and human rights. These frameworks concentrate on an overly-narrow informational base and an overly narrow view of the *means* and the *ends* of development and growth.

A.K. Sen has developed a far-reaching critique of 'welfarist' frameworks for concentrating on an overly narrow view of human rationality and well-being. Sen work has 'unpacked' the 'welfarist' foundations of a wide-range of conceptual and technical apparatus and has analyzed the limitations of this informational base from the perspective of fundamental freedoms and human rights—for the prediction of individual behaviour, the characterization of interpersonal advantage and the evaluation of the efficiency and fairness of competitive market outcomes. Amartya Sen's research agenda has moved both theoretical and empirical economics forward by stressing the importance of fundamental freedoms and human rights for the analysis of economic processes and arrangements including the evaluation of personal advantage; the efficiency and fairness of market outcomes; poverty and inequality; the adequacy of public policy and institutional arrangements; the nature of development and growth. Sen work has emphasized the development of new frameworks and approaches in theoretical and empirical economics that take account of both the *instrumental* role of fundamental freedoms and human rights in influencing competitive market outcomes and trajectories of development and growth.

Amartya Sen has advocated new approaches to thinking about fundamental freedoms and human rights. In the earlier period, poverty and hunger were often excluded from dominant discourses on fundamental freedoms and human rights. Sen has challenged this approach, arguing that: "*When we assess inequalities across the world in being able to avoid preventable morbidity, or escapable hunger, or premature mortality, we are not merely examining differences in well-being... [T]he available data regarding the realization of disease, hunger, and early mortality tell us a great deal about the presence or absence of certain central basic freedoms*". According to Amartya Sen, the idea that consequences such as life, death, starvation and nourishment are intrinsically matters of moral indifference—or have only very weak intrinsic moral relevance—is 'implausible' and fails to reflect 'complex interdependences' that arise in relation to the exercise and valuation of freedoms and rights in a society.

Besides, A.K. Sen has rejected exclusively *negative* characterizations of freedoms and rights, focusing attention away from the *absence of intentional coercion* as an exclusive condition of individual freedom, and towards the constituent elements of what a person can actually *do* or *be*. In this conceptual framework, the *absence* or *deprivation* of certain *capabilities* or *real opportunities*—as well as the denial of political and civil liberties—are relevant to the characterization of freedoms and rights, and 'poverty as well as tyranny, poor economic opportunities as well as systematic social deprivation, and neglect of public facilities as well as intolerance or over activity of repressive states' can all represent major sources of unfreedom.

He has defended the validity of expressions such as 'freedom from hunger', 'freedom from malaria' and 'freedom from epidemics'. Sen has also developed a framework for defending the idea of universalism against relativist and culture-based critiques. He has challenged the proposition that the historical origins of the idea of human rights are uniquely rooted in Western traditions of natural law and natural rights, arguing that the broad traditions from which the idea of human rights has emerged—traditions of universalism, tolerance, freedom, respect for human dignity, concern for the poor, needy and exploited, and of interpersonal obligation and government responsibility—have not emerged exclusively *in* or *from* any single cultural tradition, and have deep historical roots in non-Western societies.

POVERTY AND FAMINE

Food shortages in a population are caused either by a lack of food or by difficulties in food distribution; it may be worsened by natural climate fluctuations and by extreme political conditions such as tyrannical government or warfare. One of the largest historical famines (proportional to the affected population) was the Great Famine in Ireland, which began in 1845 and occurred as food was being shipped *from* Ireland to England because only the English could afford to pay higher prices. Many famines are caused by imbalance of food production compared to the large populations of countries whose population exceeds the regional carrying capacity. Historically, famines have occurred from agricultural problems such as drought, crop failure, or pestilence. Changing weather patterns, the ineffectiveness of medieval governments in dealing with crises, wars, and epidemic diseases like the Black Death helped to cause hundreds of famines in Europe during the middle Ages, including 95 in Britain and 75 in France. In France, the 100-years' War, crop failures and epidemics reduced the population by two-thirds. The failure of a harvest or the change in conditions, such as drought, can create a situation whereby large numbers of people live where the carrying capacity of the land has temporarily dropped radically. Famine is often associated with subsistence agriculture, that is, where most farming is aimed at producing enough food energy to survive. The total absence of agriculture in an economically strong area does not cause famine; Arizona and other wealthy regions import the vast majority of their food, since such regions produce sufficient economic goods for trade. Disasters, whether natural or man-made, have been associated with conditions of famine ever since humankind has been keeping written records.

In this context, in 1981, Sen published *Poverty and Famines: An Essay on Entitlement and Deprivation*, a book in which he demonstrated that famine occurs not only from a lack of food, but from inequalities built into mechanisms for distributing food. He argues that, contrary to conventional belief, most famines aren't created by food shortages. Harvest failures, reductions in food imports, droughts, etc, are often contributing factors—but far more important are the social systems that determine how a society's food is distributed. Absolute scarcity—insufficient food to feed everyone—is extraordinarily rare. Vastly more common is for an adequate supply of food to be beyond the reach of those who need it most. Sen's interest in famine stemmed from personal experience. As a 9-year-old boy, he witnessed the Bengal famine of 1943, in which three million people perished. This staggering loss of life was unnecessary, Sen later concluded. He presents data that there was an adequate food supply in Bengal at the time, but particular groups of people including rural landless labourers and urban service providers like haircutters did not have the monetary means to acquire food as its price rose rapidly due to factors that include British military acquisition, panic buying, hoarding, and price gouging, all connected to the war in the region.

However, Sen exposed that in many cases of famine, food supplies were not significantly reduced. In Bengal, for instance, food production, while down on the previous year, was higher than in previous non-famine years. Therefore, Sen points to a number of social and economic factors, such as declining wages, unemployment, raises food prices, and poor food-distribution systems. These issues led to starvation among certain groups in society. His capabilities approach focuses on positive freedom, a person's actual ability to be or do something, rather than on negative freedom approaches, which are common in economics and simply focuses on non-interference. In the Bengal famine, rural laborers' negative freedom to buy food was not affected. However, they still starved because they were not positively free to do anything, they did not have the functioning of nourishment, nor the capability to escape morbidity. In addition to his important work on the causes of famines, Sen's work in the field of development economics has had considerable influence in the formulation of the Human Development Report, published by the United Nations Development Programme (UNDP). This annual publication that ranks countries on a variety of economic and social indicators owes much to the contributions by Sen among other social choice theorists in the area of economic measurement of poverty and inequality.

CONCLUSIONS

A powerful, vigorous man, equally at home citing Western and Eastern philosophy, he is the first Indian—and the first Asian—to win the Nobel Prize for economics. The prize recognized Sen's contributions in the fields of social choice theory, welfare economics and economic measurement. Sen is credited with making inroads into the assessment of poverty and the evaluation of inequality. Sen's seminal contribution was in the area of squaring individual preferences with the collective good. He re-worked the assumptions of rationality to include moral constructs in order to enable the squaring individual choices with the imperatives of social justice in a democracy. Sen has focused international attention on the role of human rights in promoting human development and economic security. He has argued that civil and political rights can reduce the risk of major social and economic disasters by empowering individuals to complain, ensuring that these views are disseminated, keeping government informed and precipitating a policy response. Sen's later work illustrated that lack of capabilities and opportunities are responsible for poverty and hunger. His work on famines showed that it was not so much shortage of food as a set of social and economic conditions which deprived people of purchasing power and left them vulnerable to famines. He has carried forward the implications of this finding in his more recent work on development, and passionately advocated enhanced investment in health, education and the creation of opportunities.

References

Drèze, J. and Sen, A.K. (1989): Hunger and Public Action, Clarendon, Oxford.

———, (2002): India: Development and Participation, Oxford University Press, Oxford.

Sen, A.K. (1981): Poverty and Famines: An Essay on Entitlement and Deprivation, Clarendon, Oxford.

———, (1987): On Ethics and Economics, Blackwell, Oxford.

———, (1992): Inequality Reexamined, Clarendon, Oxford.

———, (1999): Development as Freedom, Oxford University Press, Oxford.

———, (1999): 'Human Rights and Economic Achievements', in J.R. Bauer and D.A. Bell (eds): *The East Asian Challenge for Human Rights*, Cambridge University Press, Cambridge.

Sen, Amartya (1999): Development as Freedom, Random House, New York.

UNDP (2000): *Human* Development Report, 2000: Human Rights and Human Development, Oxford University Press, New York.

Sabina Alkire (2002): Valuing Freedoms: Sen's Capability Approach and Poverty Reduction, Oxford University Press, Oxford.

Vizard, P. (2005): Poverty and Human Rights: Sen's 'Capability Perspective' Explored, Oxford University Press, Oxford.

World Bank (1998): Development and Human Rights: The Role of the World Bank, The World Bank, Washington.

CHAPTER

26

Economics and Philosophy of Amartya Sen

GEETA G. PANDYA

Here is an attempt to evaluate the characteristic features of Sen's philosophy in the light of his economic ideas.

(i) Adam Smith persuasively argued that the voluntary interaction among individuals in pursuit of their own interest in the market could result in public good. By saying this, he was not making any attempt to separate economics and ethics. He was only freeing economics from the false promises that it was unethical to pursue 'self-love'. To speak in Smith's words, "the obvious and simple system of natural liberty established itself of its own record. Everyone, as long as he does not violate the laws of justice, is left perfectly free to pursue his own interest in his own way, and to bring forth his industry and capital into competition with those of any other man, or order of men". Sen (1987) provides an interpretation of Smithian philosophy by commenting that Smith was actually talking of the enlightened self-interest whereby every individual's action was to be judged not merely on the basis of his narrow self-interest but by taking into account the interest of the society as a whole.

The framework of Sen's economics is solely based on the concepts of individual rights, freedom and choice. Sen's idea on rights and freedom is linked with his 'agency concept'. Sen distinguishes between well-being and agency. According to his philosophy, well-being refers to one's own well-being, while agency recognizes and respects the ability of a person to form goals, commitments and values, considerations of which may not be fully covered by his or her own well-being. Accordingly, agency does not mean that whatever a person values is *perse* acceptable. These valuations need to be assessed and evaluated by some criteria. Sen is highly critical of utility-based welfarist criteria which concentrate only a well-being aspect ignoring the agency aspect. Sen thinks that the perspective of freedom can be applied to the 'well-being' aspect as well as to the 'agency aspect'. Accordingly, four distinct categories of relevant informations regarding a person need to be considered, 'well-being achievement', 'well-being freedom', 'agency achievement' and 'agency freedom'. This plurality, according to Sen is reduced to a single category in mainstream welfare economics by: (a) considering freedom as only instrumentally valuable; (b) assuming that everyone's agency is exclusively geared to the pursuit of self-interest. He is critical and brings out the limitations of the principle of rationality based on 'self-interest' and 'maximisation of utility' principle.

Amartya Sen (*On Ethics and Economics,* 1987) distinguishes between two origins of economics, both related to politics, but related in rather different ways with ethics and engineering. The ethics-related approach is traced back to Aristotle's 'Nichomachean ethics'. It holds that: (a) the problem of human motivation is related to the broadly ethical questions—how should one like? and (b) is also related to the end of achieving social good or good of mankind. The ethical approach is closer to normative economics and engineering approach to economics, which Sen traces to Kautilya's Arthasastra, which takes for granted the ends. The object of economics then becomes one of finding an appropriate means to satisfy the given ends. Amartya argues that, "The deep question raised by the ethics-related view of motivation and social achievement must find an important place in modern economics".

Amartya Sen, has recognised some of the "very fruitful" contributions that has been made by the positive approach of economics. There are non-ethical views of human motivation and behaviour, characterisation of social institution in rather simple terms, and so on. Thus, positive approach helps us to understand the nature of many social relations that are very important for economics. In the analysis of complex interdependence, this approach has made very substantial strides, failure to recognise which in the opinion of Sen, is a loss to ethics as well.

Thus, Sen's concepts of individual freedom, choice, liberty—all are far away from the postulates of self-interested utilitarianism. They encounter the distribution issues and introduce a new welfare paradigm based on the norm of capability development, which re-establish a link between ethics and economics. Sen introduces universally acceptable axioms in his theory of social choice and thereby opens up the ethical dimension in economics. It is obvious that Sen is greatly influenced by Kantian ethics which emphasizes right behavior and action for their own sake independent of their consequences. Behavior and action are governed by categorical imperatives. As mentioned earlier, Sen ignores utilitarian ethics.

(ii) Sen considers the provision of minimum equal capabilities as the pre-requisite of economic development. A philosophical approach embodied in this consideration reflects that Sen demands justice for the deprived. Before Sen, he advocated for justice through the provision of equitable distribution arrangements of primary goods, on the basis of universally acceptable ethical norms. Before Sen, Rawls advised that the decisions on social choices should give the greatest weight to the lowest strata of society. Sen's poverty index is an attempt to measure the poverty of the lowest strata of the people living below the poverty line. Thus with additions of justice along with individual freedom, choice and liberty in welfare economics, Sen includes some philosophical dimensions in economic analysis. Moreover, his poverty studies, with the help of his poverty index has designated him as an economist of the deprived.

(iii) Like A.C. Pigou, Sen makes provisions for linking up ethics in economics. But, so far as tools of the welfare economics are concerned, Sen deviates from the paths shown by Pigou. Pigou discussed social welfare in terms of marginal social benefit and marginal private benefit. He advocated in favor of those production activities in which marginal social benefits exceeds marginal private benefits and discouraged those production activities in which marginal private benefit exceeds marginal social benefit. But in Sen's welfare economics, interplaying of marginal social cost and marginal social benefit have no role to play This is because Sen, like Adam Smith, deals only with the enlightened individual behavior, leaving aside the individual behavior guided by self-interest motive.

(iv) Sen shows respect also to Marxian philosophies. The basic postulate of Marxian economics is the interplay of 'superstructure' and 'substructure'. Marx called the whole economic structure or mode of production as the base or substructure; the religions, ethics, law, moral institution of society, he called the superstructure; it was the mode of production over which the superstructure was built. According to Marx, mode of production depends on: (a) forces of production, and (b) relations of production. The social relations determine individual's existence in the society and Marx opined, "It is not the consciousness of men that determines their social existence, but on the contrary, their social existence determines their consciousness". And social existence of them was determined by the property relations within which they had been at work before. This idea of Marx influences Sen's approach of entitlement relations, with the help of which Sen completes his studies on famines. Moreover, like Marx, Sen who supports liberalized and market-friendly economy, emphatically points out that even under the impact of the L.P.G. (Liberalization, Privatization, Globalization) strategy, state should come to the forefront of action and work vigorously in the fields of primary education, adult education, health care, better sanitation and for empowerment of women.

To sum up, Sen is greatly influenced by the economic ideas of Adam Smith, A.C. Pigou and Marx. But, he never followed their paths blindly. Sen's mind is rather flexible. Socio-economic condition of an economy is the prime determinant of Sen's philosophy. His philosophy is of his own. Incorporation of ethics in economic analysis is his basic philosophy and is the most important distinguishing characteristic of Sen's thinking.

CONCLUSION

The remarkable achievement of Sen is to provide a breakthrough in the new and old welfare economics by welfare judgments from existing facts of human deprivation. He makes a number of creative contributions in the discipline of economics as mentioned earlier.

Sen studies two types of deprivations, discriminatory deprivation and non-discriminatory deprivation. Sen looks at the intra-family disparities in the distribution of food. He finds that there is a good deal of evidence from all over the world that food is often distributed very unequally within the family—with a distinct sex-bias (against the female), and also an age-bias (against the children). Sen spoke against the evils of gender disparity in all spheres of life. With indicators on the aspects of health and education, he opines that there exists a relative deprivation of female compared to male which hampers the process of development. Sen's studies on poverty and famines are examples of non-discriminatory deprivation. So, Sen should be complimented for playing the twin roles—as an economist of the deprived, and as an advocator of gender empowerment.

The classical economists prescribed raising of the ratio of surplus to necessary costs in order to raise the level of economic development. Such surplus may be used either for consumption enjoyment or for capital formation. For economic development, Alfred Marshall advocated, for the maximization of net consumers' surplus, while some other neo-classical emphasized for maximization of utility. Some of the economists of the present day suggest increasing per capita real income for increasing welfare of the society. But all these studies overlook the possibility of hidden costs like ecological and such other damages which may in turn reduce the level of welfare. It is

Sen, who brings all these components in his concept of 'capability'. Sen claims that his capability index is a better index of well-being than commodities and utilities, and it is an improvement over Rawlsian approach of primary goods. For primary goods are general purpose means of resources, useful for the pursuit of different ideas of the good that the individuals may have.

Brahmananda, however, is highly sceptical on the operational aspect of Sen's capability concept. Brahmananda claims, "The heterogeneity of human beings in their desires for different types of abilities and plurality of spaces of capability, both create difficulties in operationalism of the concept of 'minimum equal capabilities' for all. The case of Kerala is a probable illustration on how the measure of poverty as defined in India cannot be positively correlated with high per capita capabilities". (Brahmananda, 1999). Brahmananda criticised Sen, on the ground that Sen does not tell anything on the financial aspect of the plan ensuing capabilities. If the government has to impose tax on the higher income group in order to ensure the level of minimum capability to the poor, then, according to Brahmananda, Sen's minimum capability is turned into Rawlsian approach of primary good which Rawls contributed in 1971, long before Sen's capability approach (1987). Moreover, Brahmananda observes also that Sen only talks about 'lack of entitlement relations' resulting in deprivations in the developing and semi-developed countries. So, Brahmananda claims that in a resource-scarce economy like India, enforcement of Sen's entitlement relations should not be extended beyond limits, and he suggests also for the legal enforcement of duties side by side with entitlement rights. Apart from all these shortcomings in two of Sen's innovative concepts, it is still to be recognised that Sen's original concept of rationality is hidden in both of his capability and entitlement concepts.

In fact, Amartya Sen is and will always be remembered not as an achiever of Nobel prize or as a Bengali economist but will be remembered as a humanist. In India, Naoroji started his studies on poverty by the end of the nineteenth century. Amartya's poverty studies reveal some similarities with that of Naoroji. For, Naoroji pointed out that internal economic drain which resulted from internal inequality, was one of the main causes of Indian poverty. Similarly, Amartya points out that though poverty and inequality are not synonymous; still poverty and deprivation result from inequality in distribution. Secondly, to both of them the poor are not inefficient and uncompetitive as is in western analysis on poverty. But, Sen extends his poverty problem in a broader way. The basic motive of Naoroji's poverty studies was concentrated only with the interest of the Indian poor.) Naoroji applied the international scale of comparison in this context, just to show how the people of India had been deprived by the British colonial administration. So Naoroji should be regarded as one of the nationalist economists. But Sen always thinks for the deprived who have been living all over the world. So we regard Sen as a humanist, or as the "practitioner of human science" (Bagchi, 1998).

Sen proves very brilliantly that human development is a pre-condition of sustainable economic development. Amartya Sen along with Mehbub-ul-Haque and many economists of the third world countries evolved Human Development Indices and we now have a Human Development Report published annually by UNDP which brings out the data related to human sufferings in the countries. They relate to quantification of data of starvation, empowerment, standard of living, gender discrimination, etc. They collect data relevant to the sustenance of the deprived.

Tagore achieved Nobel prize, his contributions touch the poverty-stricken people living all over the world. Similarly, Sen always thinks for the deprived living all over the world. So, names of Tagore and Sen will be remembered century after century not as Nobel Laureates but as humanists.

References

Bagchi, Amiya (1998): 'Amartya Kumar Sen and the Human Science of Development', *EPW*, Vol. XXXIII, No. 49, Dec. 5-11.

Brahmananda, P.R. (1999): Amartya Sen and Welfare Economics, Sudha Publications.

———, (1994): Ethics, Utilitarian, Kantian and Economics, *Indian Economic Journal*.

Keynes, John Neville (1917): The Scope and Method of Political Economy (14th ed.), McMillan, London.

Lewis, Hancy, H. (1949): History of Economic Thought, McMillan, London. Pigou, A.C. (1952): The Economics of Welfare (4th ed.), London. Rawls, J. (1971): A Theory of Justice. Robbins, L. (1935): An Essay on the Nature and Significance of Economic Science, 11th ed., Macmillan. Sen, Amartya Kumar (1962): Choice of Techniques, Oxford.

———, (1970): Collective Choice and Social Welfare, San Francisco.

———, (1973): On Economic Inequality, Oxford.

———, (1981): Poverty and Famines, Oxford.

———, (1984): Poverty, Values and Development, Oxford.

———, (1985): Commodities and Capabilities, Amsterdam.

———, (1987): Ethics and Economics, Oxford.

———, (1992): Inequality Re-examined.

Sen, Amartya Kumar and Dreze, J. (1989): Hunger and Public Action, Oxford.

CHAPTER

27

Economic Thoughts of Amartya Sen

S. SURESH

INTRODUCTION

Amartya Sen has been identified as the single most important thinker in the area of general equilibration theory and welfare economics after Hicks and Arrow by the Noble committee. He was born on 3rd November 1933, reccived the 1998 Noble Memorial Prize in economic sciences for his work on welfare economics.—This is the most significant achievement in Economics. Sen is the first Asian and the Indian to achieve this distinction of the Noble Award in economics. The Noble citation refers to : (a) Sen's contributions to social choice theory. (b) Sen's work in development economics specially in the analysis of the relation between poverty and famines, and (c) Sen's concepts of entitlements and capability development.

SEN'S EARLY LIFE

Sen was born in Santiniketan, West Bengal. Sen began his high school education at St. Gregory's school in Dhaka in 1941 in modern day Bangladesh. His family migrated to India following partition in 1947, Sen studied in India at the Visva Bharati University School and Presidency College, Kolkata before moving to Trinity college, Combridge, where he earned a first class in B.A. Honours in 1956 and then a Ph.D. in 1959. Sen had to choose a quite different subject for his Ph.D. thesis on the choice of techniques in 1959 under the supervision of the brilliant but vigorously intolerant Joan Robinson. He has taught economics at the University of Calcutta, Jadarpur University, and at the Delhi school of Economics. He was first a professor of Economics at Nuffield college in Oxford University and then the Drummond professor of Political Economy and a Fellow of all Souls College, London school of Economics, Harward and was master of Trinity College, Combridge between 1998 and 2004. In January 2004 Sen returned to Harward. He is also a contributor of the Eva Colorni Trust at the former London Guild Hall University. In May 2007, he was appointed as Chairman of Nalanda Mentor Groups to steer the execution to release the ancient Nalanda University Project which seeks to revive the ancient Nalanda University Project which seeks to revive the ancient seat of learning at Nalanda, Bihar and India into an international University.

(a) His Main Contributions

Sen's papers in the late 1960 and early 1970 helped develop the theory of (a) social—choice, which first came to prominence in the work by the Americal economist Kenneth Arrow. Sen's social choice theory, his work on Bengal Famine, his efforts to relate inequality and depth of poverty and his notions of capability had entitlement are the most important contributions to welfare economics. In 1981, Sen Published Poverty and Femines. An essay on Entitlement and Deprivation a book in which he demonstrated that famine occurs not only from a lack of food, but from inequalities built into mechanisms for distributing food. As a nine year old boy, he witnessed the Bengal Famine of 1943, in which 3 million people perished. This staggering loss of life was unnecessary, he presents data that there was an adequate food supply in Bengal at the time, but particular groups of people including rural landless labourers and urban service providers like haircutters did not have the monetary means to acquire food as its price rose rapidly due to factors that include British military acquisition, Panic buying, hoarding and price rising, all connected to the war in the region. In poverty and famines, Sen revealed that in many cases of famines, food supplies were not significantly reduced. In Bengal, for e.g. food production, while down on the previous year, was higher than in previous non-famine year. Thus, Sen points to a number of social and economic factors, such as declining wages, unemployment, rising food prices, and poor food distribution system. These issue led to starvation among certain groups in society.

(b) The Concept of Capability

Sen's revolutionary contribution to develop and social indicators is the concept of "capability". developed in his article equality of what. He argues that governments should be measured against the concrete capabilities of their citizens. Capability of human being is his ability of functioning different capacities in a society such as to enable him to achieve the components or the constitutions of his well-being. Such functioning ability concretely implies access to adequate and nutritious food. Sen has helped to induct indicators regarding the above in human development index. Sen has argued that poverty is a result of capability failures some measures, one general and probably technical education medical and health care facilities and measure of security are the only solution for eradication of poverty. Further he believed that capability development involves costs to society though the benefits may exceed the cost. If capability is deemed as a measure of surplus inhuman beings, classical economic analysis can be applied to it.

(c) Entitlement

Sen has included in the concept of entitlements items like nutritious food, medical, health care, employments, security of food supply in time of famine, etc. He considers famine as arising out of the failure of establishing a system of entitlements. He recognizes that the market can provide entitlement provided all people can get work are a reasonable wage. Sen has vigorously asserted that expansion of market is among the instruments that can help to promote human capabilities and gave the imperative need for rapid elimination of endemic deprivation. Globalization need to be put in a broader context of social and economic policies. It could be a major force for prosperity only if it is needed by adequate national policies in a conducive social and economic environment. Send has compared the Indian Index of Human Development with Chinese index of Human Development in which China is in a much higher scale. But he has compared the human development of China with human development index of Kerala, in which Kerala is better placed without any coercion inspite of low income in comparison to so many states in India. Kerala's data on human development shows the regional variation and mismatch between income and human development in Indian states. The data also shows the variation in the public action in different states in India because Kerala's progress on human development front is a result of public action and not the policies of globalization and liberalization.

CHOICE OF TECHNIQUE

Sen's Choice of Technique was a research work where he argued that in a labour surplus economy, generation of employment cannot be increased at the initial stage by the adoption of labour-intensive technique. He pleaded for adoption of capital-intensive technique in a developing country like India. His argument was that capital-intensive technique strengthens the economic foundation of the country which help in further expansion of the economy. The expansion of capital-intensive projects has a snow balling effect on development in general including agriculture and industry. The scope of expansion of employment opportunities is more in capital-based project compared to labour-based projects. This idea of Sen cannot be said to be totally new one, because the Indian planners adopted Mahalanobis capital-intensive 4 sector model in the 2nd five year plan before the publication of choice of Technique in 1960.

THE TIME SERVICE CRITERION

A.K. Sen begins with the problem of an investment planner who has to make a choice between various techniques. It is very much possible that a higher growth rate does not provide a higher level of social welfare. Sen argues after getting the 2 time series of income flows we have to apply the relevant rates of time discount. The time discount is necessary because of atleast two reasons: (a) The diminishing marginal social utility of income with the raising income level, and the uncertainty of the future. If marginal social utility of income falls quickly and becomes negligible as income raises beyond a certain level. It is possible that higher rate of growth income may not give us the higher sum of total social satisfaction.

He defines "as the period of time in which the total output, with the more capital-intensive technique, is just equal to that with less intensive technique. In the figure which Sen uses, OT represents the period of recovery as the surpluses area for the capital-intensive techniques (BCC^1) is exactly equal to the deficit area (BAA^1). H and L curves indicate the time series of consumption flows from the capital-intensive and labour intensive techniques respectively. But the investment planner wishes to consider period U which pies between O & T. If U = T investment planner would be indifferent between the two technique. He would choose technique < if U > T and technique H is U > T.

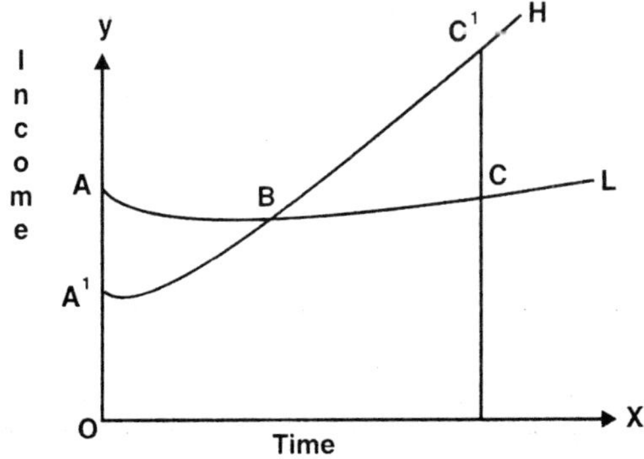

LIMITATIONS

Sen himself is aware of the limitations of this approach. According to him there is an arbitrariness involved. Since it is assumed that there is no time preference up to the end of the period U and thus each unit of income has on equal value. Thus the time factor is suddenly introduced. Sen, however, assures that such arbitrariness can not easily be avoided on account of the very nature of the problem.

OTHER ECONOMICS IDEAS

Sen was in favour of land reforms. In 1962 he opined that there was an inverse relationship between farm size and productivity. Sen believed that productivity on a small plot of land owned by a single person is higher because the owner of the land can devote personal energy to cultivation. The farmer considers the land as the only source of his income of livinghood and he whole heartedly tries to increase productivity of that plot of land. Personal care by the farmer helps to increase production. According to Sen there is a deep-seated complimentarity between various economic arguments including market mechanism and social opportunities. On the other hand, the opportunity offered by a well functioning market may be difficult to use when a person is handicapped, by, say, illiteracy or ill-health. On the other hand, a person with some education and fine health may still be unable to use his or her abilities because of limitation of economic opportunities related to the absence of markets, or over zealous bureaucratic control, or lack of access to finance, or some other restraint that limit economic initiatives. The use of economic opportunities by one person can open up further opportunities for others through backward and forward linkages in supply and demand.

REFERENCES

Jhingan, M.L., Girija, Manimekalai A. Sasikala, L., "History of Economic Thought", Vrinda Publications (P) Ltd., pp. 458-68, 2009.

Lokanathan, V., "History of Economic Thought", S. Chand and Company Ltd., New Delhi, 2009.

Amartya Sen, Development as Freedom, Oxford University Press, New Delhi, 2010.

Varshney, Ashutosh, "Why Democracy Survives", *Journal of Democracy*, National Endowment for Democracy and the Johns Hopkins University Press, Vol. 9, Issue 3, July 2008.

Leadership Review, Kravis Leadership Institute laremont MC Kerna College, Vol. 7, Winter 2010.

CHAPTER

28

Amartya Sen's Views on Economic Inequality

SHANKAR SAH

Ever since the homo-sapiens came to what Rousseau calls the social contract, possession and pilfering of provisions become one of the hungers of man to be satiated with might, either muscle power or man and money power. Naturally, the stranger ones possessed and pilfered more and more while the weak and weaker ones kept losing. And this led to, rather resulted into, inequality or disparity in the human society which is as old as the human civilization itself. The economic imbalance initially crept into with the evolution of human civilization has never been set right despite our continuous efforts towards eradication of poverty and equality which alone can bring in the desired balance. Equality has always remained a concept, an unrealized dream, and never came into existence and we are sometimes obliged to think pessimistically that men can never be economically equal just as our five fingers can never be equal in length.

Moreover, economic inequality and the gap between the rich and poor is the first social malady which every civilized society has addressed itself to. From centuries our philosophers, staticians, political thinkers, sociologists and economists have continuously been pondering and researching over the idea of inequality which has been moving people more than any other concept and which is, to quote Amartya Sen, "both very simple and very complex". Actually, the idea of inequality is a problem which leads to many further problems and intricacies. Despite so many of researches on it, we are yet to get any universally accepted concept or even a measure of inequality. And, ironically enough, some of the theories of it have created newer types of inequality rather than bringing the avowed target, that is, equality.

Amartya Sen, one of the great Economists of our times, has keenly addressed honestly to the intricate complexities in the idea of inequality and offered their very convincing explanations paving the way to further and farther investigations and findings in it.

Going into some rather broader issues concerning economic inequality Amartya Sen says that inequality is sometimes viewed in departure from some notion of rival notions of the 'right' distribution of income, based respectively on needs and desert. One may view inequality not only as a dispersion measure, but also as a measure of difference between the actual distribution of income on the one side and distribution according to needs, or according to some concept of desert on the other. That is to say, the arguments that someone should get more income than the other one since the needs of the first are greater than those of the other, or someone should get more income than the other because the first has done more work and so deserves higher reward. In simple words, whether income to a man should be according to his need, or according to his work is the basic question inherent in which (or in the outcome of which) lies the probability of inequality and that way, the defeat of our effort to bring in the cherished equality. Inequality is actually phenomenon which, it removed at one place or in one sphere, will shift to another place or sphere, or it removed in one form, develop into another. Measure of inequality is, therefore, the first concern.

Amartya Sen tries in his own honest way to measure inequality so as to have less and less of it in our society and, as stated by him in his dedication of the first edition of his epoch-making book, "On Economic inequality" he however hopes that when his children Antara and Nandana grow up." They will find less of it, no matter how they decide to measure it". This shows that Dr. Sen is very confident about his measuring of the economic inequality as also about his measures to lessen it.

Discussing the proposed measures of inequality Dr. Sen says that these measures fall into two classes—the positive ones making no explicit use of any concept of social welfare, and the normative ones based on an explicit formulation of social welfare and the incurring loss from unequal distribution. He says that part of the difficulty in using these measures arises from the fact that all these measures are complete in the sense that every pair of distributions can be compared under each of these measures. As found out by Dr. Sen, "to each such distribution x there is attached a real number I(x) which is supposed to represent the degree of inequality of x" and, therefore, "this approach is inherently defective since inequality as a notion does not have any innate property of 'completeness'." Dr. Sen further opines that "each of these measures leads to some rather absurd results precisely because each of them aims at giving a complete ordering representation to a concept that is essentially one of partial ranking."

Dr. Sen therefore believes that the most efficiently working measure of inequality requires the assimilation of all the common factors in the different suggested measures. In furtherance of the idea, he innovated Sen Poverty measure following the lines proposed by Shorrocks (1995), Jenkins and Lambert (1993) and even Shorrocks (1994). The poverty gap profile as developed by Dr. Sen comes out to be a natural way of representing the variable-measure poverty ordering Dr. Sen claims that this measure has a close relation with the key unanimity quasi-ordering associated with a widely accepted class of poverty measures.

While summarizing, Dr. Sen remarks, "How much further we can go in inequality analysis on the basis of ordinal comparisons alone remains to be seen. But it is definitely one of the possible routes through which the consideration of the broader framework of advantages and capabilities can enrich the study of inequality and poverty". (Sen, 1997) Indeed, it followed honestly and worked on the line suggested by Dr. Sen we can measure inequality and can device the ways to uproot this age-old malady of our society.

CHAPTER

29

Prof. A.K. Sen and Welfare Economics

H.N. KATHARE

INTRODUCTION

Professor Amartya K. Sen has been awarded the Nobel Prize in Economics Sciences for his contribution to Welfare Economics in 1998. Sen's contribution is substantive to all the areas he has touched; some of them are highly technical. But from the very beginning his major concern was the welfare of people; especially poor. Sen published his Ph.D. Thesis as a book on economics: Choice of Techniques in 1960. In 1970 his book Collective Choice and Social Welfare was published, which dealt with the incompleteness of Arrow's model on personal choice to social choice and established a new law in this respect. He published his book on Economic Inequality in 1973 and welfare and Rights in 1998. In his book on Economic Inequality, he stressed out that the scarcity of food is not the only reason for famine in many countries around the world.

This is principal contribution to welfare economics. Among his many books a few need to be remembered as pioneering work: Employment, Technology and Development; Poverty and Famines; Choice, Welfare and Management; Resources, Value and Development; Inequality Re-examined, Jeevan Jatra O Arthaniti; Indian Economic Development and Social Opportunity. A.K. Sen's contribution to Welfare Economics has been analyzed in this paper. His principal contribution to welfare economics that is the scarcity of food is not the only reason for famine in many countries around the world but also other reasons have asserted on it. This paper attempts to throw light on the major contribution of A.K. Sen's to welfare economics.

A.K. SEN'S CONTRIBUTION TO WELFARE ECONOMICS

Sen analysed famines with his theoretical approach to welfare measurement. He argues that famines can occur even when the supply of food is not significantly lower. In this view lack of opportunities and capabilities are responsible for poverty and famines. In other words, hunger is essentially a problem of functioning failures. Haunted by his memories of the Bengal Famines, Sen has made it his life's works to understand inequality. Being an Indian, it is his country's wretchedness that has driven him to these matchless heights in human welfare.

It is perhaps a mistake to see the development of education, health care and other basic achievements only or primarily as expansion of "Human Resources", the accumulation of "Human Capital", as if people were just the means of production and not it's ultimate end. The bettering of human life dose not have to be justified by showing that a person with a better life is also a better producer.

As above line suggest the issue of health should be viewed from two aspects:

(1) health is wealth, and
(2) health creates wealth.

The maxim that health is wealth highlights the increasing

importance of health. Health is valuable on its own. It is perhaps the supreme element of economic development. We cherish the development of world but we do not cherish less for healthy world.

According to Sen, education and health can be valuable to the freedom of a person in at least five distinct ways and these ways are as follows:

(1) *Intrinsic importance*—Education and health are valuable achievement in themselves.
(2) *Instrumental personal role*—A person's education and health to do many things.
(3) *Instrumental social role*—Education and health encourage demand for social needs.
(4) *Instrumental process role*—The education and health broadens the horizon of the people and generate benefits.
(5) *Empowerment and distributive role*—With better health and education, disadvantaged groups can better resist oppression and inequality.

There is a very close interlinkage between poverty and poor health. A vicious circle is operating here. Poverty causes poor health and poor health causes poverty. The improvement in health care can be an important step in reducing the level of poverty. When we consider a problem of health care in the context of less developed country, it is found that poverty and low income cause major difficulties in the lives of the common man. Therefore, a good health care is highly needed for human life. The components of good health care are as follows:

(1) Nutritious diet,
(2) Hygienic condition of living,
(3) Safe drinking water,
(4) Information about good health care,
(5) Existence of good health care facilities,
(6) Existence of hospitals and medical treatment facilities, and
(7) Financial ability to incur the medical expenses.

The medicine that Sen suggests for just an Indian society is of little interest to Indian politicians. Massive, efficient investment in primary health care, for instance, needs a long time to bear fruits. Longer the gap between two polls is that Indian society and Indian politician. Sen, believes globalization can be "a major force for good", but if a country globalizes fast and pays no attention to lack of social opportunity, illiteracy and health care, it ends creating serious problems for itself.

Well-being and advantage are the two headings; there are many possible approaches to them. For example, the various interpretations of utility can be seen as different ways of interpreting well-being. But there are other quite different approaches to the well-being as well; e.g., opulence or the fulfilment of basic needs. Similar exercises of comparison, contrast, scrutiny and assessment have also been done for the notion of advantage. The judgment of interest is a problem of very wide relevance to economics. It is, of course, central to welfare economics. It is also crucial for a theory of poverty for assessment of inequality, judging economic development and measuring standard of living.

Prof. A.K. Sen's economics is directed towards humanity and is intertwined with philosophy. He is not only an economist of world eminence but also a great scientist. His major contribution is not only to welfare economics but also other branches of economics and humanities. He still maintains his Indian citizenship despite his living abroad for nearly three-four decades. His work stimulates many branches of world economy.

CONCLUSION

In this paper to analyses Prof. A.K. Sen's major contribution to the welfare economics. Sen analyzed famines with his theoretical approach to welfare measurement. He argues that famines can occur even when the supply of food is not significantly lower. In this view, lack of opportunities and capabilities are responsible for poverty and famines. Haunted by his memories of the Bengal Famines, Sen has made it his life's work to understand inequality. There is a very close interlinkage between poverty and poor health. A vicious circle is operating here. Poverty causes poor health and poor health causes poverty. Sen believes globalization can be "a major force for good", but if a country globalizes fast and pays no attention to lack of social opportunity, illiteracy and health care, it ends creating serious problems for itself. His major contribution is not only to welfare economics but also for other branches of economics and humanities.

References

Ray, Biswanath (2001): "Welfare, Choice and Development", Kanishka Publisher, Distributors, New Delhi.

Sen, Amartya (2004): "Commodities and Capabilities", Published by Manzar Khan, Oxford University Press, YMCA Library Building, Jai Singh Road, New Delhi.

India Today Magazine, October 26, 1998.

Sunday Magazine, 25-31 October, 1998.

Outlook News Magazine, October 26, 1998.

CHAPTER

30

An Analysis of Sen's Approach to Welfare Economics

SHAUKAT HASEEN, MD. REHAN KHAN
AND MANZOOR ALAM

INTRODUCTION

Amartya Sen occupies unique position among modern economists. He is an outstanding economic theorist, a world authority on social choice and welfare economics; he is a leading figure in development economics, carrying out path-breaking work on appraising the effectiveness of investment in poor countries and, more recently, on the economic analysis of famines. He has greatly influenced international organisations such as the United Nations agencies, the ILO, and the World Bank. At the same time, he takes a broad view of the subject and has done much to enlarge the perspective of economists. He is as much at home writing for the Journal of Philosophy as for the Economic Journal; at Harvard, he was both Professor of Economics and Professor of Philosophy (Atkinson, 1999).

Amartya Sen had concluded his book by saying that he had a feeling that the pure systems of collective choice analysis that then existed did not seem to him to be the most useful systems to study. And that he had been concerned with the study of 'impurities' of one kind or another, for example, partial interpersonal comparability. Partial cardinality of the utility measure, restricted domains of choice, intransitive social indifference, Incomplete social preference and so on. The pure procedures, which were more well-known, he could see were only the limiting cases of systems with impurities. He found these impurities more relevant for both 'institutions' and 'frameworks of thought'. It is not that once a strong resolve is made in the mind the rest is routine. Human minds not made that way. Amartya Sen wrote on Economic Inequality in 1973. He had still not escaped from pure economics completely, even though he had already made his intentions clear. Nearly 20 years later he gave us Inequality re-examined. Not only did we then get an idea of one of the 'impurities' that he had meant to explore. (It was the one that was concerned with the question of 'What was just?' which made the conventionally used 'purer' concepts of justice look rather less usetul.) His treatment of justice became also a contribution to its philosophical discussion and we saw the subtle distinction of his concept with the one given by John Rawls. We already had his book on Poverty and Famine in 1981, on the concept of having sufficient 'capabilities' as distinct from having only the necessary endowments in 1985, on hunger and public action in 1990—his canvas has always kept on widening. But happily, he has invariably stuck to his original methodological resolve to seek out the impurities that sacramental theorisation abhors. Economists will have reasons to be thankful to Amartya Sen for just that. What conventionally were treated only as simple and monolithic conceptual cities were now given by Sen rich and complex structures—the atom often split into more fundamental particles. The most striking perhaps was the break with traditional classification of interpersonal comparability and introducing almost a continuum from non-comparability to complete comparability. Where there was no space, the interval of now provided one. Equally striking were Sen's attempts (also successes) at embedding his subtle sub-classifications and extensions in the still unfamiliar terrains of analysis—of rights, liberty, justice, equity, deprivation, entitlement, poverty, famines and public action. Many of these words now frequently appear in Sen's writings; but they either appeared or were ready to break through even within that classic formulation (Majumdar, 1998).

Sen starts with a fundamental assumption of human diversity and asks two questions: Why equality? and Equality of what? The first question quickly becomes superfluous, since "to have any kind of plausibility, ethical reasoning on social matters must involve elementary equal consideration for all at some level that is seen as critical". Thus, those who are regarded as anti-egalitarian, which normally means that they do not find equality of conditions to be an important goal, in Sen's view are supporting equality in a different way—for example, equal rights in some other dimension. Thus, we are told, while Robert Nozick does not demand equality of utility, he demands equality of libertarian rights, and a utilitarian may not want equality of total utilities but will insist on equal weights on everyone's utility gains. Sen stretches his reasoning in order to convince us that all moral philosophers of any worth base their arguments on some dimension of equality, but he succeeds in the end. His most compelling argument, apart from examples, is that it is difficult to see how any theory of justness could be morally convincing if men are not regarded as equals in some fundamental space. Now, human diversity means that if we contend that people should be equal in one dimension, we must necessarily accept that they are unequal in other respects, since we cannot expect complete concordance between different fundamental dimensions (Sen, 1992).

MEASURING INEQUALITY AND POVERTY

Measuring inequality is an old topic. Pigou (1912) and Dalton (1920) had expressed in a utilitarian framework the idea that income inequality could be measured as the distance between the actual distribution and the equal distribution. In the 1960s this approach was developed in a more general framework by Kolm (1969) and Atkinson (1970).

MEASURING INEQUALITY AND REAL NATIONAL INCOME

The key concept (even though it does not appear in the Index to Sen [1973]) is that of dominance, borrowed from stochastic dominance theory. A distribution of income is said to dominate another if and only if social welfare is greater for the former for all possible social welfare functions in some given class. As shown by Kolm (1969) and the class of social welfare functions which it is natural to consider is that of non-decreasing, s-concave functions (referred to here as the class W2). They show that, for constant total income and population, dominance of distribution A over distribution B for the class W2 is equivalent to dominance of the Lorenz curve for A over that for B. Moreover, this is equivalent to it being possible to reach distribution A from distribution B by making a series of mean preserving equalising transfers. This mathematical result links the welfare economic approach to two practical, intuitive measures, the Lorenz curve in particular being familiar to economists from first year textbooks. A firm underpinning is thus provided for a standard practice. Moreover, this formalism opened the way to further advances, such as the use of generalised Lorenz curves, and criteria which can be applied where Lorenz curves cross. It is possible to arrive at a partial order on the basis of the rule of going by the congruence of different complete orderings; for example, the shared rankings of complete orders generated by different statistical measures of income inequality.

Poverty

The bottom of the income distribution has been singled out for particular attention in studies of poverty. This is a controversial subject in many respects, including the definition of the poverty line itself, discussed below. Even however if we are agreed on the appropriate cut-off (and on other matters such as the appropriate equivalence scales), there remains the question as to the choice of poverty indicator. The almost universal practice is to count the proportion of the population below the poverty line: the "head-count", H. A good example is the widely quoted statistic, in the 1980s, of 50 million poor in the European Community.

Sen [III, 1976b], which generated a large literature. Sen found the degree of support commanded by the head-count to be "quite astonishing, since it gives no indication of the severity of poverty: people may be close to the poverty line or far below. The properties of the head-count may be seen from considering the marginal valuation of income implied by use of the head-count. Clearly a marginal euro contributes zero if it goes to a person above the poverty line. But it is also zero if it goes to people more than 1 euro below the line, since it still leaves them below and the poverty count is unchanged. The implied marginal valuation of income is very ill-behaved.

Sen's contribution was to provide an analytical framework within which these issues could be discussed, a framework that combines elegance of theory with a concern for practical application. The solution is given by the shadow price for labour obtained from formulating the problem as an exercise in constrained optimisation. The shadow cost takes account of the full economic implications of employing an additional person. Such implications include the reduction in surplus for investment as well as the loss of the output that the worker would have produced elsewhere (which could be zero). The notion of shadow prices had been well understood since the debates in the 1930s and 1940s on the economics of planning, but Sen refined it as a practical tool of investment appraisal, to be used to determine the choice of projects undertaken, showing how earlier formulations could be derived as special cases.

THE COMPLETE ECONOMIST

What then are the main features of Sen's extraordinarily impressive contribution? I have already highlighted the constructiveness of his approach: he is not contents imply to point out difficulties.

What Sen has sought to do is to open new fields for research. To take one example not covered earlier, he has attacked the revealed preference approach to consumer behaviour for its overly narrow view but has not stopped there.

For instance, he explored the implications of assuming that people having a degree of sympathy with other.

The second striking feature is the integrated view of the subject that runs through his work in different fields and links the research at different stages of his career. This is apparent from the way in which the essays on development economics interlock with those on social justice. Concern with famine is linked to that with poverty, and writing on the measurement of poverty draws in turn on his more philosophical investigations. There is a close connection between his work on individual choice behaviour and that on social choice theory; see his comments at the end of Klamer (1989). He has drawn attention to the role of social values in affecting individual behaviour, and argued that recognition of the complexity of individual motivations has implications for the formation of social judgements.

The third distinguishing characteristic of Sen's contribution is his broad perspective of the role of economics. In the introduction to Resources, Values and Development, he criticizes the narrow boundaries of modem economics.

Finally, Sen has been willing to tackle uncomfortable subjects, and to challenge conventional economics. Indeed, he does so with relish. In some cases, he has been highly persuasive, carrying the field before him. In the public arena, his research has greatly influenced the Human Development Report produced by the United Nations Development Programme. In his analysis of hunger, Sen has emphasized the importance of the press and public debate in securing effective action, and he, together with Jean Dreze and others, has contributed greatly to that debate. On the other hand, in some cases, he has not so far carried the day: for instance, the Sen Poverty index has yet to be widely adopted in official statistics. Within the discipline of economics, he has been remarkably successful in arousing the interest of the profession in the issues on which he has concentrated, significantly affecting the evolution of the subject. Indeed one of his key contributions has been to legitimize the investigation of certain topics—such as famine—that had previously been regarded by many as outside the profession's concerns. His own central position in the discipline has meant that when he has ignored the conventionalises of demarcation then graduate students have had the courage to follow.

CONCLUSION

This Paper has analyzed the contributions of Nobel Laureate Professor Amartya Sen in the field of welfare economics. It has been argued that Sen's work has expanded and deepened human rights discourse by opening up new lines of enquiry in both ethics and economics and by promoting cross-fertilization and integration on the subject of human rights across traditional disciplinary divides. In ethics, Sen has challenged the exclusion of poverty, hunger and starvation from the characterization of fundamental freedoms and human rights, and has contributed to the development of a framework in which authoritatively recognized international standards in the field of poverty and human rights can be meaningfully conceptualized and coherently understood. In economics, Sen has set out a far-reaching critique of standard frameworks that fail to take account of fundamental freedoms and human rights, and has pioneered the development of new paradigms and approaches that focus on human rights centered concerns. This development of a 'scholarly bridge' between human rights and economics has been shown to be an innovative and important contribution that has methodological as well as substantive importance, and that provides a prototype and stimuli for future research.

REFERENCES

Atkinson, Anthony B. (1999), *"The Contributions of Amartya Sen to Welfare Economics"*, Scand. J of Economics, 101(2), 173-90, 1999.

Majumdar,Tapas (1998), *"Amartya Sen in Search of Impure Welfare Economics : Finding New Space"*, Economic and Political Weekly, Vol. 33, No. 45 (Nov. 7-13, 1998), pp. 2860-62.

Erikson, Robert (1992), *"Inequality Reexamined by Amartya Sen"*. Cambridge, Harvard University Press, 1992, p. 207.

Vizard, Polly (2005), *"The Contributions of Professor Amartya Sen in the Field of Human Rights"*, CASE paper 91, January 2005.

Desai, M., (2001), *'Amartya Sen's Contribution to Development Economics'*, Oxford Development Studies, 29(3), pp. 213-23(11).

Banerjee, Ahhijit (1998). *'Amartya Sen, Development Economist'*. The Economic Times, India, October 15.

Majumdar, Tapas (1958, 1961), "The Measurement of Utility". Macmillan, London.

Nussbaum, M.C. (2001), *"Symposium on Amartya Sen's Philosophy"*, 5, Adaptive Preferences and Women's Options', Economics and Philosophy, 17 (2001) 67-88.

Osmani, S.R. (2000), *"Human Rights to Food, Health, and Education"*, Journal of Human Development, 1(2).

Sen, A.K. (1982e), *"Choice, Welfare and Measurement"*. Oxford: Basil Blackwell.

Baumol, W.J., 1965, *"Welfare Economics and the Theory of the State"*, G. Bell, London.

Klamer, A. (1989), *"A Conversation with Amartya Sen"*, Journal of Economic Perspectives, 3 (1), Winter, 135-50.

CHAPTER

31

Approach of Professor Amartya Sen Towards Welfare and Collective Choice

ARUN KUMAR SINHA

The recipient of Nobel Prize for the year 1998, the eminent economist professor Amartya Sen was born in Bengal in 1933. After completing his early education in India, he continued his studies in Cambridge, England and received his doctorate there in the year 1959. He has been professor at the University of Delhi, 1963-71, the London school of Economics, 1971-77, All Soul College, Oxford, 1977-88 and Hardward University, 1989-97. He has been awarded 20 honorary doctorates and presided over leading scientific association such as the Amercian Economic Association, The Econometric Society and the International Economic Association. His scholarly publication include a dozen of books and approximately 200 articles in different scientific journals.

Further, he has made several important contributions to the research on fundamental problems in welfare economics. His contributions range from axiomatic theory of social choice, over definitions of welfare and poverty indexes, to empirical studies of famine. All are woven closely together by a general interest in distributional issues and a particular interest in the most impoverished member of the society.

He has explained the conditions which permit aggregation of individual values into collective decisions and the conditions which permit rules for collective decisions making them consistent with a sphere of rights for the individual. By analysing the available information about different individual welfare regarding collective decisions, he has improved the theoretical foundation for comparing different distributions of the society's welfare and defined a new and more satisfactory, indexes of poverty. In empirical studies, the application of his theoretical approach has enhanced our understanding of the economic mechanism underlying famines. Besides, number of his noteworthy contributions to the central fields of economic science opened up new fields of study for the subsequent generations of researchers and scholars. Further, by combining tools from Economics and Philosophy, he has restored an ethical dimension to the discussion of vital economic problems.

INDIVIDUAL VALUES AND COLLECTIVE DECISIONS

Traditionally, the theory of social choice had only assumed that every individual can rank different alternatives, without assuming and considering anything about interpersonal comparability. This assumption certainly avoided the difficult question of whether the utility to individuals attached to different alternatives can really be compared. Unfortunately, in prevented to say anything worthwhile about inequality Prof. Sen, initiated entirely a new field in the theory of social choice, by showing how different assumptions regarding interpersonal comparability affect the possibility of finding a consistent, non-dictatorial rule for collective decisions.

In the late 1960s, his research initiated a new outlook on social choice theory. His monograph, collective choice and social welfare (1970a) had a far reaching impact and inspired many scholars and researchers to renew their interest in basic welfare issues. He also demonstrated the implicit assumptions made when applying principles proposed by moral philosophy to evaluate different alternatives for society.

THE THEORY OF SOCIAL CHOICE

The theory of social choice, analysis the relations between individual preference and collective decisions. The fundamental issues are whether various decisions in society respect individual preferences and whether different social states can be ranked fairly or evaluated in some other way. When there is general agreement, the choice made by society is usually uncontroversial. The challenge arises when different interest have to be aggregated into decisions which affect every one. That even unanimity can come into conflict with individual rights is pointed out explicitly in Prof. Sen's book (1970b).

The principle formulated by the American Philosopher John Rowls—that the social state should be evaluated only with reference to the individual who is worst off-assumes that the utility level of each individual can be compared to the utility of every other individual. Later development in social choice rely, to a large extent, on Sen's analysis of the information about and interpersonal comparability of individual utility.

INDEX OF WELFARE AND POVERTY

In order to compare distributions of welfare in different countries, or to study changes in the distribution within a given country, some kind of index is required that measures differences in the welfare or income. The preparation and the construction of such types of indexes are based on the application of the important theory of social choice, meaning thereby that inequality indexes are closely linked to welfare functions representing the values of society. After Serge Kolm and Anthony Atkinson, Prof. Amartya Sen was the first to derive substantial results in this area. Around 1970, they clarified the relationship between the so-called Lorentz Curve, which describes the income distribution, the so-called Gini-coefficient that measures the degree of income inequality and society's ordering of different income distributions. Later Prof. Sen has made valuable contributions by defining poverty indexes and other welfare indicators.

POVERTY INDEXES

A common measure of poverty in a society is the share of the population, H, with incomes below a certain, predetermined, poverty line. But the theoretical foundation for this kind of measure was unclear. It also ignored and undermined the degree of poverty among the poor. Even a significant boost in the income of the poorest groups in society dose not affect, H, as long as their incomes do not cross the poverty line. To rectify these deficiencies, Prof. Sen postulated five moderate axioms from which he derived a poverty indexes:

$$P = H\ [I+(1-I)G]$$

Here G is the Gini coefficient and I is a measure (between 0 and 1) of the distribution of income, both computed only for the individuals below the poverty line. Relying on his earlier analysis of information about the welfare of single individual. He clarified when the index can and should be applied, comparisons can, for example, be made even data are problematic. It is often the case in poor countries where poverty indexes have their most intrinsic application. Later Prof. Sen's poverty index has subsequently been applied extensively by others.

The constructions of theoretically sound indexes to measure differences in income and welfare in society is an important application of the theory of social choice. Another example of this research orientation is Sen's article entitled "Real National Income" (1976c). Here, he also uses again an axiomatic approach to explain and analyze the foundations of the concept of national income and its possible use in relevant comparisons among different countries. His main objective is to clarify the extent to which distributional indicators can be incorporated into the concept of National income. The axiom which is used to measure the income is Y(1–G) where Y is income percapita and G is the Gini-coefficient.

Prof. Sen has stressed that what creates welfare are not goods as such, but the activity for which they are acquired. This view expressed that income is significant because of the opportunities it creates. But the actual opportunities or capabilities, as Sen calls them, also depend on a number of other factors, such as health, the factors should also be considered when measuring welfare.

Further, Prof. Sen's concept of fairness presupposes that actual opportunities should be as equal as possible for all individuals; greater resources should be allotted to individuals who for one reason or another, require them in order to achieve the same capability. This reflects egalitarian view held by Rawls, who wanted to maximize the welfare of the worst off in society. Obviously such a criterion can not be applied in practice without an interpersonally comparable welfare index. Rawls (1971) mentioned an index of "Primary goods" but does not offer any suggestion for solving the index problem. However, Prof. Sen's findings provide guidelines for dealing with these maters.

DEVELOPMENT ECONOMICS

The concept of "Development Economics" assessed by Prof. Amartya Sen belongs to the realm of theory and analytical methods, even if his formulations of welfare indexes do have direct applications. But Sen has also done applied research, primarily in development economics. Virtually, almost all his works are dedicated to development economics; as they are usually concerned with the welfare of poorest people in society. In his very first articles, written in the late 1950s and early 1960s, he explained the choice of appropriate production technology in developing countries. His empirical studies proceed from his theoretical results on social choice and welfare measurement.

His well and best known empirical study is poverty and famines : An essay on entitlement and deprivation (1981). This publication of Sen is followed by discussions of ways to prevent famine, or limit its effects once its has occurred. These considerations are being briefed in a book co-authored with Jean Dreze (1989). Prof. Sen shows that a profound understanding of famine has to be based on the factors which affect the actual opportunities of different groups in society. In "Poverty and famine", he established a new approach to the problems of starvation and famine. The book has examined extremely vital problems and is undoubtedly a key, contribution to development economics.

With its emphasis on distributional issues the book reflects the recurring theme in Sen's research.

INFERENCE

Last but not the least, here it can be said that Prof. Amartya Sen has prescribed several important and valuable contributions to the field of research on fundamental problems of welfare economics. His contribution range from purely axiomatic over the theory and definitions of welfare indices to empirical studies of famine. Its unified by a general interest in distributional problems and particular interest in the most impoverished member of the society. Prof. Sen has tried his best to clarify the conditions which allows the aggregation of individual preference into collective decisions as well as the conditions which permit rules for social choice to be consistent with a sphere of individual rights. Further in his empirical studies the very application of his theoretical approach have enhanced our understanding of the economic mechanism underlying starvation and poverty in a better way.

References

1970a, Collective Choice and Social Welfare, San Francisco : Holden Day and London : Oliver and Boyd (Reprinted Amasterdam : North-Holland).

1970b, 'The impossibility of a Paretian Liberal', *Journal of Political Economy*, 78, pp. 152-7.

1981, Poverty and Famines: An Essay on Entitlement and Deprivation, Oxford : Clarendon Press.

Dreze, J. and A.K. Sen, 1989, Hunger and Public Action, Oxford : Clarendon.

1976c, Real National Income; *Review of Economic Studies*, 43, pp. 19-39.

CHAPTER

32

Socio-economic Philosophy of Amartya Sen on Gross Domestic Happiness Capabilites, Entitlement and Sustainable Development

M.P. SHRIVASTAVA AND SITA RAM SINGH

INTRODUCTION

Gross National Domestic Happiness (GNH/GDH) and sustainable development is the greatest and sole challenge of policy-makers and all concerned. Gross National happiness contains not only economic aspect but also social, ethical, welfare, cultural and moral aspects. It can be analysed in economic, ethical, philosophical, social, cultural and moral manner.[1] It is the duty of the state to provide gross domestic happiness to all.

Economic growth is a dynamic process which refers to an increase in wealth over and extended period of time. In the literature of growth theory, there are obviously many inter-temporal and dynamic optimization approaches. The concept of equitable and sustainable development has been promoted as a strategy to take care of it. Equitable and sustainable development is fundamentally an inter-temporal ethical paradigm. GNH/GDH must be sustainable rather it should not be temporary.

PURSUIT OF SUSTAINABLE DEVELOPMENT

The intergenerational equity refer to the state of being just impartial as fair to the future generation. Sustainable development being a simple idea, is open to several interpretations: It is a contestable concept like honesty or justice. The pursuit of sustainable development is the facilitation of a dynamic socio-economic process keeping in view with nature.

Amartya Sen has contributed a lot relating to socio-economic aspects which are quite significant and relevant to all particularly to India in present day context. He is the true supporter of gross domestic happiness (GDH).

Amartya Sen, more than just an economist, is an ethical philosopher and is a time lover of freedom and a humanist. He has forced mainly a poor, viewing them not an object of party requiring charitable hand outs but as disempowered fold needing empowerment. According to him, the pursuit of sustainable development is the facilitation of a dynamic socio-economic process. It compiles that socio-economic change that lead to improvement in the conditions of life should last long. (WCCD-1987)[2]

To empowering people education, health, nutrition, gender equality, safety nets in times of distress, all needed for empowering people. He has stressed the need of a positive and dynamic role of the government in improving capabilities entitlements and freedom through concrete actions viz. land-reforms and access to the education and health-care facilities.

SEN ON GDH/GNH

Prof. Sen made it quite clear that Gross National Happiness cannot be achieved merely on the basis of Gross Domestic Products (GDP) as invented by Mr. Simon Kuznets. Because GDP is the index of only economic or material prosperity and not the social, cultural, ethical, moral and other prosperity.[3] Thus, mere increases in GDP or GNP will never automatically increase capabilities and GDH. Indeed, market mechanisms, the main pillars and tools of LPG (Liberalization, Privatization and Globlisation) strategies of economic reforms cannot bring about capability development for all human beings in the developing countries or Less-developing countries. Sen argued that LPG should be market-friendly as well as eco-friendly and should state that rapid spread of primary education, substantial improvement of health care and empowerment of women are the three main pillars of socio-economic reform.

SEN ON CAPABILITIES AND ENTITLEMENT

The concepts of capabilities and 'entitlements' are the wonderful contributions of Prof. Amartya Sen. Both these approaches were primarily used by him extensively in his analysis of famine deprivation, poverty, hunger, greed and in equality.[4] This contribution forms the basis of gross domestic happiness as supported by Bhutan Prime Minister.

So far as 'entitlement' is concerned, according to Prof. Sen, "In a market economy person can exchange what he owns for another collection of commodities. He can do this exchange either through exchange or through production or through the combination of the both. The set of all alternative bundles of commodities that he can acquire in exchange what he owns may be called the exchange entitlement of what he owns." (Sen, and Dreze—Poverty and Famine p. 3).[5]

SEN ON FAMINE (HUNGER)

Sen made a comprehensive and in-depth study and analysis of famine and hunger with various angles and dealt different aspects. He further stated in Hunger in the Modern world, p. 9.[6] In each social structure given the prevailing legal political and economic arrangements a person can establish command over some alternative commodities bundles.[7] These bundles could be extensive or very limited and what a person can consume will be directly dependent, on what these bundles are. The set of alternative bundles of commodities over which a person can establish such command will be referred to as this person entitlement.

He however, clearly stated that his terminology for a person entitlement failure occurs due to loss of endowment failure of production, exchange failure, transfer failure and so on. Though, the classical economist like *Malthus* and *Karl Marks* and Indian economist like *R.C. Dutta* also undertaken indepth studies of famines yet, only failed in identifying the root causes of famines and starvation. They were concerned only with the causes of persistent misery of the people.[8] No doubt, a number of studies have been conducted on famine and starvation, but it was only Amartya Sen who advanced the plurality of causes for famine. He made it clear that famine may accur with and without food availability decline, price rising of food grains and natural disaster. He explained famine with both the approaches like[9] : (i) entitlement approach, and (ii) food availability decline approach. He categorically overviewed that famous Bengal famine could have been avoided through the exportation of food from the surplus growing areas to Bengal by the action of the state. Through the entitlement approach the economic crisis of women in jute industry of Bengal could have been easily explained.

CAUSES OF FAMINE

Sen held following causes more responsible for famine:[10]

(a) Lack of nobility of food grains from one place to another.
(b) Lack of knowledge information about the food grains by the government.
(c) Lack of purchasing power to the poor and downtrodden people.

(d) Lack of employment opportunities due to lack of income generation in the poor people.
(e) Lack of democracy, free press liberty to speech and strong opposition in the country.
(f) Lack of of transport-facilities.
(g) Lock proper management of famine relief.
(h) Lack of public works programmes for famine sufferers
(i) Lack of literacy, education and health care to the affected persons.
(j) Large scale of hoarding of food grains by the traders.
(k) No strong and proper action by the state against black marketers of food grains during famine.
(l) Reluctancy and indifference of Government in the beginning.

Thus, the famine, according to Sen takes place only due to:

SEN ON GDH AND INCLUSIVE GROWTH

Inadequacy of employment opportunities to the lower income group and poor causing which their purchasing power is quote low due to lower income.

Consequently, (i) they get quite inadequate food grains and amenities of life.[11]

(i) Literacy among low income groups, and
(ii) Poor and inadequate health care and facilities.

Obviously, Sen included nutritious foods, medical and health care, educational facilities, employment, food security in the concept of entitlement items which from the basis of inclusive growth. The entitlement approach, according to Sen is built on three basic patterns.[12]

(a) Endowment set
(b) Entitlement set
(c) Entitlement mapping

The *endowment* set deals with the combination of all

resources legally owned by a person.[13] The *Entitlement* set deals with possible combination of goods and services that a person can legally obtain by using resources of his endowment set. It refers to all possible combination. The *Entitlement mapping* deals with the relationship between endowments as well as entitlement set. *Entitlement mapping* contains three following components :

> (a) Production component: It comprises various input-output ratio, (b) Exchange component: It consists of rates of exchange, and (c) Trade component.

SEN ON RIGHT TO FOOD, NUTRITION AND HEALTH AND EDUCATION

Amartya Sen has dealt in depth the issue of food and nutritional security. He also focused on *right to food and nutrition* and health as well as education. The *right to food* is one of the basic socio-economic rights that is essential to achieve economic democracy without which political democracy is invain. *"It is an entitlement to be free from hunger"*. The term *'freedom from hunger'* lends itself to several interpretations getting two square meals a day, meeting specific calorie norms, avoiding nutrition-related ailments and so on.[14]

RIGHT TO FOOD

Article 47 of *Indian Constitution, 'Right to Food'* should be seen as *'Right to Nutrition'*. Good nutrition also depends in complex ways on a wide range of inputs like adequate food intake, clean water, basic health care, good hygiene, etc. According to Sen right to food is directly associated with the state because state is primarily responsible for *right to food,* because, state alone commands the resources essential for protection from hunger. However, it is a shared responsibility involving not only the state but also other institutions and individuals. But in making the *right to food* more secure and more just we face serious difficulties. According to Sen, in a democratic political system, allowing a famine to develop would be political suicide for the party in office.[15]

RIGHT TO EDUCATION

Likewise, *right to education* is also quite significant sound formative education both mental and physical is the mother of all virtues and sole enemy of injustice and socio-economic discrimination. It is the real breakthrough for human development. India has a rich legacy of ideas and knowledge. She was known as the preacher of the world. According to him, "education is not only for awakening the consciousness but also an essential ingredient for equalizing opportunities and empowering the common people to assert their right, dignity and self-esteem.

So far as *equality* and *distributive justice* is concerned, Sen is of the opinion that notion of justice does not imply that everyone should be treated equally unless there are relevant differences between them.[16]

With regards to equality of income, Sen argues that "The extent of real inequality of opportunities that people face cannot be readily deducted from the magnitude of inequality of incomes. Since what we can or can't do, can or can't achieve, do not depend just as our incomes but also on the variety of physical and social characterization that affect our lives and make us what we are" (1992-28).[17]

According to Sen, "The judgment and measurement of inequality is thoroughly dependent on the choice of variable (income, wealth, happiness, etc.) in terms of which comparisons are made."

The notion of *equal opportunity* finds a prominent place in the *theory of justice*. Therefore, entitlement is the right that a person exercises over goods and services. It may be acquired through the market, or it may be generated by the state in different ways.[18]

It also enables people for consuming goods and services. Sen tried to establish a sophisticated measure for poverty alleviation and for distributive inequalities and social justice.

SUMMING UP

On the basis of above analysis, it may be observed that Sen has contributed a lot relating to socio-economic issues. He suggested a number of suitable resources for achieving gross national happiness (GNH) in various ways particularly on the basis of entitlements and happiness and removing starvation and poverty. His ideas form the basis of maintaining *distributive justice* and achieving *inclusive growth*. The food and nutritional security can be maintained, equitable justice can be achieved and inclusive growth can be promoted on the basis of writings of Sen.[19]

The gross national or domestic happiness can be established by applying following four strategies on the basis of findings of Amartya Sen.

Equitable, fair, just and sustainable socio-economic prosperity.

(i) Maintaiing and conserving environment and avoiding pollution and environmental degradation.
(ii) Preserving and promoting cultural heritage and values judgment.
(iii) Providing good governance.

There are four *'mantras'* through which all related issues can be solved and challenges can be met. A human economy pursues three independent objectives of efficient allocation, equitable distribution and sustainable and inclusive development.[20] *Sustainable development* is fundamentally ethical in nature within the foundation of environomics, a base distinction is made between natural (eco-centric) and humanist (anthropocentric) moral philosophies. These strategies are gaining ground for promoting both *'intra'* and *'inter'* generational equity. It is fundamentally ethical in nature. We must preserve and conserve our cultural heritage and value judgment. But all the strategy can get success only if good, fair, transparent governance is provided.[21] On these basis *sweet and contentment* can be achieved which shall help in promoting and achieving gross domestic happiness. But these are the theoretical aspects. Sen did not highlight the practical approach relating to it. Moreover, Sen's contribution of Gross Domestic Happiness as well as sustainable and inclusive growth is indeed remarkable and quite useful. His ideas are of great significant and his attempts are praiseworthy.

GDH consists of education, health, nutrition and food security, gender equality, endowment and entitlement. But according to Sen achieving GDH is not so easy. For adequate GDH it is essential to promote equitable, fair, just and sustainable socio-economic prosperity and to control environmental degradation, greenhouse effect, acid rains, climate change as well as global warming to presence and to promote cultural heritage and value judgment and to cultural governance.[22]

He has also made it clear, as stated by the Prime Minister of Bhutan, that GDH cannot be easily calculated and examined only on the basis of gross domestic product (GDH) as propounded by the great economist Simon Kuznets. GDH can't be achieved merely through GDH/GNP. It can't be sustainable on the basis of GDP for long. For this co-operation from all corners must be sought and obtained.

There is a need to bring harmony between man and nature. The Vedas have rightly stated that the resources belong to all human and non-human and they are to be used with restraint and not for indulgence. Earth should be considered as our mother and it would be our holy duty to protect mother earth. According to *'Bhagwat Purana'* all resources should be utilized in better and proper way. The resources of earth need to be under the trust of noble people who are devoted to the mankind. The Ramayana and Mahabharata has also highlighted the role of natural resources in gross domestic/ national happiness which depends mainly on proper and optimum utilization of these resources. The *Budhist and Jain* Teachings also show that non-violence holds the key of enhancing happiness to all and also harmony between man and nature. Kautilya's Arthasastra while emphasizing the importance of money in one's life he has cautioned that the pursuit after 'Arth' (money) and 'Karma' (desire and sex) must be based on dharma (righteousness). In Manusmriti we obtain perception of land-use-planning which can benefit all human and non-human beings. The Kautilya's philosophy contains many needs and policy prescriptions to maintains and enjoy the earth in a manner everyone will be happy and prosperous. Gandhian model of development also prescribe that there is enjoy to fulfil human needs but not to rectify their greed. This alternative model has assimilated material growth with human values. It is believed that the present economic ills if modern society like exploitation, inequality and others are due to over emphasize on material growth without taking care of environmental degradation, which directly affect gross domestic happiness.

As such, gross domestic happiness is not concerned with only material happiness but all kinds of happiness viz. social, cultural, ethical, moral, educational, professional, business, and welfare of all concerned. It consists of happiness to all at every stage and on every occasion.

Notes and References

1. Sen, Amartya (1973), On *Economic Inequality*, Oxford. Clarendon Press (2nd ed.).
2. Sen, Amarya (1984), On *Ethics and Economics*, Basil Blackwell (UK)
3. Sen, Amartya (1970), On *Economics Inequality*, Oxford, Clarendon Press, (2nd edition).
4. Sen and Dreze (2004), Poverty and Famine: An Essay on Entitlement and Deprivation, Oxford University Press.
5. Prime Minister of Bhutan (2010), Delivered Lecture on "Gross Domestic Happiness" on 27th September 2010 in Magadh University Campus, Bodh-Gaya.
6. Sen, A.K. (2004), "Famines on Failures of Exchange and Entitlement." *Economic and Political Weekly*, April.
7. Sen, A.K. (1981), "Famine and Failure of Exchange and Entitlement" *Economic and Political Weekly*, August.
8. Sen, A.K. (2004), Poverty and Famines: An Essay on Entitlement and Deprivation. Oxford University Press.
9. Sen, A.K. (1981), "Ingredients of Famine Analysis: Availability and Entitlements", *Quarterly Journal of Economics*, 95:433-64.
10. Sen, A.K. (1986), "Food Economics and Entitlements", *Lioyds Bank Review*, April.
11. Sen, A.K. (1977), "Starvation and Exchange Entitlement: A General Approach and its Application to the Great Bengal Famine". *Cambridge Journal of Economics*, 1:33-53.
12. Sen, A.K. (1984), Right not to be Hungry in P. Alston, K. Tomasevski (ed.).
13. Sen, A.K. (2004), "Democracy and Right to Food", *Economic and Political Weekly*; April, 24.
14. Sen, A.K. (2005), "The three R's of Reforms". *Economic and Political Weekly*, May 07.

15. Sen, A.K. (2004), *Employment, Technology and Development*, Oxford University Press; New Delhi, 09.05.2010.
16. Sen, A.K. (1999), *Development as Freedom*, Oxford University Press.
17. Sen, A.K. (1999), Inequality Re-examined. OUP, New Delhi, p. 75.
18. Swaminathan, M.S. (2000), "Country-led Approach to Ending Food Insecurity and Poverty", *M.S. Swaminathan Research Foundation.*
19. Bidyadhar Majhi (2009), "Food Security in India *vis-à-vis* the policy of warming farm loan", *Southern Economist*, 15 January, Second Green Revolution VS: Rainbow Revolution; Deep and Deep Publications (P) Ltd.
20. Shrivastava, M.P. (2010), "Food Security and World Trade Prospectus.
21. M.J. Raghavan (2008), *American Journal of Agricultural Economics.*
22. Sen, Abhijit (2004), "Poverty and Inequality is India." *Economics and Political Weekly*; 18 and 25 Sept. 2004.

CHAPTER

33

Economics of Amartya Sen

ARINDAM GHOSH AND AGRADOOT BHADURI

INTRODUCTION

"Social choice theory related importantly to a more widespread interest in aggregation in economic assessment and policy-making (related to poverty, inequality, unemployment, real national income, living standards)" as said by Amartya Sen. Social choice theory studies voting rules for how individual preferences are aggregated to form a collective preference. Sen's Contribution to the literature enriches the theory of social choice. Sen points that there are a number of social and economic factors, such as declining wages, unemployment, rising food prices, and poor food-distribution systems, etc. behind the issues which led to starvation among certain groups in society. Amartya Sen's revolutionary contribution to development economics and social indicators is the concept 'capability' which is conceptual framework for evaluating social states in terms of human welfare. He argues that governments should measure the concrete capabilities of their citizens. This is because top-down development will always trump human rights as long as the definition of terms remains in doubt.

EARLY LIFE OF AMARTYA SEN

Amartya Kumar Sen, an Indian economist and a winner of the Nobel Prize was born on 3rd November 1933 in *Santiniketan, West Bengal.* His ancestral home was in Wari, Dhaka in modern-day Bangladesh. His family migrated to India following partition in 1947. *Rabindranath Tagore* is said to have given Amartya Sen his name "Amartya" meaning "immortal". Sen's maternal grandfather Kshitimohan Sen was a renowned scholar of mediaeval Indian literature. Amartya Sen was born to professor father Ashutosh Sen, who taught Chemistry at Dhaka University and mother Amita Sen, St. Gregory's School in Dhaka in modern-day Bangladesh was Amartya Sen's High School. Before moving to Trinity College, Cambridge Sen studied in India at the school system of Visva-Bharati University and *Presidency College, Kolkata,* where he earned a First Class B.A. in 1953. At Trinity College he received B.A. (Honours) in 1956 and then Ph.D. in 1959. He was also allowed four years to immerse himself in philosophical issues during his stay at Trinity College.

In 1981, Sen published Poverty and Famines: An Essay on Entitlement and Deprivation (1981), a book in which he demonstrated that famine occurs not only from a lack of food, but from inequalities built into mechanisms for distributing food. Sen's interest in famine stemmed from personal experience. As a nine-year-old boy, he witnessed the Bengal famine of 1943, in which three million people perished. This staggering loss of life was unnecessary, Sen later conclude. He presents data that there was an adequate food supply in Bengal at the time, but particular groups of people including rural landless labourers and urban service providers like haircutters did not have the monitory means to acquire food as its price rose rapidly due to factors that include British military acquisition, panic buying, hoarding, and price gouging, all connected to the war in the region. In Poverty and Famines,

Sen revealed that in many cases of famine, food supplies were not significantly reduced. In Bengal, for example, food production, while down on the previous year, was higher than in previous non-famine years. Thus, Sen points to a number of social and economic factors, such as declining wages, unemployment, rising food price, and poor food distribution systems. These uses led to starvation among certain groups in society. His capabilities approach focuses on positive freedom, a person's actual ability to be or do something, rather than on negative freedom approaches, which are common in economics and simply focuses on non-interference. In the Bengal famine, rural labourers' negative freedom to buy food was not affected. However, they still starved because they were not positively free to do anything, they did not have the functioning of nourishment, nor the capability to escape morbidity. In addition to his important work on the causes of famines, Sen's work in the field of development economics has had considerable influence in the formulation of the Human Development Report published by the United Nations Development Programs. This annual publication that ranks countries on a variety of economic and social indicators owes much to the contributions by Sen among other social choice theorists in the area of economic measurement of poverty and inequality.

Sen's revolutionary contribution to develop economics and social indicators is the concept of 'capability' developed in his article "Equality of What". He argues that governments should be measured against the concrete capabilities of their citizens. This is because top-down development will always trump human rights as long as the definition of terms remains in doubt (is a 'right' something that must be provided or something that simply cannot be taken away?). For instance, in the United States citizens have a hypothetical 'right' to vote. To Sen, this concept is fairly empty. In order for citizens to have a capacity to vote, they first must have "functionings". These "functionings" can range from the very broad, such as the availability of education, to the very specific, such as transportation to the polls. Only when such barriers are removed can the citizen truly be said to act out of personal choice. It is up to the individual society to make the list of minimum capabilities guaranteed by that society. For an example of the "capabilities approach" in practice, see Martha Nussbaum's Women and Human Development. He wrote a controversial article in *The New York Review of Books* entitled "More than 100 Million Women Are Missing" (see Missing Women of Asia), analyzing the mortality impact of unequal rights between the gardens in the developing world, particularly Asia. Other studies, such as one by Emily Oster, have argued that this is an over estimation, though Oster has recanted some of her conclusions.

WORK OF AMARTYA SEN

Amartya Sen in 1998 for his work on famine, human development theory, welfare economics, the underlying mechanisms of poverty and political liberalism won the Bank of Sweden Prize in Economic Sciences, i.e Nobel Prize for Economics. He became the first Asian academic to head an Oxbridge College. Among his many contributions to develop economics, Sen has produced work on gender inequality. He is currently the Lamont University Professor at Harvard University.

The theory of social choice has been developed with Amartya Sen's contribution.

RESEARCH

Sen's papers in the late 1960s and early 1970s helped develop the theory of social choice, which first came to prominence in the work by the American economist Kenneth Arrow, who, while working at RAND Corporation, famously proved that all voting rules, be they majority rule or two thirds majority or *status quo*, must inevitably conflict with some basic democratic norm. Sen's contribution to the literature was to show under what conditions Arrow's impossibility theorem would indeed come to pass as well as to extend and enrich the theory of social choice, informed by his interests in history of economic thought and philosophy.

An Essay on Entitlement and Deprivation is a book published by Amartya Sen in 1981, where he demonstrated that famine occurs not only from a lack of food, but from inequalities built into mechanisms for distributing food. His interest in famine came from his personal experience as he witnessed the Bengal famine of 1943. In his book he has shown that in many cases of famine, food supplies were not significantly reduced. In case of Bengal, food production was higher in that year than in previous non-famine years. A number of social and economic factors came into play which led to starvation among certain groups in society. His capability approach focuses on positive freedom (a person's actual ability to be or do something) rather than on negative freedom approaches, which are common in economics and simply focuses on non-interference. In the Bengal famine, rural labourers' negative freedom to buy food was not affected. However, they still starved because they were not positive free to do anything.

To Amartya Sen, then Cambridge was like a battlefield, there were major debates between supporters of Keynesian economics and the diverse contributions of Keynes' followers, on the one hand, and the "neo-classical" economists skeptical of Keynes, on the other. Sen was lucky to have close relations with economists on both sides of the divide. Meanwhile, thanks to its good "practice" of democratic and tolerant social choice, Sen's own college, Trinity College, was an oasis very much removed from the discord. However, because of a lack of enthusiasm for social choice theory whether in Trinity or Cambridge, Sen had to choose a quite different subject for his Ph.D. Thesis, after completing his B.A. He submitted his thesis on "the choice of techniques" in 1959 under the supervision of the brilliant but vigorously intolerant John Robinson. During his time at Cambridge, and according to Quentin Skinner, Sen was a member of the secret society, "The Aposties".

Indian writer and scholar Nabaneeta Dev Sen was his first wife whom he had two children, Antara and Nandana. Antara is renowned Indian journalist and Nandana is a bollywood actress. But their marriage broke up after they moved to London in 1971. Eva Colorni was his second wife with whom he had two children, Indrani and Kabir. Indrani is a journalist in New York, and Kabir teaches P.E. in the Boston area. Eva dead from stomach cancer in 1985. An economic historian, an expert on Adam Smith and Fellow of King's College, Cambridge. The Hon. Emma Georgina Rothschild is his present wife.

HONOURS AND AWARDS FOR AMARTYA SEN

(1) He received the Nobel Memorial Prize in Economics for his work in Welfare Economics in 1998.
(2) In 1999 he received the Bharat Ratna the highest civilian award in India by the President of India.
(3) In 1999 he was offered honorary citizenship of Bangladesh from Prime Minister Seikh Hasina in recognition of achievements in winning the Nobel Prize, and given that his family origins were in what has become the modern state of Bangladesh.
(4) He received the 2000 Leontief Prize for his outstanding contribution to economic theory from the Global Development and Environmental institute.
(5) He was the 351st Commencement Speaker of Harvard University.
(6) In 2002 he received the International Humanist Award from the International Humanist and Ethical union.
(7) Eisenhower Medal, for Leadership and Service, USA, 2000.
(8) Companion of Honour, UK, 2000.
(9) In 2002, he received an honorary degree from the University of Tokyo[17].
(10) In 2003, he was conferred the Lifetime Achievement Award by the India Chamber of Commerce.
(11) Lifetime Achievement Award by Bangkok-bases United Nations Economic and Social Commission for Asia and the Pacific (UNESCAP).

Works by Amartya Sen

(1) Choice of techniques, 1960.
(2) An Aspect of Indian Agriculture.
(3) The Argumentative Indian.
(4) Commodities and Capabilities.

(5) Growth Economics.
(6) *Identity and Violence*: The Illusion of Destiny.
(7) Collective choice and Social Welfare.
(8) On Economic Inequality.
(9) *Poverty and Famines*: An Essay on Entitlement and Deprivation, 1981.
(10) *Poverty and Famines*: an Essay on Entitlement and Deprivation.
(11) Choice, Welfare and Measurement.
(12) Food Economics and Entitlements.
(13) On Ethics and Economics.
(14) Hunger and Public Action.
(15) "More than 100 Million Women Are Missing".
(16) Inequality Re-examined.
(17) The Quality of Life.
(18) India: Economic Development and Social Opportunity.

CONCLUSION

Welfare economics seeks to evaluate economic policies in terms of their effects on the well-being of the community. Sen, who devoted his carrier to such issues, was called the "conscience of his profession". His influential monograph *Collective Choice and Social Welfare* (1970), which addressed problems related to individual rights (including formulation of the liberal paradox), justice and equity, majority rule, and the availability of information about individual conditions, inspired researchers to turn their attention to issues of basic welfare. Sen devised methods of measuring poverty that yielded useful information for improving economic conditions of the poor. For instance, his theoretical work on inequality provided an explanation for why there are fewer women than men in India and China despite the fact that in the West and in poor but medically unbiased countries, women have lower mortality rates at all ages, live longer, and make a slight majority of the population. Sen claimed that this skewed ratio results from the better health treatment and childhood opportunities afforded boys in those countries, as well as sex-specific abortion.

Governments and international organizations handling food crises were influenced by Sen's work. His views encouraged policy-makers to pay attention not only to alleviating immediate suffering but also to finding ways to replace the lost income of the poor, as, for example, through public-works projects, and to maintain stable prices for food. A vigorous defender of political freedom, Sen believed that famines do not occur in functioning democracies because their leaders must be more responsive to the demands of the citizens. In order for economic growth to be achieved, he argued, social reforms, such as improvements in education and public health, must precede economic reform.

CHAPTER

34

Amartya Sen's Social Choice : Theory and its Relevance

S.M. JAWED AKHTAR AND SANA NASEEM

Amartya Sen is known as "the Mother Teresa of Economics" for his work on famine, human development theory, welfare economics, the underlying mechanisms of poverty, gender inequality, and political liberalism. In 1998, Sen won the Nobel Memorial Prize in Economics for his contribution to work on welfare economics. "Social choice theory related importantly to a more widespread interest in aggregation in economic assessment and policy-making (related to poverty, inequality, unemployment, real national income, living standards)" as said by Amartya Sen. Social choice theory studies voting rules for how individual preferences are aggregated to form a collective preference. Sen's contribution to the literature enriches the theory of social choice. Sen points that there are a number of social and economic factors, such as declining wages, unemployment, rising food prices, and poor food-distribution systems, etc.

behind the issues when led to starvation among certain groups in society. Amartya Sen's revolutionary contribution to development economics and social indicators is the concept of 'capability' which is a conceptual framework for evaluating social states in terms of human welfare. He argues that Governments should measure the concrete capabilities of their citizens. This is because top-down development will always trump human rights as long as the definition of terms remains in doubt.

Sen's hero for the past 20-25 years has been a true Renaissance man, Adam Smith. And others see a similarity between the two. Richard Cooper—a fellow Harvard professor—wrote in a book review in Foreign Affairs (2000): "Most economists these days eschew moral philosophy—namely, the consideration of social justice—because they consider it too 'soft' for rigorous analytical treatment. But Amartya Sen harks back to the older and richer tradition of evaluating the considerations of economic efficiency—which dominate most modern economic analyses—with respect to their general social consequences. Such judgements require an ethical framework".

I

Of all the work he has done, Sen stresses that the most satisfying has been his contribution to the field of social choice theory, which "goes to the very foundations of democracy". As the Nobel Prize citation for Amartya Sen in 1998 explains, when there is general agreement, the choices made by society are uncontroversial. When opinion differs, the problem is to find methods for bringing together different opinions in decisions that concern everyone. The theory of social choice is preoccupied with this link between individual values and collective choice. The fundamental question is whether—and, if so, in what way—preferences for society as a whole can consistently be derived from the preferences of its members. The answer is crucial for the feasibility of ranking, or otherwise evaluating, different social states and thereby constructing meaningful measures of social welfare or helping public decision-making. For Sen, the beauty of social choice theory was not only that it was analytically exciting but also that it gave him a framework for tackling practical political issues—most notably, the best way to measure social progress. Traditionally, the economic community relied on national income statistics, such as GNP and GDP, which measure the total income or output of a society. However, Sen dismissed these figures as totally insufficient for two reasons: first, they failed to capture income distribution issues; and, second, a person's well-being and freedom depend on many non-income influences, such as disability, propensity toward and exposure to diseases, and the absence of schools. He also took strong issue with the head-count method of measuring poverty.

Social choice theory is a very broad discipline, covering a variety of distinct questions, and it may be useful to mention a few of the problems as illustrations of its subject matter. Sen used social choice theory to answer questions such as the following: when would majority rule yield unambiguous and consistent decisions? How can we judge how well a society as a whole is doing in the light of the disparate interests of its members? How do we measure overall poverty in the view of the varying predicaments and miseries of the diverse people that make up the society? And how can we accommodate individual's rights and liberties while giving adequate recognition to their preferences? How do we appraise social valuation of public goods such as the natural environment, or epidemiological security? Also, some investigations, while not directly a part of social choice theory, have been helped by the understanding generated by the study of group decisions (such as the causation and prevention of famines and hunger, or the forms and consequences of gender inequality, or the demands of individual freedom seen as a "social commitment"). The reach and relevance of social choice theory can be very extensive indeed.

II

How did the subject of social choice theory originate? The challenges of social decisions involving divergent interests and concerns have been explored for a long time. However, social choice theory as a systematic discipline first came into its own around the time of the French Revolution. The subject was pioneered by French mathematicians in the late eighteenth century, such as J.C. Borda (1781) and Marquis de Condorcet (1785), who initiated the formal discipline of social choice in terms of voting and related procedures. The intellectual climate of the period was much influenced by European Enlightenment, with its interest in reasoned construction of social order. Indeed, some of the early social theorists, most notably Condorcet, were also among the intellectual leaders of the French Revolution.

The motivation that moved the early social choice theorists included the avoidance of both instability and arbitrariness in arrangements for social choice. The ambitions of their work focused on the development of a framework for rational and democratic decisions for a group, paying adequate attention to the preferences and interests of all its members. However, even the theoretical investigations typically yielded rather pessimistic results.

When the subject of social choice was revived in the twentieth century by Arrow (1951), he too was very concerned with the difficulties of group decisions and the inconsistencies to which they may lead. While Arrow put the discipline of social choice in a structured—and axiomatic—framework (thereby leading to the birth of social choice theory in its modern form), he deepened the preexisting gloom by establishing an astonishing—and apparently pessimistic—result of ubiquitous reach.

Arrow's (1950, 1951, 1963) "impossibility theorem" (formally, the "General Possibility Theorem") is a result of breathtaking elegance and power, which showed that even some very mild conditions of reasonableness could not be simultaneously satisfied by any social choice procedure, within a very wide family. Only a dictatorship would avoid inconsistencies, but that of course would involve: (1) in politics, an extreme sacrifice of participatory decisions, and (2) in welfare economics, a gross inability to be sensitive to the heterogeneous interests of a diverse population. Two centuries after the flowering of the ambitions of social rationality, in Enlightenment thinking and in the writing of the theorists of the French Revolution, the subject seemed to be inescapably doomed. Social appraisals, welfare economics calculations, and evaluative statistics would have to be, it seemed, inevitably arbitrary or unremediably despotic. Arrow's "impossibility theorem" aroused immediate and intense interest. It also led to the diagnosis of a deep vulnerability in the subject that overshadowed Arrow's immensely important constructive program of developing a systematic social choice theory that could actually work (Sen, 2007).[1]

III

Social choice theory is "concerned with relationships between individuals preferences and social choice" (Fishburn, 1973).[2] But a great many problems fit this general description and they can be classified into types that are fundamentally different from each other. It can be argued that some of the difficulties in the general theory of social choice arise from a desire to fit essentially different classes of group aggregation problems into one uniform framework and from seeking excessive generality. An alternative is to classify these problems into a number of categories and to investigate the appropriate structure for each category.

To illustrate varieties of exercises coming under the broad heading of inter-personal aggregation, consider the three following problems:

(i) *Committee decision:* A committee has to choose among alternative proposals for action on the relative merits of which the members hold different views.

(ii) *Social welfare judgement:* A person want to make a judgement whether a certain changes will be better for the society, some members will gain from the change while others will lose.

(iii) *Normative indication:* Measurement of "national income", "inequality", "poverty", and other "indicators" defined with normative motivation incorporating interpersonal weighting in some easily tractable way.

These exercises differ from each other in many ways. For example, the typical committee decision problem is concerned with aggregating the views of its members on what should be done rather than with aggregating the personal welfare levels of members with which social welfare judgements are frequently concerned. Also, a social welfare judgement is typically interpreted in terms of "optimality", usually involving binary concepts like "better", whereas the focus of committee decisions is on arriving at actual choices in a fair manner whether or not such choices could be described as being "best" or "optimal". In committee decisions, the format for expression of views is typically rather limited. In social welfare judgments the magnitudes of welfare gains and losses are frequently invoked as well as interpersonal rankings of welfare, which are typically not applied to members in committee decisions procedures. On the other hand, the individual preferences are expressed by the persons themselves in committee meetings whereas the rankings of personal welfare in social welfare judgements are frequently made by some kind of guess work rather than direct inquiry. That is, social welfare judgements frequently involve a wider class of information but are based on less firm evidence than committee decision mechanisms.

The use of normative indicators usually involves compromises of different peoples' "interest" rather than of their "views". The focus is not on reaching actual decisions as such, but on making systematic judgements according to certain well-defined criteria. In these respects there is closer similarity with social welfare judgements than with committee decisions. On the other hand, the exercise is limited by using only that information which can be rather mechanically collected, and usually also by keeping the exercise confined to welfare judgements of a limited nature rather than presenting a total judgement about overall social welfare.

Many other exercises also fit the general description of "social choice" and have other differences. In what follows Sen focused on only two criteria of classification:

(i) Is the aggregation that of individual interests, or that of individual judgements? The first type of exercise will be marked *I* and the second *J*.

(ii) Is the intention to arrive at decisions or at welfare

judgements? The first type will be called *D* and the second *W*.

These yield four categories, viz., *ID* (aggregation of individual interests for social decisions), *JD* (aggregation of individual welfare judgements for social decision), *IW* (aggregation of individual interests into social welfare judgements), and *JW* (aggregation of individual welfare judgements into social welfare judgements).

As far as social choice theory itself is concerned, following are the main points:

(1) The classic framework, pioneered by Arrow, seems to be quite inappropriate for interest aggregation, i.e., for *IW* and *ID*. The n-tuples of individual orderings are informationally inadequate for representing conflicts of interests. The problem of intransitivity of social preference, or of inconsistency of social choice, seems to be secondary in comparison with the inability of the classic framework to distinguish systematically between essentially different choice situations. It is not surprising, therefore, that the focus of work on interest aggregation has moved towards a wider informational basis, especially in making room for systematic interpersonal comparisons. The classic impossibility results are of little interest for *IW* and *ID*.

(2) The classic framework comes into its own with judgement aggregation, and the impossibility theorems take a heavy toll on *JW*. For welfare judgement, the binary relation of social preference seems basic, and even if the requirement of transitivity is weakened to quasi-transitivity, or to acyclicity, or even to acyclicity over triples only, new impossibility results crop up.

(3) With *JD*, the situation is less gloomy in some sense, but the advantage that is gained in moving away from welfare relations to choice functions has been overestimated. Even very weak conditions of

consistency of choice bring us to the regularity properties of the base relation of the choice function, and the impossibility theorems proved for relational collective choice rules applied to its "base relation" (involving choices from pairs only).

(4) While Arrow defines the choice function in binary terms, viz., "C(S) is the set of all alternatives x in S such that for every y in S, xRy", no use whatsoever is made of this property. He also remarks: "If, then, we know C([x, y]) for all two-element sets, we have completely defined the relation P and I and therefore the relation R; *but, knowing the relation R completely determines the choice function* C(S) *for all sets of alternatives*". But, infact, the property referred to in the italicized statement plays no part in the General Possibility Theorem (GPT). While Arrow can certainly hold that "one of the consequences of the assumptions of rational choice is that choice in any environment can be determined by a knowledge of the choices in two-element environments"(Arrow, 1963),[3] the validity of GPT—and indeed of Arrow's own proof of it—is completely independent of rational choice in this sense. Impossibility theorems for relational collective choice rules, R=f([Ri]), involving transitivity of R (as in Arrow), or weaker properties than transitivity (e:g., quasi-transitivity, acyclicity, triple-acyclicity), are best interpreted by taking R as the "base relation". In this sense, the relational framework for social choice pioneered by Arrow is more—not less—general than that of functional collective choice rules involving choice functions for society over the entire environment X.

(5) There is a fundamental asymmetry in the ability of social decision procedures to cope with choice consistency conditions of two types. The "contraction-consistency properties" (e.g., α) cause problems even in the weakest form, while the "expansion-consistency properties" (e.g., β, γ, δ, ε) are easily accommodated even in their strongest form. The weakest contraction-consistency property (α(- -))

implies triple-acyclicity of the base relation, but is not implied by it.

(6) Regarding "path independence", impossibility theorems emerge easily within the framework of path independent choice functions. Factorizing path independence into two parts, the one (PI*) which corresponds to contraction-consistency (α) is seen to be the source of the problem, while the other part (*PI), which is implied by expansion-consistency ($\beta(+)$), is easily met. However, relying exclusively on expansion-consistency permits questionable social choices to be made, e.g., the choice of a pareto inferior alternative through a legitimate path.

On the impact of Arrow-type impossibility results, the score card seems to look something like this: *ID*: not disturbing; *IW*: not disturbing; *JD*: quite disturbing; *JW*: dismal.

How relevant are these respective exercises? Contrast the types of questions in each category: *IW*: "These are the interests of the different people involved. How alternative policies should be rank in terms of social good (or a specified aspect of social good)?" *ID*: "These are the interests of the different people involved. What should be done?" *JD*: "These are the judgement rankings of alternative policies in terms of social good as seen by each of us. What should be done?" *JW*: "These are the judgement rankings of alternative policies in terms of social good as seen by each of us. How do we arrive at a combined judgement giving one ranking in terms of social good aggregating all our rankings?"

JD is a practical exercise and is frequently faced (e.g., in committee decisions). *ID* is also a common enough exercise (e:g., in arbitration awards). *IW* is basic to our thinking on policy (e.g., in the formation of personal political judgements), and in a somewhat arbitrary form appears in normative indication as well (e.g., in the "measurement" of national income, inequality, poverty, or the so-called "net national welfare"). In contrast *JW* is, in some sense, a bit of a luxury. Do we need a combined judgement giving one ranking for society in addition to facing the social decision problem? There is little doubt that *JW* is of considerable philosophical interest; but in view of the fact that there is greater cause for pessimism for *JW* compared with the other exercises, it is somewhat comforting that *JW* seems to have less practical interest than the three other exercises.

It is important to distinguish between different types of aggregation exercises covered by social choice theory since they involve quite different problems. To use one general framework for all of them leads to a loss of structure which has been a source of much trouble in this field (Sen, 2007).[4]

IV

Impossibility results in social choice theory-led by the pioneering work of Arrow (1951) have often interpreted as being thoroughly destructive of the possibility of reasoned and democratic social choice, including welfare economics. Sens have argued against that view. Indeed, Arrow's powerful "Impossibility Theorem" invites engagement, rather than resignation. The impossibility results certainly deserve serious study. They often have wide_indeed sweeping_reach, not merely covering day-to-day politics (where we be rather used to incongruity), but also questioning the possibility of any assured framework for making social welfare judgements for the society as a whole. Impossibilities thus identified also militate against the general possibility of an orderly and systematic framework for normatively assessing inequality, for evaluating poverty, or for identifying intolerable tyranny and violations of liberty. Not to be able to have a coherent framework for these appraisals or evaluations would indeed be most damaging for systematic political, social, and economic judgement. It would not be possible to talk about injustice and unfairness without having to face the accusation that such diagnoses must be inescapably arbitrary or intellectually despotic.

These bleak conclusions do not, however, endure searching, and fruitful procedures that militate against such pessimisim can be clearly identified. Sen's in one of his lecture emphasizing the possibility of constructive social choice theory, and arguing for a productive interpretation of the impossibility results. Indeed, these apparently negative results can be seen to

CHAPTER

35

Empirics and Amartya Sen's Poverty Indices

PARMOD KUMAR AND REENA SINGH

Amartya Sen, the famous economist of 20th century, has been honored with Noble Prize, in Economics, in 1998. The prize relates to his path breaking authorship in "Collective Choice and Social Welfare". Sen is of the opinion that the state organization and market economy have their own distinct roles like the system of planning and economic incentives. But both market economies as well as socialist economies, cannot find solution to the problems arising out of the constraints of human capabilities. These problems relate to insufficient basic education, and health services, distortions in the system of ownership, and social classification and widespread gender discrimination. It is, therefore, essential that the process of economic reforms and the process of generation of opportunities should keep pace with each other. He is known as the philosopher of poverty. This paper analyses various empirical issues relating to Amartya Sen's measure of poverty.

Poverty is a deprivation of essential assets and opportunities to which every human is entitled. Everyone should have access to basic Education and primary health services. Poor households have the right to sustain themselves by their labor and be reasonably rewarded, as well as having some protection from external shocks. Beyond income and basic services, individuals and societies are also poor—and tend to remain so—if they are not empowered to participate in making the decisions that shape their lives. Poverty is, thus, better measured in terms of basic education, health care, nutrition, water and sanitation, as well as income, employment, and wages. Such measures must also serve as a proxy for other important intangibles such as feelings of powerlessness and lack of freedom to Participate. To better understand the nature of poverty, several related poverty concepts are employed. These include:

- *Human Poverty*: The lack of essential human capabilities, notably literacy and nutrition.
- *Income Poverty*: The lack of sufficient income to meet minimum consumption needs.
- *Absolute Poverty*: The degree of poverty below which the minimal requirements for survival are not being met. This is a fixed measure in terms of a minimum calorific requirement plus essential non-food components. While absolute poverty is often used interchangeably with extreme poverty, the meaning of the latter may vary, depending on local interpretations or calculations. Vulnerability and poverty are concepts that overlap, but, are not identical.

Deaton (2004) found that for most countries consumption estimated by surveys was less (about 86%) than consumption as reported in the National Accounts. One reason for this is that the National Accounts include items not included in surveys (for example, imputed rent) and also include expenditure on items that do not enter the budgets of the poor. A major cause of difference between poverty estimates based on the two different sets of data—National accounts and

Surveys—is that poverty estimates based on National Accounts data use GDP per head as the assessment variable. GDP, as is well known, includes many items other than personal consumption—*inter alias* private investment and government consumption.

MEASUREMENT OF POVERTY

In his book, *'On Economic Inequality'*, Prof. Sen has propounded a new technique for the measurement of absolute poverty. There are 3 methods:

(a) Head Count Ratio (HCR)

According to this technique, we first define poverty line; then identify the number of persons below poverty line; and finally, the number of persons below poverty line is divided by total population to ascertain poverty ratio, which is called Head Count Ratio. Thus, this technique involves three steps as under:

(i) *Determination of Poverty Line:* As a first step, poverty line is determined in terms of some stipulated level of income. In India, for example, an individual whose monthly consumption expenditure is less than Rs. 264 in urban areas and less than Rs. 229 in rural areas (at 1993-94 prices) is deemed as below poverty line.

(ii) *Identification of the Poor:* People below poverty line are deemed as poor. In India, 28 crore people were estimated to be poor according to the year 2000-01.

(iii) *Measurement of Head Count Ratio:* Head count ratio is calculated by dividing total number of the poor by total population of the country. Thus, in India, 26% of the population was found to be below poverty line in 2000-01.

HCR is determined as under:

$$H = q/n$$

Thus, H is obtained as the ratio between q and n where, q stands for number of people below poverty line and n stands for total population. Prof. Sen identifies two limitations of this method:

(a) This technique does not identify the gap between the stipulated level of income (corresponding to poverty line) and actual income of the poor. This implies that all poor people are simply treated as poor, differences in their income, notwithstanding.

(b) This method does not account for the intensity of poverty. Here intensity of poverty means the difference between the stipulated level of income (corresponding to poverty line) and the actual income of the poor. According by, if some income of the poor is transferred to the rich individual, there would not be any difference in the Head Count Ratio.

(b) Income-Gap Method—IG

According to this method, we estimate the gap between the per capita income of the poor and income of the poverty line. Given the stipulated level of poverty line income, income gap should be greater, lower than per capita income of the poor. Intensity of poverty is proportionate to the size of the income gap. This method involves three steps: (a) Measurement of per capita Income of the poor; (b) Determination of the level of income corresponding to poverty line; and (c) Estimation of the income gap as the difference between poverty line income and per capita income of the poor.

Prof. Sen uses the following version of income gap method for the estimation of poverty. This difference is divided by poverty line income to find out the ratio of income gap. Prof. Sen has used the following formula to measure it.

$$I = \frac{z - M_p}{z}$$

(Here, I = Income Gap; z = Poverty Line;
Mp = Per capita income of the poor).

Prof. Sen considers income gap method as an incomplete technique for the estimation of poverty. Following are some of the notable limitations of this method.

(c) Sen's Index

Amartya Sen's major point has been that the gap simplicities approach will not do. One has to take into account the distribution of income/consumption among the persons *below* the poverty line. If the gap had to be filled externally, and on a continuous basis year by year, one had to assume that the initial distribution below the poverty line would remain more or less unchanged. The intuitive finding was that the more skewed the distribution below the poverty line would remain more or less unchanged. The intuitive finding was that the more skewed the distribution below the poverty line the larger would be the Sen Gap. Sen produced a neat formula, which he termed as the poverty measure, known as the Sen Index.

$$P = [I + (1-I)\ G]\ H$$

where P is the poverty index, *I* is the measure of distribution, G is the Gini coefficient, and H is the head count proportion of the people below the poverty line. The measure of distribution generally used is the measure of the poverty line minus the mean consumption of people below the poverty line divided by the poverty line measure. If the poverty line measure is 100 rupees the mean consumption below the poverty line is 60 rupees, the mean consumption ratio per poor person would be *I*, the Dandekar gap measure as a ratio would be. If G is 0.40, and H is 40%, P would be equal to 56%. Noted that the lower the Dandekar gap ratio, the lower would be P. If G is lower, the lower would be the Sen Index. *Prima facie* any measure that reduces the skewedness of distribution below the poverty line would reduce the index. When G is 0, all persons below the poverty line have the same level of consumption, the Sen Index and the Dandekar gap ratio would be the same. Quasi-truncation of inequality is probably questionable.

DATABASE-RELATED ISSUES

Several different data gathering methods and survey techniques can also be used to collect data which can be used for poverty analysis. Since very few surveys have poverty measurement as their primary objective, poverty analysts must carefully evaluate whether surveys are conducted for other purposes and if the other (or multiple) objectives can provide reliable data for measuring poverty and changes in living conditions.

1. Population Census

The population census contains basic information on all citizens of a country. The census is carried out for all households to obtain basic information on the population, its demographic structure, and its location. In most countries, it is carried out by a national statistics institute. The right-hand variables are household demographic variables selected by the user. Apply the estimated coefficients from the above step to the census data to impute a value of log per capita expenditure for each census household. Using these imputed values to produce poverty or inequality profiles for the desired aggregation units of the census data. The technique allows calculation of standard errors for whichever welfare measure is estimated. This offers a means to assess the statistical reliability of estimates as well as comparisons across estimates for different geographic areas.

- Information at different levels of disaggregating in the country or region. Descriptive statistics of housing stock;
- Access to basic services such as water, electricity, and sanitation; and
- Employment patterns.

2. Household Surveys

Household surveys can be an indispensable tool for measuring the extent and distribution of income poverty. Once a poverty line has been determined, the distribution of consumption obtained from household surveys can easily provide the percent of population below the poverty line (the poverty incidence). At the same time, an important shortcoming of aggregate household level analysis is that it can provide only limited understanding of the intra-household distribution of resources, especially of income and consumption. While the census covers the whole population, surveys interview only a subset, generally a small fraction. This sample of households is carefully chosen so that the results of the survey accurately describe living conditions in the country, and in different parts of the country. Sampling should be based on mapping actual settlements, including newly formed informal urban ones. Sampling is most often informed by a recent population census. The actual sample size, the number of households interviewed will vary with several factors:

- A survey that aims to measure countrywide averages of income will require a larger sample than a survey designed to measure the percentage of the population with access to hospitals.
- *The level at which data are needed*: Determining the national electricity connection rate will require fewer households to be interviewed than determining regional or district rates.
- *The population*: Household surveys are much smaller than a population census and, therefore, also less costly.

An immediate problem in using household surveys for poverty analysis is that because of the burden of remembering expenditures on so many items, respondents are typically asked about few other topics. Thus, there are often few variables available from the survey that can either help explain the poverty status of the household. Another major problem with these surveys is the short period over which consumption is observed.

Generating income and non-income poverty estimates at a sub-national level is a particular challenge since most household surveys are based on sample sizes that are too small to draw accurate inferences at a local government level. Given an increased trend toward decentralization, there is a need for local government to be able to assess and track poverty conditions within their jurisdictions. One method that has been suggested is to correlate the findings of household surveys on household expenditures and access to services with census variables and to use these correlates to project poverty incidence at a district/provincial level. Another method is to correlate proxy variables, such as access to different types of household assets (housing quality, durable asset ownership) with poverty levels reported in a national income and expenditure survey, and to use these proxies to derive an indicator of poverty that can be readily surveyed at a 10callevel.

3. National Income Accounts

The National Income Accounts are also used to make income poverty estimates in several countries. This is done by applying changes in income distribution, based on household survey comparisons, to an estimate of the change in private consumption expenditures drawn from the National Income Accounts. In many countries, the National Income Accounts estimate of private consumption expenditures is substantially higher than the average consumption expenditures reported in household surveys. Consequently, the poverty head-count estimates that are derived from the use of National Accounts data tend to be substantially lower than that identified using

Household surveys: In countries such as India, major differences in poverty incidence and trends are reported depending on whether poverty head-count estimates are drawn from the National Income Accounts *versus* panels of household surveys.

4. Living Standard Measurement Surveys

The following types of household surveys are particularly useful in collecting poverty and social data for projects. LSMSs and other multi-topic surveys are generally geared toward measuring and analyzing poverty and are important instruments for poverty analysis. LSMSs collect information on such factors as: (i) household expenditures and income, (ii) health, (iii) education, (iv) employment, (v) agriculture, (vi) ownership of assets such as housing or land, and (vii) access to services and social programs. The LSMSs are explicitly multi-topic surveys. In addition to income and consumption, they collect detailed data on education, health and anthropometry, employment, migration, agriculture, non-farm enterprises, savings and credit, and community level data on public services and local prices. This coverage of additional topics is achieved by reducing the commodity detail required in the consumption module. The PLSA uses a broad range of methods developed over the last 20 years or so under the auspices of rapid and participatory rural appraisals (RRAIPRA). The methods used include matrix ranking and scoring, including wealth or well-being ranking, trend analysis, institutional analysis, and mapping and other diagramming techniques combined with semi-structured interviewing with individual informants or focus groups. The sample selection will normally consider the following: (i) ensure complementarily and comparability with existing quantitative data; (ii) capture as much as possible the diversity in living conditions among rural and urban communities; and (iii) balance sample size (number of participating communities) with depth of analysis.

5. Demographic and Health Surveys

Demographic and health surveys (DHSs) contain data on: (i) health, infant mortality, fertility, contraception practices and family planning, health attendance during pregnancy, feeding practices, vaccination, health center use of mothers and children, satisfaction with health services and cost of treatment; (ii) educational attainment; (iii) occupation, male/female; (iv) migration; (v) access sanitation, and ownership of durable goods. DHSs can be used to calculate household wealth and to carry out poverty analysis. DHSs now cover more than 170 surveys in 70 countries throughout the developing world. Country specific details of these surveys can be found at DHSs do not contain household income or consumption data; however, wealth quintiles can nevertheless be constructed that will allow for a useful poverty profile. The household wealth indicator is constructed using all available information on assets in the surveys durable goods, basic services, etc and then ranked to construct quintile distributions.

6. Employment Surveys

Employment surveys contain information on employment and unemployment patterns and fluctuations. They include questions about (i) household income, (ii) demographics, and (iii) housing features. They can be good sources for

(i) employment statistics, (ii) income-based poverty indicators, and (iii) input indicators such as access to basic services. The wage data provided in employment surveys are indicative but imprecise measures of household welfare because they do not cover the following:

- Changes in the number of unemployed who do not receive that wage;
- Micro-enterprise and other informal activity that may be important in many economies;
- Household production or wages paid partially in kind, which are particularly important in rural areas;
- Changes in household net worth used to stabilize consumption; and
- Intra-family transfers.

7. Qualitative and Participatory Poverty Analyses

Qualitative data are particularly well suited to address the question, "Who are the poor?" Qualitative data and approaches allow the community itself to analyze its own poverty and determine the most important manifestations and solution to poverty. At a strategic level, such information can be used to identify binding constraints to poverty reduction that must be addressed. At a project level, such information may be critical for the design for projects and policies aimed at reaching the poor. Participatory poverty assessment can be particularly useful for planning purposes when the degrees to which public policies affect low-income households are uncertain and, in the aftermath of periods of severe economic shocks, when changes in access to incomes, PRA uses tools for consulting the poor directly and systematically. It commonly involves qualitative methods such as semi-structured interviews with key informants and contact persons. It aims to obtain information from individuals who are thought to have sufficient knowledge about issues or groups of people. Key informants may be elderly people who know about the past situation, or women whose experiences may differ from those of men.

Sen Measure (index) is sensitive to changes in distribution parameter in the above poverty line groups, changes in the price index of wage-goods, changes in the relative prices of wage-goods due to productivity changes in the latter etc. In an unindexed population below the poverty line, inflation would move up the poverty line measure, move down the mean consumption ratio of BPL groups, and also probably increase G. Inflation in the context of natural calamities like floods and droughts would increase the poverty measure in a number of ways. In inter-temporal comparisons numerous factors have to be taken into account in explaining the changes in the poverty measure. A constant poverty measure may imply compensating changes in the different parameters. A more fundamental difficulty is that the Dandekar gap ratio requires the mean consumption of people below the poverty line. This is the total consumption of people below the poverty line divided by the poor. If initially it there had been less inequality in general in the whole population, the aggregate consumption of people below the poverty line would have been probably larger. Hence, the mean consumption is affected by the measure of general inequality and if the latter comes down, the mean consumption would be higher.

Hence, capability is prior to the attainment of the desired welfare states by individuals. (But, suppose we include Sen's capability-endowing commodities in the primaries of Rawls or we assume that Rawls' wealth and income would include the capability goods, what happens to the separate identity of capability?) Sen has gone on to argue that poverty is a result of capability failures. Such failures can occur in market economies as also in planned economies. Sen has a wide ranging critique of conventional welfare economics on account of neglect of the capability dimension. His ideas in this area are continuously evolving and further breakthroughs may be expected. One may venture on some comments on the concept of capability subject to the above.

In classical economics the goal of society is to maximize the ratio of surplus to the necessary costs. Such surplus can be used either for consumption enjoyment and/or for capital formation in physical and human categories. In standard economics in recent years the emphasis has been on the enjoyment of utilities as a result of consumption. Alfred Marshall brought in the concept of the maximization of net consumers' surpluses including non-overlapping producers' surpluses over one's lifetime. It is also common to utilize measures like per capita real income as the measure of well-being. Concepts of net welfare have also been devised. These exclude the measures of hidden costs like ecological and such damages. Sen is critical of many of these ideas. He has sought to provide an alternative to traditional welfare economics.

Capabilities of an individual imply economic capabilities. Prof. Sen is of the view that the concept of minimum standard of living would differ from economy to economy. However, in every economy, *the adequacy of the economic means cannot be judged independently of the actual possibilities of converting incomes and resources into capability to function.* Thus, he writes that an individual suffering from some chronic disease (say kidney failure or Heart attack), even when he has higher level of an income compared to some other individual, may in fact be relatively poor, because he is forced to spend the bulk of his income on his medical treatment. Hence, Prof. Sen concludes that identification of poverty in terms of income cannot be independent of the capabilities of an individual to reach a minimally acceptable level through direct income. In other words, lack of minimum capability is an equally important parameter as the lack of income for the identification of poverty line.

Prof. Sen has presented commodities, characteristics, capability and utility in the term of following chain: (Commodities—Characteristics—Capabilities—Utility). The third link of the above chain, i.e., capabilities is closely associated with the standard of living. The real indicator of poverty is the deprivation of capability. Amartya Sen, Asia's first Noble Prize winner in Economic Science for his contributions to modern welfare economics said that he would use every opportunity to bring poverty, inequality and deprivation more and more into public discourse. These problems are rampant in Europe and America also. In this view, the measurement of poverty, income, inequality and deprivation assumes relevance particularly for purposes of inter-temporal and spatial comparisons. He presented an axiomatic framework for the existing measures of income inequality and poverty. He established a one to one relationship between poverty and income inequality within the class defined as poor with reference to a single truncation of the population at the poverty line. He tries to emphasize the depth of poverty and destitution a social phenomenon completely overlooked by earlier economists who mostly used head-count ratio in their poverty measurement. We can say that a re-examination of Sen's elegant approach will be considered as new dimension of poverty, i.e., he is known as economist of poverty index which has received a new recognition since 1998. Also, there measures assume that one has access to individual income data. If ungrouped data are available, it is possible to think of standard alternative measures, such as the co-efficient of variation, to measure the relative deviation (poverty depth) of income from any arbitrary income level. More importantly, in real life situations, one cannot avoid sampling of one kind or another. If Sen's index is computed from a sample of incomes, then, what are its sampling properties, in small and large samples? This question could be further complicated when the observed incomes are subject to serious non-sampling errors. Unless and until detailed Monte-Carlo tests are carried out, it is difficult to agree with Sen that his poverty measure is far superior to the numerous measures that already exist in the literature.

A general weakness in Sen's index is that it ignores prices. Changes in price level can affect the living conditions of the poor more adversely than those of the rich. To avoid the price problem, Mahalanobis (1962) made use of the quantity of cereals consumed by households and studied its per capita distribution among various groups of households classified according to per capita total monthly expenditure in current prices.

MODIFYING THE SEN MEASURE

A stronger version of the Weak Transfer Axiom (known as the Strong Transfer Axiom) says that a regressive transfer from a poor person to a rich person must always cause the value of the poverty index to fall even if, in the process, the beneficiary crosses the poverty line. While the Sen Measure (and the generalization of the Sen Measure in equation (10)) satisfies the Weak Transfer Axiom, it does not necessarily satisfy the strong

Transfer Axiom. Had the poverty measure been an inequality index, this would have violated the Pigou-Dalton condition. The Sen Measure (and its generalization) gives too much importance to the poverty line and in the presence of measurement errors in income this importance may be largely spurious (Shorrocks, 1995). The fact that the Sen Index violates the Strong Transfer Axiom means that it is not continuous at the poverty line. To overcome this problem, define the *censored* income distribution y* = (y_1, *yM, Z,.., z)* obtained from y by replacing *all non-poor incomes* with the poverty line income, *z* (Takayama, 1979). The *continuous* version *P*(y; z)* of a (non-continuous) poverty measure *P(y;* z), is given by: *P*(y; z) =P(y*; z)*. Consequently, the *continuous* version of the Sen (1976) index is given by:

$$S^{*}=H\times f+ (1-H\times I)\ G^{*}$$

or

$$Gini = \frac{\sum_{i=1}^{n}\sum_{j=1}^{n}|y_i - y_j|}{2n^2\overline{y}}$$

where: G* is the Gini index computed over the censored distribution, y*. Such a version also satisfies the *Strong Transfer Axiom*. An important aspect of poverty analysis is to identify groups which make a particularly large contribution to poverty and whose members are especially at risk of being poor. In order to do this, we need a poverty index which *decomposes* aggregate poverty as the sum of sub-group poverty.

So to sum up, we can say that the concept of poverty is a multi-dimensional one and needs as such multidisciplinary approach. Every measure of poverty or of inequality found in the economic literature was invented to address a limited problem. There is no single index indeed which has universal validity and answers all problems of welfare administration. Any measure of poverty must, however, depend upon a general agreement on the concept of 'income adequacy' in terms of a minimum income that is absolutely necessary for meeting the personal and social needs of every person into the given society. But this concept is itself dynamic, depending upon the state of economic development and social change.

References

Anand, S. (1977), "Aspects of Poverty in Malaysia", *Review of Income and Wealth,* Vol. 23, pp. 1-16.

Bhalla, S. (2002), Imagine There is No Country: Poverty, Inequality and Growth in the Era of Globalization, Institute for International Economics: Washington DC.

Blackorby, C. and Donaldson, D. (1980), "Ethical Indices for the Measurement of Poverty", *Econometrica,* Vol. 48, pp. 1053-61.

Borooah, V.K., Gustafsson, B. and Shi, Li (1994), "China and India: Income Inequality and Poverty North and South of the Himalayas" (mimeo).

Bourguignon, F. and Morrison, C. (2002), "Inequality among World Citizens", *American Economic Review,* Vol. 47, pp. 727-44.

Chen, S. and Ravallion, M. (2001), "How Did the World's poor Fare in the 1990s?", *Review of Income and Wealth,* Vol. 47, pp. 283-300.

Clark, S., Hemming, R. and Ulph, D. (1981), "On indices for the Measurement of Poverty", *Economic Journal,* Vol. 91, pp. 515-26.

Deaton, A.S. (2004), *Measuring Poverty in a Growing World,* Woodrow Wilson School, and Princeton University, N.J.

Foster, J. (1984), "On Economic Poverty: A Survey of Aggregate Measures", in R.L. Basmann and G.F. Rhodes, *Advances in Econometrics,* Connecticut: JAI Press.

Foster J., J. Greer and E. Thorbecker (1984), "A Class of Decomposable Poverty Measures", *Econometrica,* Vol. 52, pp. 761-66.

Sala-I-Martin, X. (2002), *The World Distribution of Income,* NBER Working Paper 8933, National Bureau of Economic Research: Cambridge, Mass.

Sen, A.K. (1976), "Poverty: An Ordinal Approach to Measurement", *Econometrica,* Vol. 44, pp. 219-31.

Sen, A.K. (1998), *On Economic Inequality,* Oxford University Press: New Delhi.

Shorrocks, A.F. (1995), "Revisiting the Sen Poverty Index", *Econometrica,* Vol. 63, pp. 1225-30.

Takayama, N. (1979), "Poverty, Income Inequality and Their Measures", *Econometrica,* Vol. 47, pp. 747-59.

Zheng, B. (1997), "Aggregate Poverty Measures", *Journal of Economic Surveys,* Vol. 11, pp. 123-62.

Index